THE
ENDLESS
SEARCH

A MEMOIR

DAVID RAY

SOFT SKULL PRESS

David Ray

For Bob Bason
in friendship
David —

The Endless Search
© David Ray 2003

Book Design: Joel Tippie
Cover Painting: "Woodshed," 1989-95 by Wolf Kahn, courtesy of
Ameringer Yohe Fine Art, New York, www.ameringer-yohe.com.
Cover Photograph courtesy of the author.

Printed in Canada

Soft Skull Press, Inc.
71 Bond Street
Brooklyn, New York 11217
www.softskull.com

Distributed by Publishers Group West
1.800.788.3123
www.pgw.com

Library of Congress Cataloging-in-Publication Data
Ray, David, 1932-
    The endless search : a memoir / by David Ray.

  1. Ray, David, 1932—Childhood and youth. 2. Ray, David,
1932—Homes and haunts—Oklahoma. 3. Poets, American—20th
century—Biography. 4. Adult child abuse victims—United
States–Biography. 5. Fatherless families—United States. I. Title.
PS3568.A9Z466 2003
811'.54—dc21

                                                      2003004557

ISBN 1-887128-52-2

THE
ENDLESS
SEARCH

"They say if I do whatever they tell me to, after some time I shall be forgiven everything."

". . . And you do everything that's demanded of you?"

"What else can I do? I want to become a decent person again and be left in peace."

"Now look . . . when someone demands such a humiliating service from you and you feel too cowardly to say no, doesn't it make a split go through your whole being? A horror—something you can't describe—as though something unutterable had happened inside you?...Doesn't the picture you've made of yourself go out like a candle?"

—Robert Musil

There are some of us who in after years say to Fate, "Now deal with us your hardest blow, give us what you will, but let us never again suffer as we suffered when we were children."

—Olive Schreiner

Ah! What memories!
Myriad the thoughts provoked
by those cherry trees.

—Basho

For My Wife and My Sister with Love

1.

MY SISTER ELLEN and I tried to fix the world as we played in the Oklahoma hills close to the shack that was our home. One morning we sneaked knives and rags out of the kitchen and headed for a problem area we had noted as we roamed through the scrub oak. A network of iron rods ran from a central powerhouse set in a field to oil wells scattered around the area. The inch-thick iron rods whipped back and forth on widely spaced posts, their change of direction assisted at the base and crest of the hill by pulleys. The oscillating rods and the chugging engine in its tin shed gave out an incessant throbbing, heard day and night both on the hill and across Grampa's fields below.

Ellen and I stood enchanted, fascinated by the rods wobbling through the weeds and sliding across their greased posts. We decided we could be of help to Mr. McGregor, the neighbor who took care of the equipment. We would clean off the posts. It did not occur to us that Mr. McGregor might have slabbed the thick grease on for a purpose.

Our obsessive concern for cleanliness came from our mother, who laundered almost daily, bent over a washtub. She was at war with dirt and germs, as well as other shameful things, too vague to confront. I did not understand what germs were—maybe very tiny bugs or chiggers—but Mother's warnings were so frequent that I feared even the slightest smudge on our skin or clothes. My sister's fears had not yet caught up with mine, and she often headed for mud and dirt by instinct. I yanked her away from puddles and slapped her hand when she sat down to tamp earthen hutments for ladybugs, patting dirt over her hand, then slipping it out to leave a cave for them. My punishment left her wailing as the ladybugs escaped, taking to the air. At meals, if her hands did not meet the standards of Mother's and my inspections, I would give Ellen a version of Mother's lecture on germs. She still tried to her eat with her fingers. By age three, my favorite words were "dirty" and "nasty," "naughty" and "bad," echoing Mother's warnings. The world was full of perils.

As we roamed the hill and fields below, we often encountered Mr. McGregor in his blue overalls, with a huge black wrench in his hand. I assumed he was the same Mr. McGregor who had chased Peter Rabbit through the garden, where Peter hid in a watering can. But our Mr. McGregor was friendlier and never chased us.

We were standing one Saturday morning waist-high in weeds by the rocking pulley at the top of our hill, knifing grease away, our rags ready for polishing, when Ellen let out a scream that reached Mother's ears back at the house. Ellen threw down the butter knife and ran away before I could see what had happened. Blood spurted from her hand and her wail screamed out behind her like a siren. Throwing down my knife and rags, I ran after her.

As soon as Mother saw Ellen, she ripped off her apron and tore it into strips, then wrapped the bleeding hand and knotted a tourniquet round Ellen's arm. I watched, then followed as Mother ran with my sister in her arms down the road leading out of our clearing. The McGregor house was across the county road, and his Model A was parked in the drive. Mr. and Mrs. McGregor were standing on the porch, looking to see what all the screaming was about. As soon as he saw us, Mr. McGregor wasted no time in rushing Mother into the car.

With Ellen on her lap, hand cradling her head to comfort her, Mother called out to me. I was to stay with Mrs. McGregor. The rattling black car disappeared down the red dirt road, heading toward town. Mrs. McGregor led me into her kitchen, and resumed her baking. As she moved about she tried to distract me by giving me spoons and dishes to lick. I sat on the linoleum floor for most of the afternoon, thinking how it had all been my fault and fearing I would be punished when my father got home.

The first doctor Mother and Mr. McGregor found begged off. He had to take his son to a baseball game. The second doctor inquired about money and said he could not do anything if Mother could not pay. At last they went to the hospital where Ellen left her middle finger, and the remaining stump was stitched like a sack of grain. They returned about sunset, and my sister showed off a bandage big as a boxing glove. When the bandage was removed a week or so later, she had two black antennae, the surgical threads sticking out of the swollen stub. She waved the finger around in our faces, laughing, and days later seemed to mourn the stitches when Mother pulled them out.

When my parents had made the move to this hillside shack, the Depression was already well under way, and it made sense to live off the land. My father had worked at many jobs—as a stockboy, then assistant manager in Newberry's department store, where he had met my mother who was just out of high school and working as a salesclerk. He drove a taxi for a while, delivered blocks of ice for the Southern Ice Plant, and did a stint as a service station attendant.

Even before Ellen's birth fourteen months after mine, I had spent time in the care of my father's sister Edris, while my parents sorted out their periodic separations. They were, in fact, separated when I was born. They had made a move to Kentucky, but Mother had returned to Oklahoma to stay with her sister Peg and use her front bedroom for my birth.

I was fed a Pet milk formula which made me sick. Perhaps it was lead poisoning from the soldered seams of those cans. Mother decided I was allergic to milk, and gave up her attempts to provide either a cow's or her own. She had taken me like a gift to my father's sister Edris and the comfort of her bosomy but dry embrace. A year later, Mother nursed my new sister with no problem.

The pattern of leaving and retrieving was well established even before Ellen's birth as I was passed back and forth among relatives from both sides of the family—Aunt Peg, Aunt Edris, Aunt Ruth, Aunt Bea, Gramma Ada. After Ellen's arrival we were left and reclaimed each time our young parents embarked on another of their efforts to live together.

Our moves were so frequent, unpredictable and disrupting that the various places and people charged with our care merge in memory, a scrambled sequence. We soon learned to steal crumbs of affection from each caregiver, kneading them into our daily bread of conditional affection.

At age two weeks I was taken to Aunt Edris, the first of several stays with her and Uncle Henry in their little white house, the size of a box-car. When we stayed there later, Ellen and I slept on a pallet on the living room floor. When we visited Aunt Ruth and Uncle Mac we were tucked toe to toe on a couch. After his death, she would settle us down on the carpet with a saucer of Hershey's chocolate kisses and orange slices beside us. At Grampa Ray's farm I shared a bed with Gramma Ada's son W. T., whom we called Dub.

I would have been happy to live with Aunt Edris if Uncle Henry had not been present to torture me with his teasing and resentments. They already had two children and he did not welcome us. One of my cousins was a brilliant girl, Thelma. But her older brother, Eulys, was retarded. He had, as a small child, suffered an inflammation of the brain and an expensive operation had been recommended, but there was no way my uncle could afford it. Thelma was independent and took little notice of Ellen and me, but I was close to Eulys, goodhearted, awkward, grateful for my attentions as if I were the older cousin. Later, when I read *Of Mice and Men*, I recognized Lenny, for Eulys had been another Lenny.

Uncle Henry spent much of his time by the gate of the D-X refinery where he and other employees were on strike. Ellen and I sometimes waited for him with Aunt Edris in the black Chevrolet. The strikers had a fire going in a barrel, and when we got too cold in the car, we walked over and joined them. Aunt Edris lifted Ellen and me in turns to warm our hands over the barrel. At last Uncle Henry put down his union sign and drove us to the Red Fork church where a soup kitchen had been set up in the basement. He carried me on his shoulders, holding me by the ankles, and I bent down, clinging to his neck, as we ducked through the basement door.

It was not just striking workers who had to accept such charity as the soup kitchen offered. Few, if any, of those families hunched over their bowls at long tables were there by choice. They were like Van Gogh's *Potato Eaters*, uprooted and lost in the city. They talked of how strikers had been shot by police in Chicago, and I worried about Uncle Henry. Even if he was mean, I did not want him to be shot or beaten with a policeman's club.

Floods and droughts, strikes and soup kitchens, a poor harvest, empty pockets and foreclosed farms were concerns of the time. If a man had a car, he had to worry about how to afford gasoline. If he had children, he was obsessed with how to feed them and how not to get evicted. Landlords and bankers were feared as predators who could show up at any time, precipitating sudden flight in the night with whatever possessions could go in and on a car or a borrowed truck.

Aunt Edris wore her hair in a bun. During stays at her house I liked to watch her take out her hairpins, drop them in a saucer on her dresser, and comb out her knee-length hair. I would crawl from the pallet on the living room floor where Ellen and I were bedded down and peek through the slit of the doorway curtains into the bedroom Uncle Henry and Aunt Edris shared. Next to us the terrier Pooch snoozed, a comforting presence despite the daytime terror he inspired when Uncle Henry sicced him on me.

Teasing, or torturing, me was one of Uncle's favorite pastimes. He threatened to throw me off the bridge every time we drove across it. On the Fourth of July he tossed firecrackers at me, and he often had Pooch chase me around and around the house, under the clothesline. Aunt Edris pleaded with him to be nice to us. I was lucky not to get hit by a firecracker, but the explosions were not so wounding as his insults. "I know about the soup, but I don't know about the man," he said when he caught me playing Superman, my costume improvised from a towel Aunt Edris let me pin around my neck.

At night she carried me out to the outhouse in the rain, stepping on the wobbly warped planks that ran beside the garage and her flowerbed.

Lightning showed her face up close and I could smell her soft and sweet against me. She stood in the doorway with a flashlight while I grunted away on the wooden toilet seat, making sure the spiders did not get me.

On the hillside beyond the bridge that had become a terror, there was a gigantic chair attached to a furniture company's billboard. I dreamed I would someday sit enthroned on that chair. That would be my revenge for Uncle Henry's mockery when I announced I was Superman. Such attacks, even in jest, became part of my eternal doubts about my worth, and for the dog to be nipping at the seat of my pants as I ran around was a deep humiliation. Pooch did Uncle Henry's bidding, paying no attention to my protests, though at night the terrier lay gently enough beside us.

Being left in first one home then another became a bewildering roller-coaster ride. My parents kept trying to make their marriage work. Their most ambitious attempt may have been the farm after Grampa Ray arranged for my father to sharecrop an acreage adjacent to his own a few miles outside Sapulpa. The arrangement included the hilltop shack as a residence. Some of the fields below the hill were not yet cleared of stones and brush, but with hard work a subsistence could be eked out.

Dad was thin, sinewy, strong as he worked the fields with a mule and a plow. He dug a cellar, circling around with repeated attacks on the ground, with that mule as it dragged a sharp metal scoop. On Saturdays he took his melons, beans, tomatoes, and corn into town along with Grampa's produce. But farmers were lucky if grocers would pay a quarter a bushel for cantaloupes or tomatoes. Watermelons might fetch a nickel or a dime, even if they were the great shining diamondback globes that Grampa was so proud of cradling against his brass-buttoned overalls with the claw of his paralyzed hand.

Our unpainted shack had a dirt floor, though a porch with a plank floor jutted out in front. Sometimes the rooms without doors seemed more like a child's playhouse than a home, but Mother had set about making do with a screened fly-safe, a table and chairs, a wood-burning stove, and a few other basics. The bedroom had space for a dresser in the corner and a double mattress laid on a bedspring. For a while Ellen and I shared a crib, but most of the time we slept with our parents. Day and night we heard the powerhouse throbbing in the distance.

Our lighting was from coal oil—kerosene—lamps. Ellen and I were fascinated by mosquitoes and moths that met their end with a fizzle or a snap when they ventured across the smoke-smudged glass chimneys of the lamps. Grampa's house down the hill, though it too was only share-cropper's quarters, seemed a mansion compared with our hilltop home. His house had gas lights in wall and ceiling fixtures fed by the same bountiful supply of natural gas that provided the flame in our bedroom. Dad had pounded a pipe into the ground to tap the gas, a flickering tulip on a rusty stem.

My mother's effort to keep house in this ramshackle dwelling was a tiring and desperate business. She swept loose dirt, or even a fallen leaf that had made its way through a propped window, off the shiny packed black earth of the floor. Ellen and I, at play outside, imitated her war on dirt, and created our own little shack with walls of weeds and scrap. The patter of rain on our roof was comforting, without the bickering of our parents.

At night Mother converted her galvanized washtub to a bathtub, heating water and pouring it over Ellen and me, scrubbing our ears and any other places we had missed. We were aglow in the lamplight, ruddy with her rubbing. She was determined to get us clean, not only of grime and filth wherever she found it on our bodies, but even in the words we spoke. Germs and dirty talk, dust and smudging mud, soot and cobwebs were all intolerable and required constant scrubbing, sweeping, and laundering.

She cooked and managed to can fruits and vegetables in her primitive kitchen with its black iron stove. Dad provided firewood with his axe and a saw rig he contrived with a huge round blade attached to a salvaged car engine. Ellen and I sat on a mound of sawdust to watch as he fed tree limbs into the screaming saw.

Campers today have far more amenities than my young parents struggled to improvise on that farm. At best they could hope for subsistence. Water had to be carried in buckets from a well, and plumbing consisted of an outhouse. Dish or bath water was slung down the slope behind the house. With his .22 rifle and long-barreled .410 shotgun pistol, my father hunted for squirrels, rabbits, and possum. The fields were generous with potatoes, okra, tomatoes, beans, and corn. Mother picked greens by the bucket load, and perennial rhubarb grew in the corner of the hilltop clearing.

A boy stoops, picking greens with his mother—
This is the scene in the great elm-shadows.
A pail stands by her feet, her dress conceals
Her chill knees, made bitter by the tall man
Who now lifts a glass, she thinks, with his friends,
Or worse, seeks a younger love in the town
While she with her fading muslin apron
And her dented tin pail seeks greens, always
Greens, and wins, with her intermittent sighs,
Sympathy, love forever, from the boy.
He does not know, this sharp-boned boy who bends
To his mother, that he has been seduced
Already, that he has known anguish, bliss
Of sex—as much as he will ever know.
He does not know, here in the bees' shadow,
That he has become the tall and angry man,
The husband wounding the woman who bends,
Sighs and is ecstatic in her clutching
Of sons—bending, dark of brow, by her pail,
Stooped, brushing back the long, complaining strands
Of her hair. She is now too proud to weep,
But not to read the law, to reap greens, greens
        forever in her small, pathetic pail.

The Oklahoma hilltop was like a stage set where a man and a woman were broken in daily performances. He broke rocks and his mule, beating the beast into submission. With plow and scoop and the mule he sliced open the earth, and completed the cellar. With the same straight razor he used to shave his own chin and the necks of his brothers when they came Sunday morning for haircuts and shaves, he cut the throats of pigs. She broke her spirit over a washtub. Their efforts were as doomed as if they had tried to spoon out a pond or level a mountain with a shovel.

It was not only the daunting tasks of farming in a hard time that defeated my parents. Others, like my grandfather and my father's sister Alice and her husband, whose fields were nearby, survived the poverty and managed to live off the land, raising their family with transcendent, if hard-won, success. But they were not at each other's throats. Their fields along Skunk Creek were flooded nearly every year, but they were not breaking each other.

Over the shale of ancient seas Ellen and I floated through the night on our hilltop, often tossed on bewildering swells of overheard passion. In the semidarkness whispered secrets kept us guessing. What they said to each other sometimes seemed to mean something else. The world was full of mysteries.

At night, the blue and yellow flames dancing out of the open pipe threw scary shadows against the walls. When Mother let us run free after our bath, we would run around and jump up and down on the cool earth. Those moments in which frolicking was permitted seemed to be framed in a strict boundary of time, perhaps half an hour daily. Within those confines we could make our parents laugh. But even in such scenes there were details so odd that I held onto them knowing that some day as an adult I might be able to figure out what they meant.

Others remain forever indecipherable. Such an exchange as the following made no sense to me when I stood naked on a kitchen chair, rubbed dry and shivering in the chill after a bath. "We shouldn't keep him up with his little peter like that." What a bizarre statement that seemed even at the time. Was it a joke? Was it anxiety about some defect? Were they referring to an involuntary erection? I cannot even recall for sure which of my parents made that statement as my Mother stood there, the towel in her hands. But some day I might understand.

In the flickering bedroom flame with its shadows that could be neither controlled nor quenched, there was barely light enough to see, yet not a thick enough darkness for privacy. The sounds often seemed more those of pain than of pleasure. The smells of dank earth and musky bodies mingled in the night. Sometimes the murmuring voices of my parents seemed to come from ghosts or bad people who had gone to hell in the earth, as we were told at Sunday school in the crossroads church. The flame was fire spit from the mouth of a dragon. The gasp of Mother's intaken breath made me shudder in sympathy, tortured that I could not save her. I had seen what my father did to pigs and his mules, how he brought home the bleeding squirrels and rabbits, holding them by their tails or ears. She was pinned down, stifling rhythmic moans. I heard no counterpoint to pain, no melodic ecstasy as balance. I lay in the dark and wondered what my father would do to me if I interfered. I was alert, tensed for a fight. Of such restraint and stifling came the gasping of asthma, gulping each breath and trying to keep it silent.

My father sometimes fought with his mule as if he were Hercules wrestling a beast. One day as he was digging out that cellar with the scoop, the mule lurched away, dragging the scoop and yanking him along as he tugged at the reins tied around his waist. He yelled, dug in his heels, dodged and ducked the knife-sharp edges of the rusty scoop as it flipped end over end, just missing his head. I ran after them until he subdued the mule, then beat its hide as if it were a dusty carpet.

He butchered a pig that had been a playmate for Ellen and me, stringing it upside down from a bough as it squealed bloody murder. He made us stand back as he tugged the rope that pulled it upright. With his razor he slashed its throat as we watched the blood spurt and finally slow until it dripped on the ground. The bloody razor was the same he shaved himself with and kept honed sharp on the strop he used to whip me, three layers of leather kept hooked on the kitchen wall for easy access.

In one of his gentler moments our father crouched down at the base of a corn stalk and picked up five tiny rabbits, handing them up to me. Their eyes were not yet open. Mother helped me make a nest for them in a cardboard box in a corner of the kitchen. I fed them milk with an eyedropper. But the mewling babies annoyed both my mother and father until he took action, jumping up from the table and grabbing them. While Ellen and I followed him out begging and pleading for their lives, he took the mouse-sized creatures some distance down the hill and stomped them to death. The rabbits had their eyes open by then, and I imagined them seeing the great boot crashing down upon them.

Rabbits had offended but so did I, often. When Mother administered a spoonful of quinine for an accidental obscenity, she made me stand on a kitchen chair. I could not understand how a word could be dirty. Being in the wrong but not knowing why had become a familiar feeling. Imitating my father's profanity, I had said "damn." Much later I learned that a schoolmate had been punished for the same offense when he had mentioned Rotterdam and his ignorant father heard only the word "dam," enough of an obscenity to call for a whipping.

Even a whipping with my father's razor strop was not as bad as the quinine with its unforgettable taste and the disgrace that went with it. I rarely pleased. The days varied only by the degrees of shame brought out by carping criticism and unpredictable punishment. Angry voices fractured the air. Ellen and I never knew when the next tantrum or fight would erupt. We would leave off play to listen for clues as to what was wrong. There was no way we could help our unhappy parents.

We were still on the farm when I began first grade at the crossroads school at Pickett Prairie, two miles away. The teacher who ruled eight grades in rows of oaken desks facing her and the potbellied stove wasted no time in changing my life forever.

When I started to write, she plucked the pencil out of my left hand and jammed it into my right, clutching my fist tight around it. "It goes in your right hand," she said, and badgered me until I obediently pushed the pencil around, resisting the urge to gouge the paper. I could not figure out why the matter was so important to the teacher, and it took me some time to re-establish my control, using my right hand. At home I sneaked the pencil back into my left. Autonomy and growth were to be pursued in secret. The teacher's nagging had been about as effective as my mother's criticism of my father's drinking.

Dowell and Katherine Ray with
David and Ellen

Aunt Edris with baby David

Christmas at Grampa Ray's, with Father,
his new son and a bike

2.

THE FARM WAS rich with smelly textures and intriguing places to wander, but dangers lurked on every side—those Mother warned us about incessantly—spiders and snakes, a bull in a pasture, germs in the dirt. I was charged with the duty of protecting my little sister. I tugged Ellen away from an abandoned well and from snakes that slithered at our feet. I reached into her throat and pulled out a furry tarantula she had scooped up and popped into her mouth. I called out the warning "Hoison!" But my failure to have protected her from the rodline haunted me. She had flung great splashes of blood over the tall weeds, and it had all been my fault.

Ellen was not along when another near disaster occurred. I had gone on an errand down the hill to Grampa's barn for a bucket of milk and it was snowing heavily as I made my way back up the path, my boots sinking ever deeper as the flakes melted against my face. I strayed from the winding path and fell. But my father came looking for me. He lifted me out of the snow and carried me the rest of the way home. Mother bathed my hands in cold water as I wailed away. She was afraid I had frostbite but it had been a lucky rescue. I was not even blamed for the spilled milk or the lost bucket.

On a few other occasions my father managed to express some tenderness. One night I fell asleep on a stack of coats in a strange house where people were dancing and cavorting like the hillbillies in Thomas Hart Benton's paintings of Ozark musicians with their fiddles and banjos. I recall the midnight smell of cigarette smoke, loud jocular voices and my father lifting me into his arms. He carried me out into the night, and I shuddered in the chill as I looked up at the stars. We were in the deep declivity of a valley, walled in by hills. Was this mysterious house what my mother called a honky-tonk joint, or had they just gone to a party somewhere in the country? Rarely did he take her along. Most of his drinking expeditions, she made it clear, meant that she was left home alone.

On another night I walked at my father's side through Grampa's barnyard. We stumbled across a bulky darkness—a horse poisoned by mildewed hay. My father was carrying a lantern but its glow had not been bright enough to warn us. Now the glow was reflected in the horse's open eye. I don't know why we were heading toward that barn. Sometimes my father helped his father with milking the cows or feeding them or the horses. Now he kicked the horse for a sign of life, as if he could shock it back to its feet. Then, handing me the lantern, he knelt down and took out his knife, but then said, "We're too late. I could have got rid of that colic if we'd caught it in time." I was glad he did not cut the horse.

One day Ellen and I encountered a boy roaming the pasture where Grampa's cows grazed. He was looking for scrap metal, junk he could sell. There was lots of it scattered around—discarded wheels, pans, hubcaps, Mason jar lids, nails, and even a rusted-out abandoned Model A Ford by a roadside. The boy told us we could get rich, and I believed him. He was even prepared to sacrifice the cap gun he pulled from his pocket to show us. It did not work any more anyway. I too wanted to be rich, like my cousin George Jr., my lawyer uncle's son, who had an electric train and lived in a big house on a corner in Sapulpa.

After that encounter with the boy, Ellen and I scoured the hillsides, wandering as far as we dared, picking up every zinc jar lid and rusty nail that had found its way into a ditch or the cover of weeds. Sometimes we found a wheel. Once a month we waited by our roadside pile of scrap for the junkman's truck to chug along, stirring dust into a cloud. The coins and even an occasional crumpled dollar bill the dealer gave us seemed like a fortune. We had no idea that we were premature war profiteers, providing iron that would be shipped to Japan and melted into steel for battleships and bullets.

Our happiest moments on the farm were not on the hill but during our stays with Grampa and Ada, his mail-order wife from Arkansas. After my father's mother had died, Grampa had received a letter about a woman in Arkansas with two children who had lost her husband. Grampa wrote to her, enclosing a snapshot of a little girl in a white dress scattering corn to a flock of chickens. On the back was written in pencil, "This is my little girl with the chikens." Ada came to Oklahoma with her two children, Dub and Willa Mae, and became stepmother to Grampa's family. My father was one of ten children, including twins who had died shortly after birth.

Ellen and I had learned to hoard pleasures like a beachcomber's finds. One night I slept on Grampa's screened porch, with a pillow and a quilt rumpled over a pile of cantaloupes. The overpowering smell of the melons was like perfume. A breeze floated in from the fields. When I woke early in the morning I felt like my own man. As I peed against the back fence, I inhaled deep the scent of Gramma Ada's hollyhocks and morning glories. I felt as ambitious as my father, facing the day with his readiness to wrestle the earth into submission. But I began coughing, and an asthmatic wheezing came on.

I washed off the cantaloupe odor with Grandma Ada's strong lye soap. She made it by sprinkling ash into a greasy bubbling mix in her big black kettle set in the grass by the back door. She would stir circles with a long black pole, and later slash a tray of grey soap into blocks. But unlike the Lifebuoy our mother used, the soap smelled sour. Its grease clung to the skin and stayed on bath water as streaky scum. In the smokehouse I sat in a round galvanized tub under hams hanging from the rafters. I obsessively rubbed a chunk of that harsh soap against my belly, hoping to kill tiny red chiggers that had dug into my skin.

Dub sat watching me while he sneaked a cigarette. He had warned me that when three of the chiggers finished boring all the way through me I would die. I believed him, and lived in terror that the end was near. Each time I bathed, Dub would help look for the chiggers, then say with dramatic regret that they were still digging in. He swore he could see their little jaws at work even if I couldn't.

Others enjoyed going along with Dub's joke too much to enlighten me and relieve my panic. Nothing seemed to help. Dub poured kerosene out of a can into my palm and I rubbed it around my belly to no effect. The prayer Mother had taught us had never seemed important until this crisis. "If I should die before I wake, I pray the Lord my soul to take," was a standby request, in case my plea for God to kill the chiggers fell on deaf ears.

A plaster of Paris dog—the Victor records listening dog with tilted head and flopped-open ear, a black and white terrier—was used as a doorstop in the side bedroom, and in the morning, surprised to find myself still alive, I petted him and shared the good news, whispering into his chipped ear. But even after I found out that chiggers were not fatal, Dub tried other tricks to scare Ellen and me. He handed me a red pepper and told me to get Ellen to take a big bite. After she spewed it out and ran away crying, he told me I had most likely killed her.

Yet it was Dub who rescued me one night after I had fallen asleep on a front pew of the country church at prayer meeting. As the congregation sang the hymns, we children mumbled along, often mixing up the words we did not understand. The rafters seemed to tremble as we launched into "Onward, Christian Soldiers," "The Little Church in the Wild Wood," or "Farther Along," which told us to "live in the sunshine" and "cheer up, my brother" because "we'll understand it all by and by." There were also long spells of preaching from the pulpit.

We had come from Grampa's farm on the joggling truck, youngsters on scattered straw in back. Only after returning to the house did anyone notice that I was missing. Dub volunteered or was told to go back on his bike and look for me. Maybe I had fallen in a ditch, they thought. But I had slept on until just before Dub, with the help of the minister he had fetched, creaked open the double doors and called my name. The hooting of an owl had frightened me, but the darkness had been broken by enough moonlight through side windows for me to figure out where I was. I had little time for fear before Dub lifted me into his arms and carried me back up the church aisle and out into the night.

I bounced on the handlebars, happy on that wobbling bike in the moonlight. As Dub maneuvered the ruts, I chattered away that I had not been scared, though every shadow beside the road was a monster and we were in danger of falling into the ditch every time the bike's front wheel jiggled. But the teenager had masterly control, and his arms held me even as he avoided mud puddles and the roadside ditch.

Dub told me they had not noticed me missing until he was getting ready for bed. Since I slept in the same bed with him, he was the one who noticed—but maybe the only one.

Mother considered her family superior to my father's, who were farmers descended from seventeenth-century immigrants who had made their way from Scotland and Ireland over the Appalachians and eventually to Arkansas and Oklahoma. In their marital arguments Mother could always tar my father with the brush of his humble origins. Her family had moved to Oklahoma from Ohio, a state which seemed in some indefinable way a more fashionable background than Arkansas or Oklahoma. Ironically, decades later I found out that Mother had been right all along, since juries offering loss of life compensation in negligence cases are known to award smaller amounts when calculating the worth of a child's life in Oklahoma than in some other states. Okie babies are officially worth less in the actuarial world.

Mother never stopped singing the praises of her brother George, a lawyer and state senator. She held him and her other lawyer brother Charles up to my father as admirable examples of success. The wooden shack with the packed earthen floor provided by my sharecropper father was hardly to be compared with Uncle George's white mansion with its seventy-eight windows and a carport festooned with roses and honeysuckle. There was also a large garage in back with a pleasant apartment above, where Gramma Jennings lived. Mother regretted that she could not offer her mother such a home. Aunt Ruth paid weekly visits with lavish gifts to assert her importance in their mother's life.

On a visit to the farm Gramma Jennings was peeling potatoes when the paring knife slipped and almost severed her thumb. She dropped the knife on the dirt floor and called out to Mother. I saw that the bleeding thumb hung as if from a thread. Again, Mother had to improvise a bandage and seek medical help. At the hospital she made an important discovery, for she learned that there was a need for practical nurses. She had stumbled into her future profession.

Ellen would bear the disfigurement of her stubby middle finger from her visit to the red-brick hospital for a lifetime, but Uncle George got a settlement on her behalf from the oil company—several hundred dollars which were to gather interest for a college fund. Uncle George served as the trust fund's administrator as well. But when Ellen graduated from high school and needed the money for nursing school, there was little left. Uncle George explained that administrative fees had cut deeply into the account. He may not, after all, have been the paragon of competence that Mother often mentioned, for within the decade he had to check into a hospital for alcoholism and there were rumors that some of his wealth came from handling the oil properties of local Indians.

One Saturday in summer when Ellen and I were staying with Grampa and Ada, I rode with Grampa into town, where he was going to market his wagonload of melons. Though I loved the old man in overalls and straw hat, chewing tobacco tucked in his jaw, I felt self-conscious as we neared town. It was one thing to spend time with him in the country, to follow him about the fields and help with picking beans and cotton. But when we left the dirt section road, the iron-rimmed wagon wheels crunching up onto the concrete pavement that became a central street of the town, I would be seen sitting up on a wooden wagon with an old man my mother and her sisters called "a dirt farmer, nothing but a hillbilly." My grandfather had great dignity, but I knew people like Uncle George and George Jr. did not see it that way. I began fidgeting as we approached their street.

I looked at Grampa's twisted hand, paralyzed from an accident while he was cleaning his shotgun. I hesitated, then blurted out my lie, saying that I had promised my cousin that I would come by to see his electric train. Grampa yelled "Whoaa" to his mules and I jumped down quickly before he could repeat his offer to turn off the main street and drop me off in front of Uncle George's house. No need for that, I blurted out. I could walk right up the alley. Grampa promised to pick me up on his way back, and estimated the time.

My rich cousins—which is the way I thought of Uncle George's family—must not see me with this old man. I had seen George Jr.'s electric train with its elaborate toy town with bridges and tunnels and what seemed like miles of tracks, and I wanted nothing more than such a train. But that was my secret, to be shared only when I begged Aunt Ruth to buy me one.

For much of the day I crouched behind a bush in the alley, watching the back of my uncle's house. It was all there—the house my mother bragged about, with its fabled seventy-eight windows and rose-trellised carport and its rear garage with the overhead apartment in which Gramma Jennings lived. I was tempted to go up the outside stairs and visit her, but held back. I would no more have dared ring the bell of my uncle's white house or risk being seen by the maid than I would today saunter up to the White House door and suggest a chat with the president.

I returned to the main street and listened for the crunch of the iron-rimmed wheels on concrete. Grampa asked if I had had a good time. I described the glories of the toy train in detail.

When Grampa died and the family gathered at the farmhouse to mourn him, I suddenly realized that he had known all along about my lies. He had seen right through me, and had tried to make it easy for me to get away with it. He knew I was ashamed of him.

I wandered out into the frozen field where I had helped him hoe melons. I babbled to him under the gray skies, telling him in choking sobs how sorry I was. I clutched the barbed wire of the fence as if to keep from falling while I wept away my shame. And yet I remembered other lies I had told him to get out of work. He had gone on hoeing the rows of cantaloupes while I made up frequent excuses to go relieve myself by the creek, out of his sight. With his death he took on the omniscience of the departed. On the last day we had spent together in the muddy field, he had spoken of how we had been hoeing the melons because of the flood, and when I asked him if we would have to hoe again the next year he said, "That's for the Good Lord to decide." Then he added, "If I'm still here, and if it rains again like it has this summer."

There was no way I could make amends for my lies, not even with babbled promises that if he might somehow return I would proudly ride up high with him on his wagon and not give a damn who saw us together. I would never again be ashamed of him even if we rode right past Uncle George's house. The loss of that old man who had held me on his knees and let me fill his pipe and play with his watch chain as we sat, warmed by the potbelly stove in the farmhouse living room, was a heavy grief. And yet I was already an accomplished mourner, abandonment being a kind of death no matter how many times repeated.

Three decades later, I wandered around Grampa's farm and took the old path through the fields and scrub to the hilltop clearing. I found the ruins of our shack, scattered corner stones that had held the plank structure in place. Nearby was the caved-in cellar my father and his mule had dug out with an iron scoop. On a pile of junk and debris I found the bedsprings we had slept on in the light of gas flames. I picked up a basin, its bottom rusted out, and stood looking down into the collapsed cellar where Mason jars my mother had filled with fruit lay shattered in the ruins of a fallen and rotted shelf. I waded through tall weeds and brush and found the spot where Ellen had lost her finger. The rodlines had long since been removed, probably sold for scrap to Japan, to return as battleships. Each of the oil wells scattered about the farm had its own engine and independence now, pumping away like a giant metal grasshopper.

Except for the ravages of weather and time, the hilltop had been undisturbed since my parents had given up and moved into town. They had closed the gate behind them and weeds had grown up over the ruts leading out to the section road, the route downhill to the country store, clapboard church, and the one room school at Pickett Prairie.

At Grampa Ray's farm. David (pointing), with cousin Eulys (right) and Grandma Ada's son, W. T. ("Dub")

Grampa Ray's yard

Grampa Ray and family

3.

THE DECADE OF the thirties is justly known as one of grim poverty, hunger, deprivation of the dispossessed, dust storms, foreclosures, and the desperate westward hegira of people driven off their farms. These conditions were fully documented in literature, art, and photographs taken by the famous Farm Security Administration team that included Ben Shahn, Dorothea Lange, Russell Lee, and John Vachon.

But it did not happen! So we are told by a revisionist historian who claims that those sufferings were exaggerated by communist propagandists like John Steinbeck, who cranked out distortions in fiction that went down to succeeding generations as fact infused with the emotionality of myth. Such is the contention of Keith Windschuttle in his essay, "Steinbeck's Myth of the Okies." We should be gravely concerned, he writes, about *The Grapes of Wrath* "remaining a widely studied text in both high schools and universities," backed up by "the 1940 John Ford film that still enjoys healthy sales on videotape and frequent reruns."

Windschuttle's manipulations—this time with the pretense of correcting history—interest me, for they collide with my memories of the earth-floored shack, the rocky acreage, the diet of rabbits and squirrels and greens, and the disappointment of my father and his father when they could not get as much as a quarter a bushel for their produce.

What were men like them to do when they could not support their families? Some headed for California, as my father eventually did, believing that jobs awaited them, that the living would be easy—the same lures that led immigrants to believe the streets of America were paved with gold. But the historian refers to such events as fiction, and laments the gobbling up of the fraudulent myth by gullible millions. Steinbeck's fantasy, the historian laments, "became the principal story through which America defined the experience of the Great Depression." There were no grapes of wrath, just *The Grapes of Wrath*, pure propaganda.

It was news to me that Steinbeck exaggerated, even falsified. He had painted a picture of realities I remembered from my childhood, and I was grateful that the novelist had dramatized with compassion some of the horrors. But the historian reduces the famous exodus of the thirties to a minimalist token of wanderers who had plenty of auto courts to stay in along Highway 66.

How, Windschuttle demands, "did such a grossly false picture become so entrenched in the popular imagination?" According to his version, even the Oklahoma dust storms that I recall did not happen, though they went on for hours and choked us as we stuffed clothes and papers under doors and in cracks, and Grampa's plaster dog grew a coat of fur within an hour. I am glad to be informed that these scenes were imaginary and that bankers—decent fellows all—did not foreclose on farms, and that the topsoil of those farms did not blow away. I would be comforted to learn that our hunger pangs were imaginary and that vivid scenes witnessed of my parents trying to hold their little family together were false, and that my father's hopes for a better life were not illusory.

On Sunday mornings on the farm my father trimmed hair in the front yard for men of the family, using skills that would provide a new trade. Though Mother's view was that he took up barbering after he "failed at farming," a farmer could hardly be blamed, for all the conditions were against him. All the grapes were of wrath, and it would take a war economy and bold New Deal subsidies to assure that a man could "succeed at farming."

All he needed was a job in town, he was certain, and before long he found an opportunity to replace a retiring—or deceased—barber in the small town of Mounds. The narrow-fronted shop was on the main street.

Surely there would be a flood of customers as soon as he put out word that he had set up in business.

For our home he rented half of a brown-shingled duplex, with luxuries only dreamed of on the farm—hardwood floors, running water, and an indoor toilet. Ellen and I watched and listened as our parents discussed their plans. They were fired with enthusiasm for a fresh start, a new business, a new home.

Our arrival in town got off to an inauspicious start. My father borrowed Grampa's truck and Uncle Norman came along to help with the moving. No sooner had they backed the truck up against the porch steps of the duplex than Mother took one look inside the front door and called a halt to the unloading. Our half of the duplex was musty and littered with debris. It smelled of rats. She swept out the room, then got down on her knees to scrub the floors. She had left even the earthen-floor shack spotless, its packed black dirt glistening as if waxed. It was a rule with her, she said, that no one was going to have an excuse to think we were white trash. Moving in, moving out—it was all the same challenge. Uncle Norman and my father had to wait for her to finish before they could move the furniture in.

The barbershop was a narrow high-ceilinged room facing the main street. Both walls were lined with mirrors reflecting shelves with a few bottles of hair tonic and shampoo. The throne of a barber chair, upholstered in red leather with white porcelain arms, stood before the large front window. The room smelled of hair oil and talcum. Its wooden floors were soft and splintery and at places patched over with nailed down lids of tin cans. On one wall, over chairs for waiting customers, hung a framed reproduction of *Custer's Last Stand*. The yellow-haired general was down on one knee with his six-shooter smoking, still popping away at the Indians who had him and his blue-coated cavalry surrounded, many of his men lying around already scalped.

The Depression was getting worse. Customers who came in for haircuts or shaves or just to sit and gossip and thumb magazines spoke of the New Deal with grumpy skepticism.

"We need us a good war to get us out of this here mess," was a common sentiment.

Dad was careful what he said around customers, not taking sides in their debates. "Let 'em talk," he would tell me later, "I've heard it all."

Even before the apron was off the customer's neck and hair shaken off, even before he had managed to pull coins out of his pocket to pay, I was sweeping the floor. Dad had to slow me down. "Just wait up there a minute," he would say, holding up his hand. More than once, when a customer left, he said, "That old geezer won't be back, mark my words."

Dad sighed and dropped the mask of geniality when the shop had no customers. We could have been alone in a vast emptiness rather than the narrow little storefront with its stamped tin ceiling. More than one business had gone broke there.

"Maybe he'll come back," I said, to cheer him. I longed to help. He sat in the throne chair, gazing out the window. I sat looking through magazines like a customer, but often looked up to check my father's face. Now and then I jumped down and looked out the front window, all business. When he acknowledged my presence, his hand touching my hair, I felt a foot taller.

Dad was done in by a price war. The rival barber in the town—inspired by the techniques Standard Oil was using to "drive the little guys out of business" by lowering prices to such absurd giveaways that independent gas stations could not long hold out—started offering shaves for a dime and haircuts for a nickel, a contemptuous inversion of the usual prices. How could a loner like my dad compete with that? Dad did not, like the rival barber, have friends to count on. Many men paused on the sidewalk and looked in, but few entered. My simple arithmetic tells me that my father would have had to give twenty haircuts or ten shaves to make a dollar.

In the shop I looked for opportunities to help, sitting with waiting customers, swinging my legs that did not reach the floor, eager for a chance to run forward with a broom. And I was always available for errands—a trip to the corner service station to bring back ice-cold bottles of soda pop fetched out of a deep metal case, or running back to the duplex to tell Mother that Dad was too busy to make it back home for lunch, one of the many lies he put me up to. On those occasions I would return to the shop with a paper sack with sandwiches—lunch-meat on white bread, Wonder or Rainbow—and always Dad's extra onion, which he ate like an apple, a preference Mother found obscene.

I too preferred the sandwiches at the barbershop to the hot lunches at home. At either place, Dad seldom missed his favorite radio program—*Bob Wills and His Texas Playboys*—which was broadcast at high noon. But the program offended Mother, and they always argued about it. That argument over hillbilly music often turned into a kitchen sink fight about everything else too. Mother would turn to Ellen and me and say she should not be surprised at our father's behavior. She should have known better than to have married him. Everybody had warned her not to, including his own father. "That old dirt farmer," she would say in sympathy, adding the burden of Grampa's disappointment to her own.

Ellen and I could never decide which side we were on. We could not see why she had to get so mad about hillbilly music, but we agreed he was mean to hit her, or us. And yet it left us feeling just as bad when he stormed out rather than throwing a tantrum.

To Mother the music was conclusive evidence that Dad came from a class far below her own. "It's hillbilly music," she declared.

"I can't help it," Dad would say, "and I don't want you to turn it off, you hear?"

Turning the dial down and then off might as well have been an invitation for him to slap her.

"You see there," she turned to her witnesses. "Did you see what your father did to me?" Sometimes she had bruises to show for days.

"Do you want another one?" he would say, but then in disgust push back his chair and stride out, slamming the door behind him. Mother burst into tears and wiped her eyes with a tea towel.

"We should go and live with Aunt Peg," she would say. At other times it was, "I'm going to send you children to Colorado. Your Aunt Ruth is out there and she says she'd love to have you live with her."

I knew Aunt Ruth had gone to Colorado on vacation, a repeat of the previous summer, when she had brought us back some red rock samples, but she was no more going to get a house in Colorado than she could bring Uncle Mac back from the dead. We had loved staying with Aunt Ruth when Uncle Mac was alive, for he was kind to us. He would come home with candy hidden in the fold of his sweater and the brim of his hat, laughing as we stood on his shoes to reach up to grab at the candy. I would pull his arm to bring him down to our level, and did not realize that he was cooperating. After his death in a skid row hotel fire, we occasionally spent a night or two with Aunt Ruth in what she called her bachelor girl apartment in Tulsa.

For one who exerted such power over the lives of others, Aunt Ruth was an amazingly small, doll-like woman. She bragged that her size three shoes had to be purchased off mannequins, since such tiny feet as hers were rare. She was proud of her ability to charm and tease salesmen to part with show window items meant only for display. She told us she was famous in shoe stores all across the state for those unique tiny feet. "Butter 'em up," she laughed about her technique in getting men to please her with gifts, after she coaxed them into shopping with her.

She always came bearing gifts, and never let you forget it. A game of jacks for Ellen or a yo-yo might as well have been made of gold. Taking credit for clothing us, she reminded our parents of their inadequacies.

"What happened to that red pinafore I gave Ellen?" she asked my mother.

"It wore out," Mother said. "And Ellen grew out of it. I threw it out, or maybe I gave it to the Salvation Army, I don't remember."

Ruth was furious. A gift of hers could never have worn out or simply not been wanted. The obligation was to take it and keep it for eternity and thank her forever. Anything else was an unforgivable betrayal.

Bitterness about gifts often dated back to a funeral or a wedding. I once asked Mother why their oldest sister Peg and Aunt Ruth would have nothing to do with each other, and if I had not known Aunt Ruth, I would never have believed the reason.

On her wedding day Aunt Ruth discovered, shortly before the ceremony, that she had a run in her white stockings, so she told her older sister to run down to the drugstore and buy her a new pair and put it on her, Ruth's, charge account. Aunt Peg undertook the errand and returned with the pair of white stockings, but said she had paid for them herself as an extra wedding gift. Aunt Ruth never forgave her. She was the one who paid. She was the one who controlled. She was the one who decided how things should be done. She was the one who never quit bragging and complaining that she paid.

Some who tangled with her — including at least two of her brothers and two of her sisters — banned Ruth from their homes for life. They had many tales of arguments she had provoked. She reminded everyone that though Gramma lived in the apartment provided by Uncle George their mother was nevertheless sorely neglected and would have died of grief if she, Ruth, had not shown up once a week to take her mother out for a meal, and sometimes to stay overnight with her. Gramma sometimes appeared with blue curly hair after a trip to the beauty parlor. The sight always surprised Ellen and me. Gramma looked uncomfortable, as if a nest of Christmas tinsel had been fitted upon her head.

Ruth also reminded everyone that she alone remembered to put flowers on their father's grave every Memorial Day. She alone had loved the departed, and no one knew how much. Not only that, they were the most expensive flowers she could find. I knew this claim to be true, for I had once accompanied Mother and Aunt Ruth to their father's grave site. When Aunt Ruth discovered that Mother had brought along more impressive flowers than she had, she made a second trip back to the florist's to exchange her offering for a pot of taller lilies.

At weddings, my plucky and diminutive aunt felt no obligation to hold her peace when the minister invited the gathering to offer reasons why this man and this woman should not be joined together. Ruth might say it only in loud whispers, but she could always come up with something. Whatever the occasion, she made sure she was the center of it, and could not understand that she was not. As for her solemn predictions of doom for a marriage, they usually came true. Her curses were lucky, her talent to blight and disrupt boundless. Marriages did not have much of a chance in our family. My father's side had better luck, but not much.

Aunt Ruth stood just an inch short of five feet, though the high heels on those tiny shoes often brought her up to the five-foot mark. Despite that stature, she always seemed to be looking down at everyone, and her lips were often pressed prim and firm in disapproval of crimes and character defects. She wore rouge, and her powdered cheeks had the soft fuzzy texture of a pink powder puff. Her frequent reminders that she had been a beauty queen in high school and had stood on a float in the graduation parade seemed to provoke new makeup sessions, as if to show us how she had looked years before.

She deplored the way her younger sister neglected herself, seldom wearing any makeup at all. Ruth would force her own mascara and rouge on Mother. "There, that's better, isn't it? You look a thousand times lovelier now." Mother looked doubtful, but she seldom disobeyed her domineering sister. Ruth's advice for her to leave my father hung over the marriage like storm clouds. She nagged Mother about what a heel she had married, and how she should "just up and take the children and leave. Why should you put up with his drunkenness and abuse?" He did not provide properly for her and never treated her right. My father was as bad as her husband had been, she said, and look what had happened to him. She had wisely made Uncle Mac leave because of his drinking, and when he died in the skid row hotel fire, his hellish fate was a final confirmation of his villainy. "That's what I get for marrying a Catholic," she observed, "just like Peg."

As my ability to make judgments developed I began wondering why Mother put up with Aunt Ruth's meddling rather than banish the troublemaker as others did. Mother knew all about her sister's reputation, but she did not protest a visit when we lived in the shack on the hill, even though Ruth would predictably be critical of the conditions she would find.

Somehow they would manage, Ruth insisted. She would not mind the humble accommodations, primitive though they were. She would be happy to sleep in a tent. Even that cellar my father had dug with the mule and the scoop would do just fine. She would not mind bringing a bedroll and sleeping in the cool, damp cellar under the shelves of

Mason jars filled with green beans, tomatoes, peaches, and the rest of Mother's canned goods. Through the fog of years I can hear Aunt Ruth voicing her demands quite effectively by protesting that she had none. Martyrdom ran in the family, and she was the champion.

She not only needled and provoked—she openly picked fights with my father.

"If you ever come and visit me," she said as she watched him sitting at the rickety table sipping his coffee, "you won't be allowed to slurp like that."

"I ain't considerin' a visit," my father said.

"Dowell!" My mother overlooked her sister's aggression, but picked on Dad's grammar. Both sisters nagged at him about saying "ain't" and about his profanity. Even "damn" was too much for them. One "Goddamn" could ruin a day.

Aunt Ruth took on my father as a major rival for control. One of the most frightening scenes I recall from the farm was the tug-of-war they fought over a rifle. Her virulence about the man was so intense that I long ago concluded that she must have been fervidly in love with him.

The fight over the rifle climaxed one of Aunt Ruth's visits on the hill. She claimed my father had borrowed the .22 from her. He claimed that it had long been his hunting rifle. The dispute led to a fight that started on the porch. They both grabbed at the rifle, trying to pull it from each other. Soon they were standing in the clearing in front of the shack. Mother was as terrified as Ellen and I were. Dad and Aunt Ruth twisted at the rifle and kicked at each other's shins. Aunt Ruth was much shorter than Dad, but that didn't keep her from a desperate fight, and she at last made him let go of the gun by biting at his hands.

I always assumed that my father had the superior claim to that rifle Aunt Ruth wrested from his clutch, but many years later, after Aunt Ruth's death, I saw evidence that her claim might have been valid. The family had gone directly from the cemetery to my aunt's lockbox in the bank, dividing coin collections and stock certificates and cursing Aunt Ruth's stepdaughter for having got there and almost cleaned it out first. Where were her fabulous jewels and her collection of silver dollars?

Having married a man she was proud of having "buttered up," my aunt had been a wealthy widow in her later life, leaving Mother a surprisingly generous legacy.

The mourners headed for her house, and within minutes were carrying out to their cars furniture, mirrors, dishes, coffee pots, and even the potty chair Aunt Ruth had required in her last years. Exhausted by the display of greed that reminded me of a similar death watch and property grab in *Zorba the Greek*, I plopped down on the living room sofa, prepared to move when they got round to carrying it out. Assorted family pictures still hung on the walls, and Aunt Ruth's photograph album offered a distraction. I picked it up and opened it on my knees just as the coffee table disappeared from under it.

There were many snapshots of Aunt Ruth as a teenager. Unlike my mother, who had usually worn dresses nearly indistinguishable from flour sacks, Ruth was almost always dressed up, and often stood beside one of her many boyfriends before a car or an impressive boulder. There was a picture of her in her graduation queen outfit, complete with crown and regal gown, a wand in her hand. She looked like a stand-up Shirley Temple doll as she rode a flower-decked float through Sapulpa's Main Street. I recognized the storefronts.

I turned the wide black pages with their double rows of yellowed snapshots and was startled to see a series showing, according to the captions, the Young Women's Rifle Club. Aunt Ruth and several other girls dressed like her in white short skirts and Balkan-style blouses were in various postures of rifle practice. The gun Aunt Ruth held looked very much like the one she had fought my father for. Maybe I had solved the mystery of the rifle and the furious struggle on the hilltop. At the same time I wondered if there was more to the story.

"Don't you want anything?" my sister asked me as she passed in front of me with a box of dishes.

"I don't think so," I said. But then, looking about the room, I made a choice. "I'd like to have the footstool," I said. "Do you remember it?"

"Which footstool?"

"That one," I said, "there in the corner."

"What's so special about it?"

"It's the one that was in her apartment in Tulsa."

"You mean when we slept on the floor," Ellen said.

"Right."

"Funny you remember it."

"I can almost smell those oranges and taste the chocolate, those Hershey's kisses. I think we were happy."

"Maybe, for a while," Ellen agreed.

The footstool was square, about a foot high, with maple legs and a needlepoint cover. My sister and her husband had already carried out a large upholstered chair and wedged it in the trunk of their Cadillac, tying it on with binder twine. The chair and footstool had survived Aunt Ruth's move from Tulsa to live in a small town with her second husband, an insurance broker who looked and spoke like Will Rogers. Uncle Harold frequently stretched his neck out of his collar, a show of discomfort that was possibly his self-reminder not to talk back to Ruth.

All through their marriage, Harold bought Ruth anything she wanted—anything to keep her happy was his policy. He seemed happy with the arrangement, and she was grateful that he had rescued her from a tedious office job in Tulsa pasting up layout pages for a church newsletter. It was a lucky day, she often said, when Harold strolled into that office by mistake, just looking for a restroom. To Aunt Ruth he was a bonanza—someone to lead around on shopping expeditions. The sexy charm of that runty, spindle-legged woman who chattered endlessly about her tiny feet and how she kept her husband happy only now and then provoked a dubious glance from Uncle Harold, as if he never ceased to be amazed by the wonders of a woman who could collect so many shoes.

In Tulsa, Ellen and I had sometimes visited Aunt Ruth in her skyscraper office. Over the front entrance with its offer of both swinging and revolving doors was a great sculptured figure of Atlas, crouched and straining with the near-unbearable weight of a globe on his back.

Father visits at Aunt Edris's

4.

NOT FAR FROM the duplex my dad found for our life in Mounds, a fat woman with several children had set up housekeeping in an abandoned warehouse by the railroad embankment. She reminded me of the Old Woman Who Lived in a Shoe with so many children she didn't know what to do. Those kids had toys scattered about in the weeds, some even abandoned in the ditch, Disney pull toys—long-eared Pluto the hound and big-eared Mickey Mouse and quacking Donald Duck. Though that wealth of toys caught my envious eye, Mother saw an opportunity to help the needy. With our new home in Mounds, she had worked at regaining the respectability she had nearly lost by being a sharecropper's wife. She could hold her head high again, she said, often noting that there were plenty who were worse off than we were.

She cooked up a tasty stew with a soup bone. She rationed servings for Ellen and me so she could take what seemed to us most of the meal to that poor family. She proudly carried the pot through our backyard as Ellen and I watched from the kitchen window.

> And I smile to see my mother still,
> cradling the steaming soup, straight down
> the hill, to the wretched poor who huddled there
> while we at home, brother, sister, sucked the bloody air.

I had taken close notice of that fatherless family, living in the warehouse of corrugated tin. I glimpsed through the open sliding door the concrete floor and many items of furniture cozily placed. The fat mother often sat in the sunlight in a large easy chair, fanning the flies from her face.

But I did not see the needy family as Mother did. I made plans to steal my favorites of their toys: a small round water trough and pump like those on ranches, and a blue Shirley Temple dish their dog ate out of. With a vicious bark, his rope allowing him to guard the bowl quite successfully, the shaggy black chow seemed to read my thoughts. It was an insult to give that blue bowl to a dog, and I waited until he went to sleep.

Though I succeeded in stealing both the toy pump and the blue Shirley Temple dish, Mother quickly discovered my crime. The unoccupied half of the duplex had been left unlocked and for some time my friend Harley, the sheriff's son, and I had been using it as a hideout. I kept the stolen items tucked up inside the fireplace. Mother caught us at play, just as I was pissing in the trough to provide for the little pump. She banished Harley and inflicted heavy doses of shame on me.

She ordered me along on an expedition to the warehouse by the tracks. I had to return the pump and trough and the blue bowl as well. She stood by while I apologized to the fat woman and her gloating children. Then, when Mother found out the bowl had been used for the dog, she insisted that I apologize to the dog as well. I knelt down and said I was sorry. The chow licked my face and began to slurp water, not stopping until he was licking Shirley Temple's face and curls in the bottom of the bowl.

At least my contrition turned a snarling dog into a friendly one, but I did not walk that way again. When I wanted to climb the railway embankment and hike along the gravel, I took a different way, pulling Ellen up the steep slope. At other times Harley walked the tracks with me, balancing on one rail while I took baby steps like a tightrope walker on the other. Sometimes we heard a distant train, dropped to our knees and placed a penny on the rail, then waited to retrieve it as a thin copper coin not even the friendliest store clerk would accept.

Harley and I were fascinated by hoboes we encountered. We watched for them to jump off boxcars and lollop down a slope with their worldly possessions wrapped in a bedroll. They would sleep in the woods for a time, then move on when they felt like it or when the sheriff urged them.

The town offered many diversions. On summer evenings, men played "donkey baseball," riding donkeys around as they played the game. On Saturday nights movies were projected on the brick back wall of the grocery store. Families brought blankets and quilts and spread them on the ground. Shirley Temple and Hoot Gibson movies were fine, but my favorite film concerned convicts planning an escape. Sirens wailed as searchlights fanned out in search of them. Bloodhounds and guards chased them stumbling through the woods. Machine guns rattled away from guard towers. A corridor of dusty, wavering light from the projector collided with the searchlights seeking the convicts, seeming to scan us as well. Not for a moment was there any doubt where my sympathies lay. I would have loved to help the prisoners dig their tunnel, or flee with them through the wilderness.

One night we watched a version of *Huckleberry Finn*, whose friendship with Tom Sawyer reminded me of Harley and myself. Mother objected indignantly to a silhouette shot of Huck as he stood on a bluff and like a *mannikin pis* made his contribution of a thin arcing stream fall, as from a garden hose, to the river below.

Anything below the waist was taboo with Mother. She watched our bodies with intent suspicion. If she noticed the slightest irritation or heat rash on me as she bathed me with a washcloth, she would ask if I had been doing something I shouldn't. I had no idea what she meant, but her taboo against my playing with or even touching myself kept me wondering. It was more than just a concern for cleanliness. But Harley and I could at least imitate Huck's playful piss as we walked the rails beyond town. We could pee off a bridge in a contest. Which of us could loft the stream higher and farther before it dropped to the creek below?

On May Day the schoolyard on the hill was turned into a carnival, with a maypole dance right out of a Goya painting. I stood clanging the triangle in the second-grade rhythm band, proud as a prodigy. There were fireworks displays on the Fourth of July—a rich man opened the tall iron gates of his estate for the festivities. Ellen and I sat on a bench with Mother, watching the spectacular Roman candles and bright blue and red and yellow sprays of rockets. Mother suddenly sprang to her feet, slapping at her felt hat which was smoking from falling cinders.

Harley and I sometimes visited an old lady who had a talking parrot on her screened-in porch. Age had turned the widow into a hunchback crone. She often invited us in, offered cookies, then informed us with a mischievous smile that we could use her toilet if we wanted. The bathroom off the kitchen was a green jungle of potted plants, hanging and shelved, as if in a greenhouse. The toilet was a shining cylinder that looked far down to a small mirroring pool below. As she saw us off from her porch, she apologized for the weeds in her yard, which she called a jungle, but we ignored her hints that we might help with the problem.

After school and on weekends Harley and I prowled the town's outskirts, sneaking up like Indian scouts on the covered wagon of a grizzle-bearded tinker who was conducting his business in a vacant lot. Far from being frightened, he was welcoming, having spotted us with uncanny peripheral vision. He asked what we wanted to be when we grew up.

But he had a better idea than either of us could come up with. "Get yerself a wagon and a petrified man," he said, then invited us to climb up. He lifted canvas flaps back from his doorway and demonstrated in the shadows what appeared to be a man made of stone.

"When I take him out to the County Fair or a carnival," he said, "I charge a dime for people to see him. Them dimes add up." On a later visit he suggested we take a closer look at his petrified man, and told us never to tell his secret—that it was made out of plaster of Paris. "It ain't likely you'll find yerself a petrified man," he said, "but you can sure make yerself one."

We decided it was good advice. While Harley and I debated the possibility of becoming partners and running away from the second grade and getting ourselves a petrified man, the old loner hitched up his donkey, kicked his embers into the dust, and left town. We arrived one Saturday morning to find only flattened weeds and the grey ashes of his camp fire. We tried tracking the ruts of his wagon wheels, but gave up when they led onto the main highway, where the mud trail thinned to nothing. We were hurt that the old man had not told us goodbye.

Harley sometimes led me into his father's office where a gun rack held several rifles. If the sheriff was not sitting behind the desk with his boots up, Harley would sneak down one of the guns, pull its hammer back, and blow the barrel clean. We took turns aiming guns in every direction, including at each other, and were lucky we did not blow our brains out.

Through a side door was a concrete corridor running past three or four small jail cells. One of them was usually occupied by a dejected drunk or a hobo who had been caught panhandling or wandering around town. The bunks with bare webbed metal springs had no mattresses, the yellow-stained toilets no lids, and the only food was bread and water. The sheriff had explained that the meager meal was meant not only to teach jailbirds a lesson but to keep them from thinking they could stick around for free room and board. If a hobo looked too hungry to survive such torments, the sheriff would take him to the edge of town or to the railroad tracks and see that he boarded a boxcar.

Harley assumed he would be sheriff himself when he grew up. "Nope," he said, "you don't get no bacon and eggs in jail." That sort of talk made me wonder if Dad had been fed only bread and water all those times Mother said he had been in jail.

"It'll do a lot of good for them tramp jailbirds," Harley said, trying to match his father's tone of stentorian authority. "Maybe they'll think twice before they come around here." He scorned the alcoholics his father made a habit of arresting.

When we came across bottles along paths around the town dump, Harley suggested we fill them with urine and place them where a drunk would find them and mistake them for whiskey. We filled up several bottles and recapped them, placing them near the railroad tracks and along paths. We went back and forth on the question of whether a hobo could tell the difference between the taste of our piss and his favorite whiskey. Now and then one of the bottles we had left would turn up intact but emptied, proof that we had fooled one of the hobos.

One morning we met a disgruntled hobo who had inspected one of our bottles rather than drinking it. Somehow he connected this odd discovery with the two boys coming down the path.

"Get out of here, you brat bastards!" he yelled and swung at us, though we were well out of range. After that, we had no heart for such tricks.

Harley's father referred to us as his deputies. He told us his secret for catching bootleggers—he noticed when a car driving through town was sunk too low on its rear axle. It was amazing how many crates and boxes of liquor could be extracted from a car trunk. The sheriff made piles of the bottles and broke them with a hammer in public ceremony. But I knew from Harley that his father kept a good supply for himself and his friends.

My father was getting restless. He was talking of moving on, maybe to Tulsa. There would be more people, more customers, he was sure. Once again Uncle Norman showed up with Grampa's truck to move the furniture. It was late in the evening, a sneak departure. I worried about Harley. If the landlord fetched the sheriff, as Dad feared, because we were running out on the rent, Harley might have to decide whose side he was on. He might show up with his father like a deputy, so I kept a watch out for him while Dad and Uncle Norman loaded the truck. They had already loaded the barber chair, but rearranged things so that it stood facing backwards, set up high. I wanted to sit up in it so I could act as a lookout.

It was nearly midnight and had begun raining, but Mother delayed departure for she was once again scrubbing the floors. She had already washed windows and tidied up the yard, hoping to please the next tenants. She had generously given a few items to the fat lady down by the railroad track. No matter how poor we were, she said, we could always help others who were worse off.

About midnight we pulled out of the yard. Uncle Norman did not turn on the headlights until we got out of town. Rain streamed down, and Mother wailed that the furniture in back was getting soaked. I tried

to comfort her, though the gearshift knob joggled against my knees
every time Uncle Norman shifted gears. The truck slipped around in
mud that had sloshed over the highway. Windshield wipers flailed away.
I cast harried looks back through the rear window to see if the sheriff and
his son were chasing us. I expected bullets to crash through the glass at
any moment.

I never saw Harley after that night. In movies we called picture
shows, best friends always went searching for each other, even if it was
only to have a gunfight when they met up again. But I did not know
which one of us was Billy the Kid and which was the sheriff.

Dad made a deal to work in a shop near the Farmers' Market in Tulsa.
"It won't be my own shop," he told us, "but I have my own chair and
they got a good trade goin'. That old boy I'll be working for seems like a
pretty nice fella and they ain't so hard up around here that they got to
war with one another and drive a man out of business."

Mother was already disputing his claim to ownership of the chair,
reminding him that he had purchased it with a loan Uncle George had
arranged, using Ellen's settlement from the oil company. According to
her, he should already have paid back that hundred dollars.

Dad was ever hopeful, and enjoyed stopping by his favorite diner, the
one he had taken me to when we took our produce in from the farm
near Sapulpa. In those earlier visits he had set me up on the counter saying I was his boy. The friendly blonde waitress would chat with Dad
while he worked his gums with a toothpick. Sometimes she handed me
a penny from the cash register to use in the vending machine that poured
out a handful of peanuts with papery red skins, fragile as beetle wings.

Chanking one peanut at a time while the voices happily flirted on, I
would have gladly stayed for the afternoon, or even bedded down in a
booth the way we had at the market stall whenever we arrived before
daylight. After breakfast in the diner he had carried me piggyback to the
vast tin-roofed market, putting me down in our wooden stall. I was
always glad to see that nobody had stolen our produce. My job was to

plug a watermelon and pluck out a juicy red-tipped chunk, offering it up for a free taste. A slurp of approval meant triumph for my salesmanship.

Now we were back at that same diner, and the same blonde waitress lingered at the cash register, subsidizing my peanuts, penny by penny, as I learned to be patient, waiting for Dad.

From the two-storied yellow tenement on North Lewis Street where we had an upstairs apartment, we did not have far to go to school. The brick building was directly across the street, and the crossing for students was in front of our house. I had a new ambition—to be a school crossing guard wearing a webbed halter and holding up a stop sign like a ping-pong paddle.

When our parents argued, Ellen and I were afraid Dad might fulfill his threats to leave. Mother dared him to go right ahead. It would have been hard to sort out what we were most afraid of, his hitting her or her yelling at him or one of them leaving and not coming back. She too sometimes made the same threat.

"You kids better not be naughty or I may not come back," was one of her favorite lines, even when she was only off on an errand to the grocery store. Her technique worked, for we sat in the yard or on the driveway as if chained. We dared not get dirty, run around, or make noise. Naughty was such an all-encompassing word that complete paralysis was the only way to avoid one offense or another.

The chance she would make good her threat seemed reasonable enough to fuel our whispered speculations. She had, after all, left us plenty of times with other relatives, and we never knew for sure if she would come back to get us, nor had we been sure when we were left somewhere if our father would return, whether it was from the harvest fields or such an expedition as Mother accused him of, something involving drinking and other women like that blonde in the diner, or something involving a stickup or a hijacking.

On a hot summer afternoon in Tulsa I set out on my regular mission across vacant lots, kicking dust on the sandy path. With an empty milk bottle, I headed to the drug store for a quart of root beer from the soda fountain.

The interior was cool and shadowed, the aisles between rows of shelves cluttered. With hardly a word, the pharmacist manning his soda fountain took the bottle from me, placed it under a tap and pulled a porcelain-handled lever. The sweet brown root beer poured down until it foamed over. He clapped on a cardboard lid and handed the bottle down, giving it a wipe. I settled the bottle carefully in my arm, for I had dropped and broken one just like it on an earlier trip.

The man looked worried as he handed me a note. "Give this to your mother," he said.

All the way back, dragging my feet, I resisted the temptation to unfold the note and read it. I sensed the inevitable.

When I handed Mother the note she looked at it and broke into sobs. She managed to read the short message aloud: "I have got a ride West on a watermelon truck and won't be back this time."

I was assailed by a storm of new considerations. If she had meant what she had often said—that we would be better off without my dad—why would she be taking it so hard, this announcement of his sudden departure? I stood wishing I could do something to make her stop crying. She wept as if she had never called him names or dared him to get out.

They were strange, these grownups, they never knew what they wanted.

5.

IN THAT FIRST leg of his move westwards, Dad only got as far as Blackwell, Oklahoma, where he took a job in a smelter. Later he went on to Hutchinson, Kansas. Then, after the war, on to the promised land of California. Ellen and I got updates on him secondhand, by hearsay, passed on by my father's sisters Alice or Edris or Beatrice. Mother was proud that my father's own family sympathized with her and saw her as the wronged woman she was. She would try to keep up contact with them, even if my father was only to be spoken of as a black sheep, a deserter, a drunken womanizing heel. On more than one occasion I heard him called a skunk, which made no sense at all to me. He had always smelled good, of barbershop lotions and tobacco.

Mother's bitterness was so unyielding that I wondered how she could have been talked into teaming up with him in the first place. They had rarely worked together, except for hard labors on the farm, had more often struggled against each other. Reports of their battles would never die, some of them vivid tableaux forever frozen in my mind. There was enough bitterness for a lifetime and enough left over to hand down to future generations.

My father's presence was magnified by his absence. He was as big as Gulliver, my view distorted by my helplessness. When he placed me across his knees and whipped me with his hand I seemed no larger than a floppy doll. A numbness later set in. Something had died in me. The generations could have been Russian dolls, one inside another inside another. Even when I had no evidence of what my parents must have gone through in childhood, histories they preferred to keep secret, I knew that they too were dead dolls, hollowed out. Something in them— and something in me—had been so paralyzed that we could not grow beyond childhood.

Mother kept a photograph of her sister Dorothy, who had died at age ten. Dorothy was laid out in a white gown and covered with long-stemmed lilies. Like her, even the living in our family seemed somehow locked in childhood, frozen in the earth or inside ourselves.

Perhaps neither of my parents had anything left over from their struggles. In a poem called "Genitori," I imagined them freed of the fear and perplexity they had provoked, converting them into beneficent figures. The desire to rescue them was unquenchable.

> As a Buddhist tried for months
> to visualize a gold Bodhisattva on the air,
> I benignly conjure up this couple,
> his arms about her, free of trouble.
> They're young and smiling, apple clean,
> whose embraces gave my shining hair,
> and she is both his piano and his cello,
> which are played with fingers, light
> arpeggios now and then, rough gutsy
> rubbing on the belly when it's night . . .
> In the decades later they still obsess us
> so that daily we forgive them and daily
> don't, and in a field may find them still,
> blue in paired flowers, their love transposed
> and borne beyond a billion rocks, and time . . .

Such craving made things worse for my own healing, for I needed to be free of them. It is hard to get the message that there is no way to recover what was not there. My meditations were usually broken by memories of betrayal. The work of trying to reshape is as futile as a caterpillar's trips around the lip of a jar, locked on its own trail. When we finally forgive, it may be only after we have exhausted all other options.

My father came back to Tulsa a time or two, disappearing into the apartment house for a talk with Mother. Ellen and I sat on the sidewalk in a pretense of play, alert to the voices rising and falling from the upstairs apartment. They had both made their positions clear. She would take him back if he would change his ways. He would return if and when he damn well pleased, maybe never. We now and then heard the term "for the sake of the children." She used the word "children" and he referred to us as "kids."

The friend who had driven him waited at the curb, drumming his fingers on the steering wheel, like the driver of a getaway car. When my father came out of the yellow building my mother glared at him from the upstairs porch, her arms crossed over her chest in disgust with both of these men, as if they had indeed robbed a bank. My father wore the black bow tie he had always worn in his barbershop. He carried his fedora. His shoes shone, black and glistening, as he stood above us and put the hat on.

He bent down and offered me a dime. "You take care of your Mother and your sister, d'ya hear?" he said. "And both of ya do what your Mother tells ya, d'ya hear?" He reached in his pocket and got another coin out for Ellen. She was more delighted with hers than I was with mine.

"Don't spend it all in one place," he advised, standing up. We did not get up as he walked on to the car. I already knew it was a crime to show much interest in him. Mother was watching.

After the black coupe disappeared, dipping through the tunnel under the railroad tracks, I fingered the dime and considered not spending it. But I soon led Ellen to the little store next door. We pondered our choices in the dusty glass of a display counter. There were wax candies shaped like dwarves and bright colored jawbreakers, but I passed up the pleasure of cracking a hard-shelled globe for the tasty goo within and pointed to a model plane kit—three flat pieces of light balsa wood held together by a red rubber band. I fitted the wing pieces in place to make my glider. Outside, I waved Ellen back while I launched the plane. I pitied her for wasting her dime on a perforated cardboard sheet—a paper doll with a wardrobe to be cut out and pressed into place, held on by little white tabs.

But the tail of my prize glider soon popped off. On its second flight it swooped and dipped, then nosedived and struck the sidewalk. Ellen still had her paper doll, but my plane had a busted wing. I kept the red rubber band, and gamely took the broken pieces of balsa back to show the storekeeper in hopes he might offer another. He shook his head, "Too bad!"

Mother's efforts to be the perfect single parent seemed to run off a tricky power supply. No matter how many times she left us with relatives or strangers, she held onto the hope of reclaiming us.

Everything was my father's fault. There were many ways she referred to this missing man who had accepted the ride west on a watermelon truck. "Your father" was rare. "That heel" was not infrequent. "That man I had the misfortune to marry" would do when she had time to spell it out. She tirelessly related his crimes, bad habits, and selfishness. He did not care enough about his appearance to get rid of the row of blackheads across his nose. His manners were terrible, he never cared about anybody but himself, ran around with other women, and spent too much on beer. He left us alone to go out to honky tonks and carouse. He went out to restaurants and treated himself to T-bone steaks with French fries while we went hungry. She never left out the French fries.

"I caught him once," she would gloat. The triumph in her achievement seemed to override the pain she described.

The listener would lean forward. "What was he up to this time?" The rocking chair squeaked, Mother sighed. The space was cleared for her tale.

"I just happened to look in that diner when I walked by after work."

He was unemployed, in that period before they tried farming. "And what do you think I saw?" She would wait for a guess, then go on.

"Him! Sitting there at a booth with one of his women. He looked out and saw me and then he jumped up and ran out the back door. He always was a coward."

"What did the woman do?"

"Why, I have no idea." Mother washed her hands of that person's problems. "He was the one I wanted to throw scalding water on."

Her stories, though doubtless true, took on the glow of a fairy tale. She often told how, before my birth, when my father had picked her up after her shift at the department store, she had noticed a large red heart-shaped box, tied with a shining ribbon. Thinking the gift was for her, she reached to untie the bow. "Don't touch them chocolates, they're for my girlfriend," she quoted him as saying.

"That was nothing," Mother said. "I was used to him doing me wrong, but he didn't have to commit those crimes. He'd have gone to jail if it wasn't for my brother George. He had to do everything he could to keep him out."

"Yes, I heard about all that."

But nothing could stop her telling the story again. Her lines never varied more than a phrase or two from performance to performance. There was no question of forgiving or blunting the worst.

My father's crimes were too gross for forgiving. Ellen and I deserved to know the whole story—she would not temper it just to give him a free ride. She gave no quarter. It did not occur to her that we might have been better off with some illusions about him.

"It was just like him to try to hold up somebody he knew. Sometimes he acted like he didn't have the sense he was born with." I do not remember anyone, even my father's brothers or sisters, trying to defend him to her. "It was getting dark," Mother said, "and he stuck that pistol in a man's stomach and said 'Stick 'em up,' and guess who it was?" Again, she would wait a beat, a dramatic pause. "His boss from the ice plant!"

It was not clear to me whether she was criticizing my father for taking a pistol and committing the holdup or for bungling it.

"He could have at least gone up to Tulsa where he'd more likely run into strangers." Exhausted at last, Mother gave thanks for small favors. "Thank God my brother kept him out of jail," she repeated, adding, "On the other hand, maybe it would have been better to let him go to prison."

If Mother was right in her claim that even his own father had denounced my father, nobody had ever expected much of him.

"He was always different," one of his sisters said. "All the rest of us seemed to figure out what was right from wrong, but Dow always did seem a little crazy in the head. Sometimes I wonder."

But she never said what it was she was wondering. And he had not been all bad, had he? If he were so terrible why had my mother fallen in love with him back in high school? What had been the charm, the appeal?

I saw his crimes differently—as proof that he loved his family enough to protect them from starvation, even if it meant taking up arms. Montaigne tells us that a man has a natural inclination not to be a thief, but that this instinct can be overridden by the determination not to be hungry. My father's first crime, Mother told us, was rustling a cow. In her version the theft was from Grampa.

My father's stepbrother Dub remembered the details somewhat differently. Dub remembered the theft of a neighbor's heifer as being settled by Grampa's offer of a payment of $10 to the neighbor. In any case, the District Court of Creek County Complaint charged the two men with stealing "one pale red cow, branded with a figure '2' on the hip," fixing their bond at $1,000 each.

Under the front page "SPOTLIGHT NEWS TODAY IN SAPULPA" column of the *Sapulpa Herald* for Monday, August 21, 1933, the following report appeared:

PRELIMINARY HEARING IN LARCENY CASE CONTINUED

A preliminary hearing for Dow Ray and Olen Rayburn, charged jointly with larceny of a cow, was continued for 30 days upon agreement of attorneys in the justice of the peace court of Paul C. Davis.

. . . The two are accused of stealing a cow owned by J. E. Scott.

I often wondered how many of Dad's holdups and hijackings were real, and how many were inventions of Mother's dramatizing. I was not sure if I had invented, dreamed, or remembered the events described in my story, "The Hijacking," in which, as a child, I accompanied my father in the theft of a truckload of tires. The story ended with my witnessing his arrest, much like the newspaper account of officers coming to the door, although I had not yet discovered archaeological evidence found in the *Tulsa Tribune* for January 16, 1937:

TULSA ROBBERS LOSE RAPIDLY
POLICE SETTING UNUSUAL CAPTURE RECORD

Tulsa's police war on robbers pounded on all fronts today as officials announced arrest of four men, three of them identified by victims of holdups in the preceding 48 hours . . . .

D.A. Ray, former taxi-driver, 2104 S. Thirty-eighth west av., was said to have been identified by J.A. Briggs, 1428 E. Second st., as one of two men who took $8.27 from him as he walked near his home Thursday night . . . .

. . . Ray was taken into custody at his home by Officers C. O. Davis and Roy Houseour.

If the sleepy four-year-old fantasized the arrest, so did the editors of the *Tulsa Tribune*. If my mother imagined the trial, so did the judge and jury.

In the District Court of Tulsa County, Oklahoma, D. A. Ray was charged on 4 February, 1937 with "Robbery with Firearms." According to the indictment:

. . . said D. A. Ray, on the 14th day of January, A.D., 1937 . . . did unlawfully, wilfully, forcibly, and feloniously, take, steal and carry away, from the immediate presence and person of one J. A. Briggs, and without the consent and against the will of the said J. A. Briggs, certain personal property, to-wit: $7.00 in good and lawful money of the United States of America, being the property of the said J. A. Briggs, said taking, stealing and carrying away being then and there accomplished by said defendant upon and against the said J. A. Briggs, by means of force and fear, said force and fear being then and there used by said defendant in the manner as follows, to-wit:

> That said defendant, did then and there unlawfully, forcibly and feloniously, threaten to shoot the said J. A. Briggs, with a certain revolver or pistol, then and there had and held in the hands of said defendant, if he, then and there resisted, and did then and there threaten to take the life of the said J. A. Briggs, or do him great bodily harm, if he, the said J. A. Briggs, then and there resisted . . . and thereby producing in the mind of the said J. A. Briggs, fear of immediate and unlawful injury to his said person, and said fear so produced in the mind of the said J. A. Briggs, was sufficient to and did overcome all resistance on the part of him, the said J. A. Briggs . . .

There was another indictment for a robbery on the 15 January 1937, yielding "$8.61 in good and lawful money of the United States of America," committed by my father and a certain J. A. Thompson who, "within the jurisdiction of this Court, did unlawfully, wilfully [sic], forcibly, conjointly, and feloniously, while acting in concert each with the other" robbed "the person of one Irwin Hopper . . . by means of force and fear." With fulsome redundancy the account charged that

> said defendants and each of them, did then and there unlawfully and feloniously, take, steal and carry away, the property aforesaid, with the felonious intent then and there upon the part of said defendants and each of them, to deprive the owner thereof permanently and to convert the same to their own use and benefit . . .

My father did some jail time, but on March 12, 1937, was released by the motion of the assistant county attorney, John Conway. Whether Conway's motion resulted from the intervention of Uncle George is not a matter of record. The other defendant, J. A. Thompson, was sentenced to fifteen years in the State Prison at McAllister.

Children do not really care much about right and wrong so long as their needs are met. John Holloway, in *A London Childhood*, wrote of the time he realized that the toys his doctor father brought back from the hospital were, in effect, stolen, for they had been meant by the donors to be given to pediatric patients. But they were wonderful toys, and he seemed amused that his father felt obliged to sneak them home late at night. So long as he was thinking of his son, trying to make him happy, all was in order. As amoral as that boy, I would have been happy to go along any time, any place, as accomplice in my father's crimes.

For Ellen and me any contact with Dad—or even secondhand word of him—was of mythic proportions. After his final departure Mother had gone for a visit with him. Ellen and I hung on her every word as she described how it had gone.

"I was a fool for letting him talk me into it," she said. "He claimed he had a good job now, working in that smelter in Blackwell, and why didn't we talk it over again? I wound up in that filthy boarding house where he was staying, and he tried to get me to come in his room and talk things over. Well, I knew better than that, you can be sure. I insisted on him leaving the door open, and you should have heard him carrying on about how silly that was. But I knew him far too well to trust any of his tricks. He begged me to take him back. He used every argument he could think of. 'For the sake of the kids,' he said, can you imagine that, after the way he did me?"

He did not care about us, she always affirmed, and yet there it was from her own lips, an odd crumb that kept nourishing us long after we took it in—his very own words. He had wanted to return *for the sake of* his two children. Ellen and I would look at each other as if to say, "That means us!" He cared about us after all! But we could not let on to Mother that we saw it differently than she did.

Mother's pride had determined the outcome. She had put him in his place.

"You should have seen that awful smelter," she said, "with its stench to high heaven. It was the filthiest place I ever saw, what with smokestacks spewing out black smoke and God knows what all. It was just like him to pick a place like that. Serves him right, that's what I say."

Whatever drove my father, his energetic reconstruction of his life time after time may have indicated an undiagnosed condition which he tried to medicate with drinking, flight from stress, and new relationships. An unshakable illusion of *la vita nuova* drove him, as it has driven me. Just eighteen days after his divorce from the woman he had abandoned with his first two children, his first son by his second marriage was born.

6.

WITH DAD GONE from the second-floor apartment in Tulsa, Mother decided to board Ellen and me with Aunt Peg in Sapulpa. We should have felt quite at home, returning to our birthplace, even now and then romping around on the same saggy bed. The older of Mother's sisters, Peg was the only Catholic in the family. Widowed and left with several children, she had plenty of sympathy for Mother's complaints about my father's drinking. Her husband's fatal car wreck had involved alcohol.

Years later Mother was reminiscing about the Depression era that contributed to our staying with Aunt Peg. "That morning you were born, my brother Jim was smoking out on the porch. He took bets with the twins on whether you would be a boy or a girl. Jim's birthday was the next day, so he said if you were a boy he was going to kill you if you didn't wait a day to be born."

An odd remark, I thought, for Mother to remember and to quote — a threat on my life even before I was born, and blaming me for choosing the wrong day.

From the window of that front bedroom where we had been born, Ellen and I looked across Lincoln Street to the Indian school surrounded with a tall fence topped with barbed wire. The distant figures playing outside the large white building raced one another to climb aboard a spinning roundabout, grabbing at the rails. They stood on the octagonal platform as it spun around fast enough to make them dizzy, then jumped off, staggering about with arms flung out.

Sometimes we crossed the street and peered through the high chain link fence. None of the children came over to speak to us, but we could not have accepted even a cordial invitation anyway. Barbed wire topped the fence—slanted inwards. I wondered if it was to keep them in or keep us out. My cousin Bobby told me it was to keep them from escaping.

In their fire drills, the children popped out of a hollow tubular chute running down the side of their building. Though a serious occasion— practice for disaster—the drill offered entertainment. Their laughter rode the air like flocks of birds. It puzzled me, and seemed somehow wrong that they were having fun. When we had fire drills at Washington School, marching out of our red brick building where I was in the third grade and Ellen in the second, our queue was sullen and spiritless. The teachers barked out orders, insisting that we imagine flames licking out of the windows. Glumly we obeyed, then stood watching the three-story building, wishing it would catch fire.

Mother was living in a nurses' residence next door to the hospital. She promised to come for us at school and take us downtown to the movies, as well as visit us at Aunt Peg's house. For a few weeks she kept her promise to show up on Tuesday afternoons, though sometimes she was too busy or had something she needed to do with a friend.

Our thoughts of Mother were always associated with the hospital where we knew she could be found. There was only one way to get a nurse's attention, and that was to cry out with pain, find something terribly wrong. But when cousin Bobby picked me up and threw me across the living room, shattering my elbow, Mother did not hear about it right away. Bobby threatened to kill me if I told anyone, so I put up with the agonizing pain for three days, until my wincing caught Aunt Peg's attention as I was trying to dry the supper dishes.

Mother came running and took me to the hospital. After a cast was put on my arm, she took me next door and showed me her room in the nurses' residence, apologizing that she was not allowed to keep her children with her. The cast on my arm held her attention, giving me a temporary status that would disappear as soon as it was removed.

When an infected hangnail on my thumb developed gangrene, she took me to a doctor who scraped the bone without anesthetic. She helped hold me down, shushing me with orders not to cry, to be strong, her little man. At least I had her attention for a while. In our family, illness was the language spoken well before my entry on the scene.

But infections and broken bones were not enough. The only way we could keep mother was to eat her up, swallow her whole. She was inside me where I could keep her with all her pains, and mine too. I had learned this technique by gasping with asthma from my first days. Like Proust's Marcel, I longed for my mother's kiss, "for a communion of peace in which my lips would imbibe her real presence and the privilege of falling asleep." I would breathe her back.

> Strangely
>   my mother's sad eyes
>   did not show up
> on the X-ray
> though I had long since
>   swallowed
>   all her sorrows
> and they should have been
>   right there
> where the pain IS
>
> nor my father's
>   old loves
>   which should have been
> THERE
>   cavorting
> heedless of fluoroscopic
> voyeurs
>
> nor was the little boy
>   loveless and snotnosed
> who'd been entombed

for sure
there
years ago
in sight.

Perhaps he hid
behind the spleen
behind the ribs
Oh he is out of hiding now
and is drumming drumming
drumming my heart.

No one had given our mother any attention except under desperate circumstances. Why should she in turn be moved by anything less? And how could we compete with her patients in the hospital, or with children she sometimes took care of as a nanny? On her visits to us she proudly showed snapshots of those children—a baby in a carriage, another child or two near her as they stood on a sidewalk or she sat on a park bench, her hand on the handle of a carriage as if to keep it from rolling away. Sometimes she was pictured in her white uniform cradling an infant in her arms, and I would feel an aching shudder of envy invading my chest. Yet she seemed to think we should share her fondness for these children.

Whether my mother embraced the children of strangers or my sister and myself, I think of her as Dorothea Lange's "Migrant Mother, 1936." Though she did not accompany my father on his trek west, the hilltop shack in Oklahoma had been as basic as the migrant peapickers' camp Dorothea Lange encountered in California. Mother must have felt just as helpless and impoverished. The woman photographed at the nadir of her misery strangely survived, and so did my mother. Neither they nor their children anticipated such a future as they lived on into a war-born prosperity. The migrant mother in the photograph never forgave Dorothea Lange for memorializing the most miserable time in her life.

When I look at photographs like those of Walker Evans or Dorothea

Lange, I appreciate how helpless Mother must have felt as she tried to keep her children with her but saw no way to do so. She was never quite so desperate, perhaps, as the mother in Dorothea Lange's photograph. But like the woman shown in her gunnysack dress she had done the best she could. Both women were victims of troubles so inextricably compounded by hard times that their hopelessness was far beyond their control. Yet much of the futile work of my childhood was trying to bring a smile to Mother's face.

With the frequent moves of our childhood, it was as if Ellen and I had been sentenced to bounce down stairs. Every move, as if by some rigidly enforced law, turned out to be a worse situation than the one before with the exception of the brief period in Mounds. There, for a while, we lived an almost normal life. But no home was more than a temporary camp, and Mother's efforts to keep house were often a foredoomed absurdity — sweeping the dirt floor of the hilltop shack, scrubbing the floors of the Mounds duplex so that neither landlord nor tenants would think ill of us.

Nothing was predictable. Everything was possible. My father might return — that is why I kept watching the road. If he came back they could fight some more. But with one smile he could have wooed our forgiveness.

On return stays at the farm, landed as boarders in Grampa's house, Ellen and I learned to play relatives off against one another. I would stride around with a bluff boldness and say to my grandfather or Ada or Aunt Bea, "When we stay with Aunt Peg, she gives us apples and bananas all the time and she's a lot nicer to us than you are." Later we would add, "If you aren't nice to us we'll go live with Aunt Peg."

It was all a bluff. When we were left with Aunt Peg while Mother lived in the nurses' residence in Sapulpa, I would brag about how nice my father's people had been to us on the farm, hinting that Ellen and I would go right back there if we were treated unkindly. I made the farm sound like paradise, a land of Cockaigne where we never had to do any chores. I pointed out that what little we did we got paid for, citing Grampa's rate of pay—a penny a hundred for swatting flies, a nickel a bushel for picking green beans, a dime a load for the long canvas bag we dragged between rows of cotton.

As I told it, we spent most of our time at the farm gorging on home-made ice cream, as if at a Fourth of July gathering, every day if we wished, and we had free run of the fields where we could pluck toma-toes and melons and eat at random. I praised Ada's berry cobblers, as if meals at the farm were mostly tasty desserts. I bragged of the technique Dub taught me—lifting a melon that had ripened on the vine, dropping it back on the ground to smash it, then scooping out only the delicious red heart and gobbling it, leaving the rest, then going on to another.

"We could eat a whole row of watermelons if we wanted to," I said, not mentioning that after the one occasion when I had overindulged I had made frequent trips to the outhouse all night.

One Fourth of July, cousins I had never met turned up from Texas and Arkansas with their parents for a family reunion. My father was miss-ing, but his brothers Norman, Orville, McKeel, and Olen were there, along with his sisters Alice, Edris, and Beatrice, as well as Gramma Ada's teenagers W. T. and Willa Mae. My mother came out from town—she stayed closer to my father's family than to her own querulous brothers and sisters.

The fenced yard was turned into a picnic ground. We children played tag and jump rope and kept far too active to get to know each other—perhaps that was the purpose. Like Tom Sawyer begging to paint the fence, we each pleaded for a chance to turn the handle cranking out ice cream in an oaken bucket. The ice cream was streaked with fresh peaches, and we stuffed ourselves with potato salad, ham and beans, and slices of watermelon, spitting out seeds and letting juice drip on the ground. We got into a seed-spitting contest. Eating and laughing broke down our reserve, and by late afternoon we were friends. I was inspired to lead an expedition through the barnyard.

The furniture my parents had hauled from place to place had been left for storage in the hayloft of Grampa's barn. We climbed up the steep wooden ladder and I proudly displayed the items, brushing straw off a bureau and pulling drawers open. Surprisingly, many personal possessions had been abandoned—my mother's jar of Indian-head pennies, my father's .410 pistol, rolled balloons that I later realized were condoms.

That was the last time I saw the furniture in one place. Later, on brief visits to the homes of my father's brothers or sisters, I would spot the Victrola, the bureau, the wooden icebox, my mother's kitchen cabinet with the built-in flour bin and sifter. Failed marriages leave good pickings for gleaners.

My efforts to play relatives off against each other seldom paid off. Our words got the amused and tolerant gaze of the unconvinced. Whether landed on my father's side of the family or tossed back to my mother's, I failed to persuade. Behind my transparent boasting, claiming an intimacy, a loving atmosphere, an eager willingness to care for Ellen and me, everyone seemed to see right through me. But my lies were good practice for a lifetime of "cracking hardy," keeping up a front, hiding depression with a mask of cheer and geniality which, when successful, might convince others that I was a mindless fool. "The trouble with depression," a friend once told me, "is that you have to spend most of your time smiling."

My desperation was too apparent, and it followed me to other landscapes. When, much later, my son Sam saw me reading a book entitled *How to Be Loved*, he asked me what it said.

"It points out," I replied, "that people only love those who don't try too hard to be loved."

At age fourteen he had already come to understand enough of the world to point out the obvious contradiction. "Then if you care enough to read that book," he said, "nobody will love you. You shouldn't read it, then. Maybe you ought to throw it away and just not give a damn." He laughed and ran out, seeming not to give a damn himself.

Sam was right. Love is freely given or not at all. I have always sought it desperately, only to become an addict courting disappointment, a professional orphan seeking rescue. I kept going back to Mother's empty breasts and longing for Father's return, despite all that had been said of him, and all I found out for myself.

Freud's views on the father conjure up visions of a fearful figure, the aggressor in the inevitably witnessed primal scene. So why should I have longed to bring back such a threatening presence? No matter what, I never gave up trying to reshape my parents' behavior into the love we needed. I must have overlooked something. I kept looking. My father's sister Beatrice once wrote me: "I remember an incident when you were a baby. Your family was staying with us for a while. There was an upstairs and I was carrying you downstairs—I was 8 years old—and fell with you—bumped your head. I was so scared and Katherine kept crying 'Oh, my baby—my baby.'" Aunt Bea went on to joke, "That's what your problem has been . . . " The big news for me was not her explanation for all my craziness, my neuroses, my politics, but that here was a clue suggesting that my mother had once cared enough to lament "Oh, my baby—my baby!"—to call me by that name and to weep for me.

I was dumbfounded, astounded, just as with that evidence of my father's love that Mother unintentionally conveyed when she boasted of turning down my father's pleas for reconciliation "for the sake of the kids." She did not have a monopoly on that pious phrase after all. That my father had wanted to keep his family together, that he cared about his two children, canceled out a multitude of his crimes.

We could never summon omniscience enough to account for their behavior. Love was hardly factored in. Rage—theirs and mine—made more sense. Much later, in psychoanalysis, I would probe both patricidal and matricidal urges that might have disposed of my torment by killing one or both of them. I have no problem understanding the murder of parents or the displacement of rage onto other victims. At times, though, I turned that rage toward myself.

"We are the commotion born of love," poet Charles Madge wrote. In the commotion of mind we would do anything to entice back either or both of the *genitori,* or find them in surrogates or the avatars found in dreams. When a poem of mine about a woman in a hospice was published in an anthology, the editor of the book, which was otherwise about grief for dead parents, expressed surprise that my mother was still living, and his comment made me realize that I had for most of my life grieved my mother as if she had died long ago.

> On a visit to the hospice I notice
> a woman playing the piano, trying
> to learn, and it comes welling back—
>
> the hunger for love never offered.
> Mother did not play the piano,
> and was never able to love me,
>
> but if I had loved her enough,
> nothing else would have mattered.
> I'd have taken no note of her failures.
>
> And what matter if she could not
> love me? I look back over the years,
> seeking the date of the great power
>
> failure, when our hearts froze
> and were left in cold storage.
> Maybe it was the year we fled
>
> to the cellar, the sky black
> with dirt and rubble. Or maybe
> it was one of those nights her sobs

outlasted the rain or she moaned
in the arms of a lover and I
could not help her, this woman

who still tortures me with her ghost,
who has learned to play the piano.
And I cannot help her with that either.

Mother with David and Ellen

7.

WHILE WE WERE boarded at Aunt Peg's my third grade year, I became a nervous clock-watcher as I sat in the classroom on Tuesdays, Mother's day off. If she kept her promise, she would show up to take us to the movies. After she missed a few times, I was afraid she would not turn up after lunch.

I sneaked looks toward the door. The teacher told me to settle down. "I won't excuse your absence anyway, if your work's not finished." She was all business except when she wanted to get off on a sidetrack, telling us about how her hot water heater had blown up or how she and her mother had once taken a trip to South America and almost fallen out of a boat into the Amazon River.

She pulled down the wall map and pointed with a ruler to show us right where she had the scariest experience of her life. "They've got man-eating fish in those waters," she told us. "Ten minutes in there and we'd have been eaten down to our skeletons." She spread out a *National Geographic* and showed us a picture of piranha fish. Several of the children were fascinated, but she was not fooling me for a minute. I doubted she had ever been to South America. The business about the hot water heater exploding seemed pretty bad, though, and back at Aunt Peg's I kept my distance from the one in the bathroom. I was afraid it would go off like another such bomb. Its heat helped when Ellen and I were getting dressed on cold mornings, but I did not want to take any chances.

Sometimes Mother would show up in her nurse's uniform, sometimes in her red plaid dress. It must have been her favorite, she wore it so often, and I envied Ellen her joyful greeting when she ran and pressed her head against Mother's stomach, hugging her hips, feeling the flannel softness of that dress against her face. I held back.

Her arrival was a double victory—we could go to a movie, and I could indulge a smirk at the teacher, who looked as if she would love to keep me from leaving. But the principal had given permission. Mother and I would walk down the hall and pick Ellen up from the second grade classroom, then we were free of school for the day, Hallelujah! I worked at not showing my excitement. Outside we crunched across the gravel, past the jungle bars and teeter-totters and swings on the playground. Mother, holding our hands, chattered on about her busy week as I numbed my face to hide my criminal joy at our reunion. She now and then asked about our schoolwork.

For once I had one-upped my classmates. They should, in fact, be jealous of us. Our mother had come and got us and the school could not keep us. That was special, and I could hardly keep from shouting out about it to strangers on the bus. But my mother's attention strayed from us to the driver, Gerald, who was her current boyfriend. Soon, though, we slipped into the cool shadows of the Criterion, safe for a few hours in the darkness. *Billy the Kid* was my favorite movie. *Gone with the Wind* was Mother's, but she said it was for "Adults Only," so she went to that one with another nurse and told us about it later.

Mother sat between Ellen and me. Eventually we would have to come out, sometimes into startling sunlight, other times into pouring rain, both rude awakenings. The following week, though, we might not be spared the humiliation of waiting for Mother's arrival through the long afternoon until the four o'clock bell rang. The teacher threw me a knowing look. She had warned me that Mother might not show up.

Mother came by Aunt Peg's house one day and said she wanted to take me for a walk. We left Ellen behind. I guessed what she wanted to talk

about. While she was building up to it I looked up to her and kept saying, "Fine, Fine." Then we stopped by a railing along a steep slope. The
sidewalk was torn up and tilted, but she seemed to think that was a good
place to stand. "Look at me," she said. I wanted her to get to the point
and get it over with.

"Do you know what a divorce is?" she asked. I told her I did. Then
she went ahead and told me anyway. "A divorce is when two people
don't love each other any more," she said. That phrase sounded strange,
for I had never seen much of a sign that they loved each other. This
moment had been a long time coming, and yet it was a shock.

"Your father won't come back this time," she said. "The divorce will
come through in a few weeks. He wrote me and said he wanted it, and
I told him if that's what he wanted I'd give it to him." I could tell she was
ready to cry, but she stopped that by dabbing her eyes and nose with an
embroidered handkerchief.

"You're the man of the family now," she said. "You'll have to be."

I wished she had not said that. I shuffled around, then asked her if
we could sit down on that tilted sidewalk.

"It's better to walk along," she said, and took my hand.

Her rouge was smeared on her cheek and my glasses were blurry. I
knew I had better straighten up or I would be crying too, not something
the man of the family was supposed to do. I should, however, find a way
to get a new dress to replace the red plaid.

"Your father ran out and left me with my hands full," she said.

I was wondering what I could do about it. A kid could not get much
of a job.

"You're old enough to understand," Mother said, "even if your sister
isn't. I don't want you to tell her yet. I'll tell her when she's big enough."

That was how our family told each other things—tell somebody not
to tell someone else and they will be sure to pass it on.

A man passed us. I hoped he would not think I had made my mother
cry. It was not any of his business anyway.

"He's got a new woman," she said. "I think they left Tulsa together. I can't prove it, but I'm pretty sure," she went on. "He doesn't love us and never did. And now you don't have a father." Now she was back to lies. I felt more comfortable with that.

"Don't worry, Mother," I told her.

"I don't know how I'll support you kids. He doesn't care enough about his own children to send anything."

"Yeah, I know, Mother. That's all right. We'll stay at Aunt Peg's and she'll take care of us."

"Peg's patience runs pretty thin too. She's got enough of her own to worry about."

We had heard a lot about Aunt Peg's troubles since she became a widow. She was not home much because she had started a cafeteria and worked long hours. Ellen and I had learned not to be in the way. We did most of the cooking and housework.

"I'll tell you when the divorce is final," Mother said. "You have a right to know. You and Ellen can stay with Aunt Peg for the rest of the school year. The alternative is a foster home and I'd rather not."

"Yeah, me too." I had no idea what a foster home was—maybe something like the Indian school. I was scuffing up my shoes on the broken sidewalk.

"Maybe Uncle George could give you some money," I said. It seemed a logical suggestion, since she had bragged so much about how rich he was.

"I can't ask my brother for anything. It was bad enough he had to keep your father out of jail so many times." I looked around. There had been a recent flood and debris was everywhere.

Shortly after this conversation, a strange thing happened—my handwriting changed radically. Teachers had always praised its elegance, and even called visitors over to admire it. Whereas previously it had been neat and balanced, now all of a sudden it was as shaky as an old man's and the script did not even slant in the same direction for two sentences in a row. I had two kinds of Ds and two kinds of Ss and could not seem to make them stay alike. I could not get back to the way it had been.

Mother's worry about money troubled me. I hoped she would find someone to marry. The only possibility I could think of was Gerald, the bus driver, who seemed to take an interest in Ellen and me. I got to know Gerald better and learned that he had started his own city bus company with two used school buses which he had painted chocolate brown. He told us we could ride free whenever we wanted to.

I looked forward to any trip downtown that was an excuse to ride the bus. The fare had been only a nickel, but free was better. One day I took a trip to the dentist, whose office was upstairs over the Criterion. Like Mother, the dentist was fond of his x-ray machine. "Another x-ray," he coaxed, aiming the smudged yellow cone. A chattering inside sounded like beebees rattling around. The chubby dentist smelled like cinnamon as his belly pressed against me. I could not wait to climb down from his chair.

Just as I hoped, when I boarded the bus Gerald waved aside my nickel. As the bus rattled and jolted along he told me that he was thinking of enlisting in the army, that maybe it was not the right time to be starting a bus company.

Not long after Mother's announcement of the divorce, Aunt Peg decided she could not keep us any longer. If Bobby and I could not play together without broken bones, she said, she could not be responsible. Ellen and I bounced down another step. We had run out of relatives as caregivers. Now we would find out what foster homes were.

With the father's flight from the scene, the mother gets to write the histories, plant her version, and her children grow up with that account and often no other. In time it becomes as fixed as a fairy tale and unshakable. If the father was a scoundrel in her eyes, so will he be in theirs: distortions, lies, and projections rooted deep as dreams or myths. Chances are that retrospective attempts to correct the record will not have much impact other than distressing the searcher. The boy deprived of a role model and the girl missing her father need a balanced picture, not the distortions of a funhouse mirror. But brainwashed, they become committed to her cause with loyalty that even a later challenge with documentary evidence cannot shake.

The children may never forgive the father. If he too had his heart broken by the marriage—and in my father's case, by lifting those stones out of his field to grow potatoes and beans—his children might never know it. If he struggled to be a breadwinner and was defeated more by economic forces than by his character defects, the mother's version will seldom be tempered by such realities. I heard that my father was "a heel" when I still thought the word meant something on a shoe or the end of a loaf of bread. It did not make much sense.

Custodial parents of either sex seldom tell of their own failures. I know a man who was proud, when his children were small, that he got them to tell their mother on a visit that they did not love her any more and never wanted to see her again. The self-righteous father was proud of his total possession, not only of his children's bodies but of their minds. He had plenty of trouble with them later, the payoff for his arrogance.

The more pitiable Mother was in dramatizing her plight, the more Ellen and I felt an obligation to rescue her. But even for her we could not censor out our dreams and fantasies. The child learns to wear a mask, hiding divided loyalties. But when Aunt Edris, working in her kitchen as I sat on the table, my legs swinging, offered the balm of explaining my father's absence without reference to anything but economics, I felt absolved. He had not left, after all, because of my unworthiness. Pausing with her quilted mitten on her hand after she reached into the oven for a pan of steaming biscuits, Aunt Edris said, "You father's out working in the harvest fields and I bet he's sorry you can't be out there helping him." He would be back, she assured me, but did not say it would be only to get his things and leave again.

A boy never knows when he might need a father to help him fly his kite or go fishing with him the way his playmates' fathers go fishing with them—the way Uncle Skeet, whose face was as wrinkled as an old turtle's, once took me along turtle fishing under the rusty bridge on Skunk Creek. A boy never knows when he might need a father he can brag about to his schoolmates, as if he can take the man for granted, the way they can. He never needs his father more than when mocked for not having one—no answers for the schoolyard jeers, nothing to fight back with. The earth opens at his feet.

8.

MOTHER CAME ALONG for the ride when a social worker from the welfare department drove us through Tulsa to Mingo Corners, a crossroads with a few houses, a school and church, a tavern, and a grocery store with gas station. Nearby was a popular riding stable with its name painted on the barn roof. The social worker pulled her car up beside a picket fence and led us through a gate where our new foster mother, Gertrude Greeley, a runty divorcée in slacks, was waiting for us. Her three daughters tiered in ages from eight to fifteen—Dorothy, Martha, and Charlene—stood beside her. The two older girls were already taller than their mother.

The space was "tight but just right," Gertrude told Mother and the social worker as she showed us through the house. With new playmates the place was bound to be an improvement over the earlier foster homes, which had been cramped. In one place we had slept in a pantry. At Mingo, Ellen and I and the two younger girls were to sleep in the back bedroom in one large bed. Gertrude and Charlene, the fifteen-year-old daughter, shared the front bedroom. The small bathroom was between the two bedrooms.

Gertrude neglected to tell the social worker that her father, Pops, was also crammed into that little square box of a house. Pops, a bald and grumpy but dignified gentleman who commuted to his job in Tulsa, was usually settled in place under his covers on the living room sofa by ten o'clock, with the corner radio turned down low so that only he could hear the nightly news, which Gertrude found annoying. Pops seemed consistent—he had no use for any of the children he waved and flailed away, as if they—we—were flies or mosquitoes. But when he babbled about Venezuela, where he had worked on an oil rig when he was young, he expected us to settle at his feet and listen respectfully. We were glad when he did not show up for the pork and beans or Kraft macaroni and cheese or sandwich suppers, for we did not have to feign interest in his adventures.

Pops would fiddle with his hearing aid and glare at us with his bulbous eyes as if never quite sure we were there, or even what we were. Before the news was over, he would chase us out of the living room. We would retreat to the back bedroom. If Gertrude was out so she could not yell at us to settle down, Pops would intrude without knocking. His hearing problem had not kept him from getting aroused by our noise.

On summer nights when all the doors and windows were open and the breeze blew through, the house seemed like what Gertrude said it was—a cozy little ship, "tight but right." But before long, things did not feel quite right. Mornings brought trouble, with Gertrude, Pops, and Charlene arguing. Gertrude complained of headaches and snarled at her father when he called them hangovers and reminded her what time she got in the night before. Gertrude, in turn, took Charlene to task about what time *she* got in.

The girls quarreled and when Gertrude got mad at them she often took it out on Ellen and me. Before long she was not waiting for us to have breakfast before ordering us out of the house, while lamenting what a fool she had been to take us in. Our welfare allotment did not pay for half what we ate, she lamented.

In the evening Gertrude arrived home tired and irritable, sometimes after a few beers. Her daughters knew where to find her. Sometimes Ellen and I would venture with them into the smoke-filled tavern on the corner, where a jukebox provided twangy versions of "I Don't Want to Set the World on Fire" ("I just want to start / A flame in your heart"), and "Don't Sit Under the Apple Tree with Anyone Else but Me" ("No, No, No, Don't . . . ").

Still in her welder's coveralls, Gertrude shuffled around the dance floor with one of the tavern familiars. Charlene and her boyfriend Bill Bean were often there too, dancing cheek to cheek. Bill towered over her in his Levis and dung-caked cowboy boots, smelly from his job at the stables where he took care of polo ponies. Between dances, the group filled up ashtrays and emptied beer bottles in a back booth.

Gertrude reminded us often that making airplanes was a serious business. As a welder working on B-17 bombers at the Douglas plant two miles away, she was out to win the war. She also told us of mishaps at work, how a test pilot had ejected and come right down on the barbed wire–topped fence around the factory. "It was a bloody mess," she said.

When Gertrude was home a tense quiet reigned, and her two younger girls would play card games or jacks in whispers. But when she and Pops were gone, the girls dressed up and danced around in Gertrude's dresses and nightgowns which touched their ankles. The oversized high heels wobbled. Wide sleeves hung and flopped at their wrists. Then they would step out of the shoes and jump around on the saggy bed in the back room, and run wild and hollering through the house.

The girls backed teasingly into the closet, their dressing room, for another change under jangling hangers. Gertrude's shining silky dresses were just the right pinks and lacy reds for their strip show. Their sister Charlene was usually out with Bill, probably in the tavern or the hayloft. We had seen her picking hay from her hair. Once, when running around the rooms of the little house, we surprised Charlene as she sat on her bed, bare-breasted, mending her bra. I had glimpsed her once before, bending over the bathroom sink, washing her hair. I tried to think of a way of making the same mistake again, bumbling into the bathroom at the wrong time to get a closer look.

I ran with the girls round and round the rooms, yelping like a cowboy. Charlene held the bra up to cover herself and pretended to be indignant, but the frail garment was lacy and transparent, and she seemed to be teasing. In bed I sometimes would caress Martha, but she had only button-size bumps on her chest. Our furtive caresses under the covers after lights were out were inhibited by her flannel nighty and my pajamas.

Gerald occasionally drove Mother to Mingo for a visit. One evening we stood by his car in front of the house, listening to a boxing match on the radio. The announcer, breathing heavily, sounded as if he himself was taking the blows. It was hard to wait until after the fight was over to get Mother's attention. I wanted to tell her the news about my pet coyote, Foxy, a pup another boy and I had found in the state park a few miles away. We had made a house for him out of scavenged bricks and tin sheets, although Gertrude had forbidden us to keep him. Foxy was tethered to a stake when he was not penned in his house with orders to be quiet.

The fight settled it, Joe Louis was still the world champion, much to Mother's distress. But at last, with flashlight in hand, I led her and Gerald to see my pet, only to discover that Foxy had escaped. He had yanked up the stake, broken down the tin sheet barricading the door, and run away. Foxy had made a cute pet, and it was fun to stroke him and hold him against my cheek. We had shown him off in the schoolyard. But he had grown quickly, and had begun nipping our hands with sharp bites. It was just as well that he had run away, and I hoped he would find his way home back to his mother.

My own mother gave us more bad news. Gerald was going into the army. We would never see him again, although Ellen and I had agreed on his suitability to be our stepfather. He was the last of her nice guys.

Over the radio on a Sunday, December 7, we heard the news of Pearl Harbor. Pops pulled his hearing aid out of his ear and shoved his bald head right up against the radio, trying to make sense out of the news. He turned the volume up as high as it would go. I ran out of the house to search the sky in case enemy bombers showed up.

I took a long walk in the wind, treading the crusty frozen grass of the highway shoulder. I felt I was in the presence of something momentous—something going on over the horizon—something that would touch all our lives, we knew not how. But nothing special was within range of my searching eyes. Someone had laid a plank down over the frozen scum on a ditch, and I stomped across it.

I kicked at everything I could find to kick—a brick, gravel, a rusty pipe. I did not like the silence. I walked along the road and when I reached a railroad crossing I turned around and returned to Mingo, but did not want to go back in the house. I climbed onto the jungle gym in the schoolyard. Like a contorted monkey I reclined inside a cube of pipes and watched the sky from that cage, feeling an emptiness I knew I would never forget, a day on which it seemed strange that nothing terrible had happened.

After I heard that my father had joined the Seabees, my fantasy was always the same—that he would return, looking for me. "Climb in," he would say, and we would be together again as we had been when he was plowing his field. I heard that he was married again, that he had a new son, that he had moved to Kansas. If I ran away, how far would I have to travel, and was he still in Kansas or did the Seabees send him off to war? There was much to puzzle about. I was not even sure if a Seabee was a soldier or a sailor.

On April Fool's Day, I felt flattered to be included in an invitation for the fourth grade to play hookey from Mingo school. The invitation, whispered around the classroom, came from the biggest bully and it seemed highly desirable to be included in his plans. It would at least keep him from beating up on me.

A gang of a dozen or so, we trekked a dusty section road to an iron bridge spanning a creek. We scampered down a weedy bank and, expecting our teachers to be in hot pursuit, crouched under the bridge. The boys smoked cigarettes made of coffee grounds, cornstalks, and tobacco garnered from butts along the highway. The girls admired our courage and pondered the taunts of the bolder boys, urging us all to skinnydip in the muddy waters despite the chill.

We were having a grand time, or pretending to. Most of the girls and boys stripped down to their underpants and shivered with goosebumps as we waded out of the shadows of the bridge and cottonwood trees into the dappled shallows. The fun was interrupted by the class tat-tletale calling down from the bridge. He had resisted the pressure to come along, and now he had been sent as teacher's messenger to call us back. He leaned so far off the bridge that we dared him to jump on over the rail and join us.

We ignored his warnings, but then he yelled that the teacher had told him we would not be punished if we returned right away. Admitting surrender, we waded out of the water and put our clothes back on, the girls telling us to turn our backs. We stumbled up the creek bank and trudged back to school, dragging our feet, kicking up dust.

But the promise had been a lie. The principal waved the boys into his office and told us to line up. Each in turn obeyed the order to step forward, take down his pants and bend over the desk. The stinging strokes on bare buttocks stung sharper because we were still damp from the creek waters. I could not help jumping up and down as the hickory paddle, long as Dad's razor strop, flailed away. It was a humiliating event, exacerbated by word that the girls had got off more easily, a token spanking. Whatever exuberance I had enjoyed by being accepted into the company of classmates playing hookey was wiped out.

One girl in our fourth grade class, Eve, already had a reputation as a precocious flirt. Some of the boys bragged that they had seen her naked. One day after school she asked me to walk her home so she could show me her horse. We set off out down the tar road and over the railroad tracks. Her home was in the woods not far from the state park, where my friend and I had found the coyote, and a lake where we had watched stinking gar fish gasping in puddles after a drought. Eve led me down a graveled driveway past a metal mailbox and detoured us toward a barn. We slipped through a half-closed sliding door. In the shadows inside she motioned for me to follow her as she started up a wooden ladder. The smell of hay reminded me of Grampa's farm.

Upstairs in the loft, under the high pitch of a shingled roof with many chinks throwing silver nails of light into shafts filled with galaxies of dust motes, Eve pushed me down on a hay bale and stepped out of her panties. Holding her dress up to her waist she plumped out her belly as she watched my face to see my reaction.

"You sure act dumb," Eve said, just as a voice from outside called her name. "It's my Dad," she said, grabbing her panties. In a jiffy Eve was again the good little girl. She ran to a loading door, pushed it open, and called out, "We're up here, Daddy. I'm showing my friend how much hay we feed the horse."

At nine Eve was a cool and glib liar, prepared for a life defended with quick wit and deception, the bravado of the faithless, the abused, the disenchanted. But I hardly knew all that. I followed her down the ladder, then shuffled away, stepping fast and as if deaf to avoid her father. The next day after school I saw her invite another boy to walk her home. One by one she was taking her male classmates into her world.

The rusty bridge over Mingo Creek became my observation post, for I was still waiting for my father to return. I often went there after school and sat by the road or stood on the bridge, staring down the road, checking each car that approached. I gave up hope only when the car rumbled over the bridge, leaving me coughing in a cloud of dust.

After fifteen-year-old Charlene got pregnant, Gertrude took out her frustrations on Ellen and me with even greater intensity. Like us, Gertrude knew that the hayloft of the riding stable was where Charlene got together with her boyfriend. Nobody, even Gertrude, seemed surprised when the inevitable happened, but she was furious that her lectures to Charlene had been ignored. Gertrude sought scapegoats for her rage.

"Why don't you kids just get out of my way?" she demanded, not waiting for an answer. She simplified her life by locking Ellen and me out of the house, not bothering to give us breakfast or even letting us fix our own. Her two younger daughters may have been torn between their loyalty to Ellen and me and their hope of not being locked out themselves, but they stayed at the table.

Ellen and I wound up in the schoolyard across the road, perched in the branches of a mulberry tree, munching a breakfast of berries. We seasoned those dusty berries with hate for Gertrude, whom we now thought of as a witch. Defeat fed hunger and hunger fed bitterness.

I might have put up with the situation indefinitely, too proud to complain. But Ellen, with the candor of a beggar, wandered into the corner grocery store and told Mrs. Collins, the storekeeper, how things were. Mrs. Collins sent Ellen to fetch me. In the store she led us through a curtained doorway into her living quarters and gave us breakfast. She also called up the welfare department, setting in motion yet another move.

We were taken to the Children's Home on the West side of Tulsa. It was mostly an orphanage, we were told. We were wards of the court and had run out of foster homes. There was no other place to go.

Decades later, I learned that my sister may have told Mrs. Collins more than I knew. Perhaps the reasons we were taken out of the home were more complex. But the welfare department files were destroyed after seven years—a state rule—and my sister would tell me nothing beyond, "You don't know what went on in that back room with that old man." Even after half a century, she broke into uncontrollable sobbing.

9.

FROM THE CHILDREN'S Home we marched to school along the street, the boys in brown corduroy knickers and tartan socks, the girls in pinafores and blouses. We were well aware that if we tried to run away, our clothing would make it easy to catch us. I was self-conscious about the scrutiny of passing motorists, afraid they would mistake me for one of the orphans. I kept my face turned away. One morning I was inspired to stick my arms in two empty spaghetti boxes swiped from the kitchen garbage bin. It would be obvious that I was different. After all, the other kids did not have square hands.

I told my homeroom teacher that my sister and I would not be staying long at the Children's Home. She doubtless saw that I was as much homeless dog as boy. I lapped up the praise she gave me for my plaster of Paris plate featuring a relief map of Europe, the white Alps erupting out of green and pink land masses surrounding the blue Mediterranean. I was tempted to tell her about my ambition to make a petrified man, as suggested by the tinker back in Mounds. What I read in her eyes as she smiled at me was confirmation that she did not confuse me with those damn orphans and castoffs of society. Although I arrived at school with them each day, that was a misfortune that she seemed not to hold against me. It was just the sheerest bad luck, a grotesque misunderstanding.

Other kids had trouble accepting their status as well. They engaged in banter about what had happened. Some of the orphans would not admit that their parents were never coming back. They made up stories about fathers and mothers who were on long journeys. If a victim of harassment fought back, he was challenged to prove his mother was not a whore or his father was not awaiting execution in some prison. The blame kept shifting. Sometimes the orphans were the low ones on the totem pole, and at other times they made their case that it was not their fault that their parents were dead. They challenged us with "Why did they put you in here?" or "I bet your mom hates you." There was no chance of any of us forgetting even for a day that we had been abandoned, whether by willful neglect or by death, due to our basic unworthiness. All the terrible things that had happened—as squalid and violent as newspapers and rap sheets could testify—had been our own fault, no one else's.

Although I had no idea where my father was, and he would not be drafted until the war had gone on for nearly two years, I bragged that he was fighting the enemy, though I hedged on whether he was serving in battles against Hitler or the Emperor of Japan. I worried about him when magazine and newspaper pictures showed men under fire. With a postcard from Blackwell my father could have allayed my worries.

> Seated on the dormitory floor
> I searched for his face in *Life*,
> *Look* and *Liberty*, spreading
> the pages for all to see. Fathers
> were wading across rivers
> with rifles held high, and one
> of those men could be mine.
> But those soldiers were in
> the Pacific, not Europe,
> said my worst orphan foe,
> pointing out that I was not
> even looking in the right half
> of the world to find a father

In our dormitory bunks in the south wing of the building, some boys would whimper through the night. Two of us were gasping asthmatics. Boys awoke from nightmares. One was a sleepwalker and had to be carried back to his bunk by a matron, who ignored all but the most desperate cries. They spanked boys who wet their beds or got up too many times to pad down the hall to the bathroom. We were supposed to stay in bed as if strapped in.

Some kids had frequent stomachaches, numb fingers, headaches, twitches of facial muscles. Some moaned and groaned in the night, and cried out in terror. Pains flickered around their bodies like lightning. Ellen told me it was the same on her side of the building. Half the girls cried themselves to sleep and others sneaked into other bunks in order to find a friend to hug through the night.

One Saturday we were told to climb into the station wagon chauffeured by Anson, the cook's husband, who also worked as a handyman. We headed into town for our immunization shots. We were taken to a doctor's office in a downtown skyscraper and lined up to receive the injections. As the queue advanced and we entered the inner room, I was surprised to see that the nurse was my mother. It was a strange moment. She had not visited us for weeks. But here she was in her white uniform! I wanted to rush forward and give her a hug, but something in her expression told me not to.

She was committed, it seemed, to a stony professionalism and could not show us any special concern. As she told me to move on, I held the wad of cotton she handed me against my stinging arm, and vented my bewilderment with a sigh. This was the mother I had longed for. But she showed no sign that she was even glad to see her children. It was a great mystery.

Perhaps she was playing a game—it would have broken the rules to show how glad she was to see us. But it was no more amusing than pranks like the one Uncle Henry played one day when he and Aunt Edris visited the hilltop shack. We were in town on that Saturday, and they decided to surprise us with a trick called the Seven Devils. They carried our furniture out of the house and turned it upside down, dumping laundry and the contents of drawers in the dirt. Mother said the yard looked as if a tornado had hit it. There had been nothing funny about the malicious prank, and Mother had wept.

I hated the Children's Home more than ever—the corduroy knickers, and the hot cooked turnips dumped on our plates every Tuesday. They were nauseating, so I slipped them into my hand and, when nobody was looking, dropped them in a potted plant behind me. A matron once grabbed me off my chair without warning and pulled me into the hall for a whipping. As if my father had taught her the technique, she held me with one hand and beat me with the other. I was glad she did not have his razor strop.

Another survivor of the Children's Home in Tulsa, the writer Lloyd Van Brunt, remembers being hauled often into the basement for whippings, but I had that honor only once. Most misdemeanors were dealt with without elaborate ceremonies of punitive sadism requiring a trip to the basement. Matrons teamed up for those sessions, as two of them did one day after my red-haired enemy Donald and I were caught fighting in the boys' playground. Donald and I were forced to whip each other with belts, much to the amusement of the matrons. First Donald had to whip me until I cried, then I had to whip him until he cried. It was more of a humiliation for him, I hoped, because he was the biggest boy in the place, and I had been brave to fight him. In the playground we had been charging at each other like bulls, locking horns though we had none. It was a wonder we did not get skull fractures. My hatred of Donald was grounded in envy. Christmas was just another "visiting day."

> As I sat in the hall next to my aunt
> I watched Donald, his eyes lit up
> as he sat by his fat gramma,
> his "only living relative"—we knew
> that term—and I heard her say
> "I'm sorry, Donald, it's all I have."

It was a giant red apple, a "delicious"
which she had polished until it gleamed.
Donald, how I hated you for having
a gramma like that, who brought you
a red apple glowing with her love.

I followed you for days
but you wouldn't put it down,
and we fought at least a dozen times,
duels nearly to the death, over other things.

Ellen and I were not allowed to join each other in the corridor running between the two wings of the building without the excuse of a visitor. On visiting days Aunt Ruth might turn up. But her gifts were
loaded. She would tell us our mother was too busy to come along, but
never said it in a convincing tone. We accepted the gifts, but not one of
them was the equal of Donald's apple.

It was not just the apple that made some of us hate Donald. Taller
than the rest of us, the ruddy freckled boy had a bush of red pubic hair
that he showed off like a personal achievement, scoffing at the rest of us
for having nothing more than fuzz.

At night I lay on my bunk and stared across the miles towards Tulsa's
skyscrapers. The spotlights on the tallest changed colors every two or
three minutes, working through the rainbow. I indulged my Superman
fantasy of stepping out the window, my cape flowing in the wind as I
flew across the sky and landed atop that tower. Then I would slide down
the building and search out Mother. Sometimes the fantasy carried over
into my dreams.

At the Children's Home there were no father figures other than
Anson—only the mannish matrons. We called them "slap-happy"
because they seemed eager to slap us around. There were rules against
using too much soap or toilet paper. Each boy had to make his own bed
and pass a matron's inspection. He would get a belting or a slap if the
mitered sheets were not perfect at each corner. Shoes had to be kept

shined and lined up when not on feet. Lockers lined one wall, and they were subject to inspection. Assignments of cleaning chores had to be carried out promptly. Mopping the bathroom one Saturday, I found myself berated by a matron for two reasons at once. I had used too much of the odiferous Clorox and I had opened the window without permission. The matrons also swooped down on us for horsing around in the shower, a large facility running the rear width of the bathroom, and they permitted no talking after lights out.

Even if we had memorized all the rules controlling our every hour, the matrons would have come up with new ones. Rules that made no sense brought another hazard. If we asked any questions, we were disciplined for insolence, "talking back." Boys and girls were allowed to play together for half an hour after supper each evening in the front yard, but even then the rules were elaborate. Matrons policed choices of playmates. They preferred that brothers and sisters not talk to each other, even in those supervised half-hour sessions. Ellen and I were caught and punished for talking through the fence separating the two playgrounds.

On Christmas afternoon, Bob Wills and His Texas Playboys, in cowboy boots, Stetson hats, and bright kerchiefs, set up their sound system in the dining room, cleared for a concert. This was the band my father loved, the music he and Mother had argued about. I sat cross-legged on the floor, as close as I could get to the fabled musicians. They started out with "San Antonio Rose" before launching into Christmas carols. Now and then Bob Wills leaned into the microphone with the familiar "Take it away, Leon," giving way to the steel guitar. The children were thrilled to be treated with such attention by the famous band. Bob Wills paused between numbers to ask what we wanted to hear next—"You Are My Sunshine," "My Adobe Hacienda," and "Mexicali Rose" were called out. At last I summoned the courage to request my father's favorite, "Take Me Back to Tulsa."

After a vigorous session of music and stomping, Santa Claus appeared with a great bag full of gifts which he passed out to all the kids. I caught the whiff of whiskey as he bent to hand me a present, so pretty I did not want to unwrap it. I kept thinking my father would have loved to be there, but when I turned around, it was Mother I saw standing in the doorway. Strangely, she too seemed thrilled to see Bob Wills. She did not complain about the hillbilly shrieks and was happy to share the candy in my gift box. I broke away from her to run out with the others, taking advantage of Mrs. Spessard's permission to wave goodbye to the band as they departed in their bus.

I hung around Anson, the genial handyman, as much as possible. As chauffeur of the wood-paneled station wagon, he sometimes let me ride along with him on some of his errands, trips to stores or to take someone to a bus or train. The privilege was special, against the rules. He would pick me up behind the kitchen and I would hunch in the back seat until we were out of sight.

I confided in him that I was in love with Mary Lou, whose straw-colored hair was clipped like thatch. Her blue eyes twinkled in her freckled face with a triumphant disregard of the sadness of orphanhood, and her bouncy steps often broke into a skip. I had seen her do handstands and cartwheels in the front yard play sessions. We had become friends while sharing kitchen duty, which included setting the table, helping serve dinner, clearing dishes, washing up, and in general helping Hilda, who heartily encouraged our innocent flirtation as we dried dishes together. Usually the boys and girls could not get close enough to speak to each other, so even standing next to Mary Lou was a thrilling intimacy.

On occasion Hilda sent us to the basement larder to fetch something. What I considered our romance consisted of accidental touching as Mary Lou and I bent over grocery boxes or a potato bin. Since even Ellen and I had to conduct our conspiratorial whispers by sneaking up to the fence between the separate playgrounds, the closeness to Mary Lou seemed a greater triumph over the rules.

But there was a worry. A child was discharged from the Children's Home on reaching a twelfth birthday. For an orphan like Mary Lou that meant being transferred to the Francis Willard Home for girls. I asked Anson if I could go along when he took her there.

I spent the week before Mary Lou's transfer trying to devise a way she and I could escape together. I knew it would mean betraying Anson, but decided he could deal with the problem. But when we made the trip, and he turned down a dusty road on the far side of Tulsa, I knew it was too late. Anson and I walked Mary Lou to the front door of her new home. I carried her suitcase up the porch steps. When a woman came to the door, Anson introduced Mary Lou, who was ushered inside. I missed my chance to kiss her goodbye, as I had planned. On the way back in the empty station wagon, Anson and I were as mournful as if we had left a loved one to be executed. And I lost Anson, too. The trip to transfer Mary Lou was the last time he invited me to ride along in the station wagon.

With the closing of that screen door, Mary Lou had disappeared from my life, although I still nursed a fantasy. I had it all worked out, where we would meet—under the big clock in the lobby of a Tulsa sky-scraper—on her twenty-first birthday. I pictured the ultimate in inti-macy—taking off our clothes together for a bath. We would get married in secret, though, since it would be too embarrassing if people suspected us of doing that sort of thing. We would play and frolic together, naked most of the time, then hug and kiss all night. But we would never be as careless as Charlene and her cowboy lover.

What I knew about sex hardly prepared me for realism. I remem-bered the animals on the farm, and confusing glimpses of my parents when they were behaving oddly. The truism that American kids get their sex education "in the gutter" was borne out by huddled conferences with other children in a culvert at Mingo. Sometimes the misinforma-tion was grotesque. One boy bragged that he knew for sure that men bled like women, but that the Modess sanitary pad had to be worn "on their assholes." There was conflicting opinion about which hole babies came out of. Had I pursued anatomy research with Eve in her hayloft, she might have enlightened me on such matters.

Sundays at the Children's Home were not only visiting days for rela-tives but also open house for charity ladies or citizens who wanted to inspect a public institution. They had to see everything, including how politely we sat in the dining room, and how we mumbled the compul-sory prayer. Sometimes, led by Mrs. Spessard, the director, these chatty

voyeurs trooped through the building, inspecting the dorms and shuf-
fling down the second floor hallway where they paused to look into the
bathroom.

One evening the women in fur coats crowded into the doorway,
gawking the length of the room where a dozen or more of us were show-
ering. Their tour seemed timed to climax with this entertainment. They
gave us their full attention, whispering comments that provoked us to
cover ourselves with washcloths and crowd toward the back of the cur-
tainless shower. Some of the boys managed to produce remarkably
opaque layers of soapsuds within a minute or two.

A girl about my age was among a group of women. She stood gawking, thunderstruck. I felt like wadding up my washcloth and throwing it,
or maybe sticking out my tongue. But I saw that she was staring not at
me but at Donald with his bush of red pubic hair and his hefty penis,
the largest among us. Later I could not forget her blushing face. I was
left with the surprise that it was not only boys whose eyes could burn
with curiosity. The odd thought occurred to me that it would have been
nice if she had stayed behind and joined us in the shower.

For all our fighting and rivalry, the children I knew in the Children's
Home already shared a common heritage, a conviction that they were
not worth much, that what had happened to them was their fault,
regardless of their arguments otherwise. Dodging that reality would
become a lifelong crusade, trying to vanquish detractors despite being
convinced that every insult and degradation was deserved.

We had too often been told we were nothing—not Superman, not
even the man. Uncle Henry had spoken with an authority I could never
refute. The effort to regain dignity would taint every relationship. I was
already asking too much from others, as if begging for a bit of charity
here, another there, hoping to take in enough to assure survival. I have
seen this in the faces of beggars, craving unconditional acceptance
where even a dime is unlikely.

The abandoned child never leaves off the hope that the discontin-
ued life will be taken up right where it left off. The parents will return,
whether from an errand or from death, and life together will be

resumed, though on better terms, as if the time apart had only been for learning new respect for one another. Then what a relief it would be to quit relying on strangers who never give enough!

Eileen Simpson, in her book called *Orphans Real and Imaginary*, wrote that "emotional damage is never easy to measure, but mothers who are alive but psychically absent impose filial burdens which knot their children's feelings in a way biologic orphans are spared." Simpson mentions "artificial orphans" who sometimes "refused to recognize their mothers when they reappeared." But when we returned from school one afternoon and found Mother waiting for us, standing outside the front entrance by the round flowerbed, chatting with Mrs. Spessard, while a man we had not seen before sat waiting in his car, Ellen and I approached, as watchful as stalking dogs. Mother bent down to hug us, but emptiness struck like a stomachache.

"Big surprise!" she announced. She was taking us back to live with her in the little town where she had a new job. Our lack of enthusiasm puzzled her, but Mrs. Spessard assured her that children are always surprised by good news. Had I been asked the day before how I would feel if Mother came to get us I would have been overjoyed. But now I held back. We had been to too many schools already. Mary Lou would not know where to find me if we disappeared. Why did Mrs. Spessard not tell Mother to go away? Why did they not give us some warning? At last Ellen and I each gave Mother a sullen hug and we were marched toward the car to meet her new boyfriend.

The matrons had gathered up our things, cleaning out our dormitory lockers. Our bags were in the car before we got back from school. Mrs. Spessard in her perennial blue dress with white polka dots—I had never seen her in any other—stood outside by the circle of roses and waved us goodbye as if she had always been that friendly. Ellen and I did not wave or look back at her as we were taken out the front gate. We had been in the Children's Home for only a few months, but it seemed an eternity, long enough to learn that we belonged with orphans.

Mother had a new boyfriend—not Gerald, who had disappeared into the army. Who was this new man called Doc, driving his restored Model A Ford, bragging about it, as if I cared? I leaned forward and asked him if he would mind going back so we could say goodbye to our friends. He gave Mother an annoyed look and she turned around and told us not to be ridiculous, there wasn't time, and we would really like Nowata.

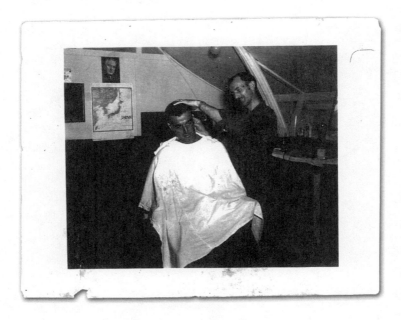

Father serving in World War II

10.

THE TRIP TO Nowata did not feel like the answer to our prayers. I did not like Mother's friend at all. Doc was no substitute for Gerald, who had disappeared from our lives. The last time we had seen him was in Mingo the night of the Joe Louis-Max Baer fight, when my coyote Foxy had run away.

Maybe a warning about our impending move would have helped, or even a pretense at involving us in the decision. But Mother had already worked everything out. Ellen and I waited for the next surprise. So far, each of our moves had been a descent to a worse situation, as if we were fated to bounce down steps, never up.

On the one-hour trip north, Mother was glad enough for all three of us. She chatted breezily on about Nowata, how we would just love it. She said it was a shame school had already started, but we were smart enough to catch up fast. The school in Nowata was every bit as good as Tulsa's and we were bound to like it, that was the important thing. I was not so sure.

The bumpy, much repaired highway took a big curve, ascended a railroad overpass, then offered a choice of a street angling left, a direct shot to the town's center, or the continuing main route along the highway. We took the road left past the cemetery and soon rattled along wobbly brick-paved streets. Streetcar tracks still ran along the center of the main street, offering interurban service to Coffeyville, Kansas, twenty-five miles north. Doc and Mother gave us a quick guided tour of downtown Nowata. With a rev of power matching Mother's breathy enthusiasm, we roared uphill past the post office, climbing to the highest cross street.

Doc pulled up in front of a tall white house towering above a retaining wall. Ellen and I lugged our suitcases up the cement steps and past a withered apple tree in the front yard. Inside, we took the stairs past two landings to the third floor. At the far end of the hall Mother opened a door and we were introduced to our new home—a large room with a wide maple bed, a rocking chair, a small desk and chair, a bureau, and a tall window beyond. From there we could see far out over fields beyond the outskirts of town.

Mother's eagerness to retrieve her children may have been too impulsive. She was living in this one large room, which we would now share, sleeping with her. She had been lonely, she told us. Maybe we would help cheer her up. The novelist Wallace Stegner, remembering his childhood stay with his sister in an orphanage, was not able to clarify his feelings about this period until he approached the age of eighty, long after his mother's death. "When you found how miserable we were in that home," he addressed her spirit, "you took us out and brought us back to the only safety available, your father's house in Iowa. I can imagine what that cost you in humiliation."

We were soon following a new routine with new rules. The bathroom halfway down the hall was as large as our room, with linoleum floors and a long claw-footed bathtub. We bathed in Mother's soapy water, me in the first shift, Ellen in the second, for there was not enough hot water to run separate baths. Mother came in to make sure we did a good job washing our ears and backs. Her inspections were a matter of pride. She scrubbed where we had missed, then followed up our baths with enemas to make sure we were clean inside as well as out.

For the enemas she filled the coral-colored rubber hot-water bag with soapy water until it bulged fat as a football, then hooked it to the wall. She held the rubber tube, dipped its black nozzle in Vaseline, then had me lie on my side on the floor, knees up. She insisted that I wait as long as possible after the bag was emptied. That wait, with its suppressed urgency while I became bloated, seemed to last an hour.

After our first night with her, Mother decided there was no need to use the hot-water bottle as a bed warmer. With Ellen on one side of her and me on the other she said she was warm as toast. I felt proud to be of such service and soon added still other devotions, nightly polishing her white shoes, and rising before daylight to walk her down the hill to her early duties at the hospital. Before long we were slipping and sliding, our steps the first in virgin snow catching dawn's buttery light. Her laughter when we fell offered rare and welcome relief from her grim mask of constant worry. We were like playmates and even threw snowballs. But she left frivolity at the hospital door.

Sharing a bed was nothing new. Oddly, the Children's Home with its crowded dormitories in separate wings of the building had been the only place Ellen and I had ever enjoyed the privacy of our own beds. In the hilltop shack we had slept with our parents. On Grampa's farm I had shared a bed with Dub, both of us encased in scratchy woolen long johns. At Aunt Peg's and Aunt Ruth's and Aunt Edris's and Aunt Bea's, Ellen and I had been bedded down together. In the Greeley home we had slept in the back room in one bed with the two younger girls. Even when we had spent a few days in St. John's Hospital in Tulsa to have our tonsils out, Ellen and I had slept together, defying the separation the nuns had imposed by settling us in opposite cribs in a shared room. As soon as the nurse had left and lights were out, I crawled over the side rails, crossed the room and climbed into Ellen's crib. In the morning, the nuns put me back where I belonged.

On my way to surgery, when two nuns were wheeling me on a gurney and were about to roll me through the gaping doors of an elevator, I flung back the sheet and jumped down, breaking into a run as my feet hit the floor. I headed at full stride toward light flooding through the front entrance and almost made it to the revolving doors when one of the nuns scooped me up in her arms and carried me back, kicking and screaming. The fat penguins in their black and white habits held me

down, clucking compassion as the elevator doors closed and the fright-
ful box lifted us. I was still screaming as they wheeled the gurney into
the operating room. Under a great klieg light I went down fighting, a
mask of ether shoved over my face. I fell back, down a black whirlpool,
and woke up with a throat full of pain.

Whatever fear of elevators signified, I was as frightened of them as
of any mad dog. When Aunt Ruth took us Christmas shopping in
Vandever's department store in Tulsa, she tried her usual bribery to
overcome my terror. Knowing how much I wanted an electric train like
my cousin George's, she promised me one just like it if I would get in
the elevator. The bribe tempted me, but the fear was uncontrollable.
She tugged me toward the elevator as the uniformed operator waited
with the door open while he and shoppers observed the attempted
bribery. Each time the bronze doors slid closed with a boing boing and
the elevator swooped upwards, my exasperated aunt upped her offer.
She would buy me not only the train but several accessories. Finally
she took me up the stairs and we crossed the second floor to the toy
department and looked at the large display, which included everything
George Jr. had plus extra locomotives and trackside buildings. Then
she took me back downstairs and tried once more to get me into the
elevator. But all the efforts to entice me only triggered spells of wheezing. Even into my adult years I considered anyone who voluntarily
stepped into an elevator crazy.

For all her efforts to provide us with a better situation, Mother only
plunged Ellen and me into a deeper level of hell. No social worker had
approved her plan to bring her ten and eleven year old children to share
one bed on the third floor of a firetrap rooming house. After a few weeks
there, we moved to an apartment over a double garage—four small
rooms with plasterboard walls and a screened-in porch on four-by-four
stakes. Canvas blinds rolled down inside the screens, and Ellen and I
sometimes slept there. In the garage apartment, as in the rooming
house, I tried not to look over Mother's shoulder when I obeyed her call
to come in and wash her back as she bathed, warning me not to peek.
And when she came in as I was taking a bath and told me to stand up,

she did not take note of my embarrassment as she had me peel back my foreskin to prove that I had washed properly.

My mother dated several men during this period. One by one they came into our lives, and Ellen and I viewed them as potential replacements for our father, although they were no match for Gerald. But as suddenly as they appeared, they departed. I disliked all of them, but I liked their cars. Doc, the balding older man with a mustache, had a refurbished Model A Ford. Bill had an elegant tan limousine with whitewall tires. The Greek who owned the lunch counter and the pool hall had no car so far as I knew.

They brought their bottles and their gifts of flowers or chocolates or ice cream and disappeared into the bedroom or the screened-in porch where the canvas blinds were tied down only for lightning storms or privacy. It was all too easy to hear the squeaking of bedsprings, occasional scraps of talk: "Did you remember to bring a rubber?" Mother asked one of them, her whispers resonant though the closed door. The pathos of my mother's search, the desperation of it, the dreary pattern of it, lingered long after the men had left.

Sometimes Mother or her date gave us money and sent us off to the movies. But Nowata's theatres let out early, and we still heard and saw far too much when we got home. Intelligent as she was, our mother seemed impaired in her ability to choose men. Each was a step down from the last. With few, if any, exceptions they were alcoholics. Mother hoped to change the men she dated, and never seemed to meet one who did not need reforming. Her efforts to please men were a diversion from her need to protect herself and her children, and we could not protect her. Sometimes, as Ellen and I tried, it was as if our roles as children and parent were reversed. Mother often seemed as absent from our lives as she had been while we were in Tulsa.

Mother now and then apologized for the men she brought home. At least one of her boyfriends she introduced to Ellen and me as our "uncle." He was a stocky little man with a sailor's cap and high-cuffed khakis. To this day I do not know whether she asked us to call him "uncle" as a courtesy, the way the term is used in India for children to convey respect to an adult family friend, as a euphemism, or as a semantic shortcut to get us to accept him. Could we have overlooked or forgotten a relative? We were mystified as to how to react, but he soon disappeared.

On evenings in Nowata when she had no visitor, Mother would take fifty cents or a dollar from her purse and say, "Take this and go on down to Chubb's and bring me back a pint of hand-packed black walnut. And get me a *Redbook* if the new issue has come in. You can get yourself a Hershey bar." Fatigued from her work at the hospital and propped up in bed, a pillow hugged between her knees, she comforted herself with the magazine and ice cream, licking the spoon after each bite.

She reminded us it was unfair to expect her, after a busy day at the hospital, to keep house or cook when she got home. We tried harder. Ellen learned to cook spaghetti, and more often to heat up Kraft Dinner, a dreadful yellow goo of macaroni and cheese. She taught herself to bake, and we drank her first effort at making a chocolate pie. She kept a flat dish of red Jell-O in the icebox. We tried to keep the apartment clean. We took over the laundry, washing clothes and sheets in the bathtub and wringing them tight. We tried not to bother Mother when she was resting, or to ask for a taste of the ice cream.

She suggested I get a paper route and set to work stitching a canvas shoulder bag for me, using the sewing machine in the nurses' lounge in the hospital basement. The after-school paper route kept me out until after dark, but we were still too much in the way, and Mother complained about our "not minding." One evening she settled us down for a serious talk and told us that the doctors—Wagner and Wheeler—had told her she had six months to live, and that therefore she would appreciate it if we showed more respect and tried to help her more.

The death of Grampa may have set off her anxiety. Mother was sure there had been some kind of psychic contact between her and the old man. She claimed she had awakened in the night at the very moment of his death. She was also upset when she learned that her former brother-in-law, my Uncle Norman, was missing in action in Germany. In this case her psychic powers misled her, for she presumed Norman was dead, but he turned up after the war at a Fourth of July reunion on

Grampa's farm, his leg mottled with scars. In a poem I tried to capture in a metaphoric incident his shaky post-traumatic stress.

> My uncle,
> Great Norman,
> Whose leg was full of
> Finest German shrapnel,
> Broke three chairs and a table
> When the kids
> Set off firecrackers
> On July 4, 1946,
> Just after apple pie.

Mother often told us about her work at the hospital. It was not all just bedpans and sponge baths, she said. She also helped in surgery. One time, the doctor handed her a bloody leg he had just amputated and told her to dispose of it. She wrapped it, carried it out back and dropped it in the rusty trash barrel by the alley. Her variety of duties impressed us.

As if part of our genetic legacy, hypochondria ran in the family. Aunt Ruth was the champion in getting attention from doctors. She had nearly thirty surgeries to brag about. Whether because of or in spite of them, she lived to her ninetieth year. "They go in so often they oughta put a zipper in," her oldest brother, my Uncle Skeet, once wisecracked. He himself refused to go to a doctor, preferring self-medication with alcohol.

One complaint—a tummy ache or a fleeting pain—and Mother would take us to the hospital for x-rays, a blood count, and fluoroscopy. Armed with a key, she had access to weekend use of the equipment. She did the blood counts in a tiny passageway, sitting on a stool and peering into a microscope, pressing a metal counter with her thumb. She would lean aside to let me get a look at the various cells. When I had yet another of my frequent afflictions of boils—under the arms, in nostrils, on my buttocks—the blood was mine, the diagnosis scary. She reminded me that her father had died from this sort of affliction.

When she stood me against the glass plate of a fluoroscope, the glow illuminated her face like a Renaissance Madonna tinted with reflected green of radiant grass. I tried to peer over the machine to see what defects she located within me. Whatever they were, she always seemed to fear the worst, and her fear was contagious. Radiation was still considered a blessing that could not too often be employed for fun or profit. In a shoe store we children seldom passed up an opportunity to slide our feet into a slot and peer down at our glowing metatarsals. We were only a year away from the wonders of Hiroshima and Nagasaki.

11.

AT TIMES MY hunger for a father leapt past Mother's choices to include others. At school, a casual wave from Coach McCoy as he headed across the schoolyard to lunch could provoke a vivid fantasy. Over the meal he would praise me to his wife, even suggesting they have me live with them. If he and his wife adopted me, though, they might have to move fast, for I had the same thoughts about the teacher of our manual training class. Under his tutelage I crafted a wooden lawn chair with two left arms. His tolerance of my incompetence, giving even that sorry production an approving grin and a high grade, encouraged me to think he liked me. I needed little invitation for my fantasies, which landed on friendly faces as randomly as pollen.

When Mother started dating the Greek who had a lunch counter at the Oasis bar and pool hall, she suggested that I might work for him, so I took on a second job for two dollars a week—two hours after school and all day on Saturdays. I worked behind the counter, serving up chili and mulligan stew, handing across Tabasco sauce and bowls full of crackers. The customers, many of them drunk from their time at the bar across the room, sat on low stools, huddled over their bowls, dribbling on their beards, and licking grease or mustard from their hands. I tried to keep them supplied with plenty of napkins.

Nick, the Greek, was a thin fellow with a mustache and a stained apron wrapped at least twice around his waist. He ordered me about, directing my duties as fry cook at the grill when he wanted to take a break and cross the room to get a beer at the bar. Most of the time I was busy as a waiter and dishwasher, standing over the deep steaming sink. The plumbing was primitive, so I carried buckets to the back door and slung the dirty dishwater into the alley.

When I mopped the cement floor, Nick told me to stop at the invisible line in the middle of the room—he was not responsible for the tavern across the room or the pool hall in back. After sweeping up the cigarette butts and other litter, I mopped the entire floor anyway, just to be nice to Lee, who tended the bar and would soon replace the Greek as my mother's suitor.

Lee, a big man with a beer belly hanging over his belt, his shirt stained with snuff, conducted business at the bar with genial authority, keeping the peace with a pistol he occasionally pulled out of a drawer. Most of the time he was friendly enough, his hands splayed out on the bar as he stood before a vast dusty mirror and shelves crowded with liquor bottles, mostly decorative, since Oklahoma was a dry state.

Only 3.2 beer was legal, but Lee had a reputation as a bootlegger. The bar and shelves behind him offered potato chips and peanuts, the cellophane bags hanging like dusty fruit, as well as pickled eggs and pigs' feet in large jars. Framed Elks and V.F.W. certificates and group pictures of Lee and his buddies lent prestige. Now and then he lit up a cigar from one of the open boxes, or plucked down a can of Copenhagen snuff for himself, opening the tin and pinching out a dab.

Lee was a big man who had been a blacksmith before a stint in the army. His first wife had died of cancer, and he had a son, Charlie, a sailor exactly five years older than me—we shared a birthday. Charlie had lied about his age in order to join the navy. He and his father did not get along and he had been eager to escape, as I learned on Charlie's first visit home. Though only in his forties, Lee had lost all his teeth and had a sharp jutting jaw. His dentures pained him, and therefore were often left atilt in a glass. Without the teeth, he often cupped his palm over his mouth, talking through his fingers. On the special occasions when he put the teeth in his protruding jaw gave him a skull-like appearance, his sallow skin almost jaundiced.

Lee seemed an unlikely choice for Mother, who had snubbed the hillbilly tastes of my father. But she liked to point out that she had not met Lee in the Oasis. Women did not, in fact, go to the Oasis. Her acquaintance with this man destined to become our stepfather went back to more innocent encounters. She had met him in his role as volunteer fireman.

As she left work at the hospital, Mother walked past the firehouse, a yellow brick building with two wide doors facing the street, the prows of red fire engines gleaming inside. The volunteers, including Lee, would sometimes be sitting in front, and would make flirtatious remarks as women passed by. Lee had struck up a conversation with Mother, and after a time had invited her out.

Before long Lee was dropping by regularly at the garage apartment. From the beginning, his presence kept me alert and suspicious. It was one thing to see him at work behind the bar, where he sometimes offered me a Coke or 7-Up as thanks for mopping his side of the room. But even on his first visit to our apartment, I tensed with an instinctive aversion, watching with disapproval as he pulled Ellen onto his lap with grabby hands, a familiarity she did not invite.

Ellen slapped at his hands and wriggled away, off his lap, but Mother would reproach her. "Be nice to him, Ellen," she insisted, and before long she was telling us that Lee would soon be our stepfather and we had to show him more respect. In Lee's rattling tan DeSoto, we paid a visit to the edge of town where a weathered clapboard house leaning like the tower of Pisa was pointed out to us as our future home. We got out of the car and looked through the downstairs windows, the glass discolored by sun, with swirly patinas like the scum on oil. When I exclaimed that there was no floor inside, Mother told us new flooring was already ordered—yellow pine, tongue and groove.

The toilet was an outhouse reached through a muddy lot fenced with chicken wire. Lee kept a flock of dirty geese there, fed with donations of garbage from the Greek's lunch counter. A faucet behind the house was the water supply. I was not thrilled at the prospect of this move.

The wedding ceremony took place in the Court House. After a snapshot session on the front lawn, Mother and Lee rumbled down the brick streets in the DeSoto, heading to the Ozarks on their honeymoon. Cans tied to the back bumper bounced and rattled behind the car, the chivaree mischief provided by Lee's pals from the Oasis, the V.F.W., and the Elks Club.

When the couple got back from the Ozarks, we moved into the house at the edge of town. Ellen and I shared the upstairs room. Several steps of the stairs had rotted out, so we had to be careful. When the new downstairs flooring was near completion Lee had a falling out with the contractor, and the job was never finished. The flooring left off a foot or so from the back wall of the living room. The virginal lumber soon became smudged and warped. With the cold of winter, the narrow boards contracted. Soot and lint gathered in the widening cracks.

In a corner area of my upstairs room, where the roof sloped down nearly to the floor, there were bundles of clothes, suitcases, and an old camelback trunk—the legacy of Lee's former wife. Lee's green foot-locker from his service in the infantry tempted my curiosity. It held blacksmithing tools and magazines devoted to mechanics. Rust, oil-stains, and holes left by insects testified to age and neglect, but I was intrigued to find a few nudist magazines like the ones he kept rolled up in the back of the DeSoto's glove compartment. The bodies in those issues of *Sunshine and Health* and *American Sunbathing* were air-brushed, hairless and sometimes nipple-less dolls posed on lake docks or at picnic tables or leaping in volleyball games. Breasts seemed arrested in midair like planetary globes. Men seemed to have suffered a dissolving of their nether parts by a puff of bleach painless enough to permit their goofy smiles.

Lee and others, including his employer Lee Iseli, had a troubled history with the law over liquor sales. The Oasis was known, according to a February 1947 State and County Petition for Injunction and to Abate a Nuisance, as a place of business with "a general reputation of being a bad place where intoxicating liquors are sold and drunk, and where rowdyism and boisterous conduct is carried on, and that men in a drunken condition congregate in front of said place of business and offer insulting language to women passing along the street."

Lee had to appear in court to answer charges the County Attorney filed after a violent incident in the Oasis.

"The plaintiff alleges and says that in the building located on said described premises and apart from the beer concern charged with the illegal traffic in intoxicating liquors, is a pool hall, which is not separated from or screened off from the bar and that portion of the building in which said intoxicating liquor is sold, and in connection therewith, also is a restaurant or cafe where people are served with edibles, and that as a result of the illegal sale of intoxicating liquor, to-wit, 3.2 beer, and the pool hall and cafe, a large number of people congregate inside the building and up to and around the bar and buy and drink and consume large quantities of beer and become intoxicated, and engage in profane, loud and boisterous language and quarreling and threatening to fight, and that on the night of February lst, 1947, at a time when a large number of people were present and assembled in said place of business, trouble ensued between one, Albert Harrison and others to the petitioner at this time unknown, and that said Albert Harrison challenged the bar tender to fight and invited him to come out into the alley to fight and otherwise creating a disturbance in said place of business, and on the 2nd day of February, 1947, being Sunday, and in the afternoon, when there was a large number of people congregated and assembled in the building, the said Albert Harrison appeared in the building and demanded to be served with beer, and Lee Pape being in charge thereof, refused to serve him beer, and a quarrel and trouble ensued, which resulted in a threat and challenge to fight, and the said Lee Pape grabbed a revolver, to-wit: a French 44, 1917 Model, and fired a shot at the said Albert Harrison and slightly wounded him."

There is some evidence, not all of it clear or accessible, that Lee had a violent history well before he met Mother. After the shooting, which had the town talking about little else, Lee was charged with assault with a deadly weapon. While out on bail, Lee took us to the Oasis and showed us the bullet holes on the door.

Lee was acquitted. Ellen and I endured embarrassment at school, and worried about rumors that the shooting victim and his friend threatened revenge. Lee claimed self-defense. His version was that after being refused service, Harrison went out to his car and returned with a gun. Lee also claimed that he had only meant to disarm the man, who, according to the newspapers, "was nicked in the left side by a .45 caliber slug." The Court documents described the gun as a .44. It could have been either, as Lee kept one revolver in the drawer behind the bar and another in the glove compartment of his DeSoto.

Iseli closed down the embattled Oasis but managed to get a license to open another tavern for our stepfather to manage. On the main highway at the edge of town, the new Oasis, which was to be called Lee's Place, was meant to capture the business of truck drivers and passing motorists. Behind the building covered with white asbestos shingles, with neon beer signs in its windows, was an old streetcar, mounted on cinderblocks. The streetcar served as a storeroom, with beer boxes stacked as partitions. There was also a tiny room added at the rear, a mattress on its floor.

As manager of the new tavern, Lee decided to make the business a family affair. Mother gave up her job at the hospital and committed herself to helping full-time at the restaurant and tavern. Ellen was expected to work after school as a waitress. Mother cooked hamburgers and French fries, as well as T-bone specials served on oval plates, which she passed through the wicket window behind the bar.

Mother invited Uncle Skeet to come and stay—a make-shift arrangement by which her brother, a frail and wrinkled old man at fifty-five, never without a tailor-made cigarette dangling under his droopy eyes, helped around the tavern and was allowed to sleep there. He had been having a hard time and Mother was proud of rescuing him from skid row by this arrangement. She limited him to only a few beers a day, although Skeet was watchful for opportunities to empty a neglected glass or bottle here or there as he cleared the booths. Nagging him about his

shirttail hanging out or his open fly, Mother never failed to let her oldest brother know that she was ashamed of him.

Lee's new place reminded me of the corner tavern in Mingo—a bar,
wooden booths, and a dance floor with scuffed and warped linoleum.
The jukebox tunes got in my head as I tried to do homework in a booth.
I spent far less time than Ellen and Mother at the tavern, preferring to
go back to the house when I finished the jobs that had replaced my
employment with the Greek. In addition to the after-school paper route
for the *Nowata Star*, I took on a Saturday job as janitor and caretaker of
the Church of God. I was responsible for cleaning the church, mowing
the lawn, and showing up Sunday mornings to press a button activating
the electronic carillon that blared out an hour of religious melodies
from the loud speakers mounted on the steeple. "Onward Christian
Soldiers" bonged through the neighborhood.

One Sunday morning parishioners complained that grass along the
sidewalk was not trimmed neatly enough. The minister cited that complaint as his reason for firing me, but did not let me go without inform-
ing me that he could not give me a second chance for another reason. I
was already on the road to hell and damnation. His son had seen me
going into a Saturday matinee downtown, where Western movies and
Green Hornet serials were shown. Although my job did not require me
to join the Church of God, he could not have anybody associated with
the church pursuing such sinful ways in public. As far as he was concerned, picture shows were the work of the devil.

I kept my mouth shut, hiding my sense of injustice. Not only did I
spend a nickel on the movies every Saturday, I often did so in the company of the minister's son, the tattletale who had betrayed me.

I found another job as helper on a Rainbow Bread route, riding
along on the truck's running board, hopping off at stops in front of grocery stores. I rushed in with a cardboard bin in hand, a large but easily
managed weight because the loaves of bread were as light and airy as pillows. I dropped the bread route when an opportunity came up to
become the town's Special Delivery messenger, but took with me for life
the knowledge that I should never choose a loaf of bread from the front

of a shelf, but reach far behind where the fresh bread is placed.

The post office job obliged me to check in at 6 A.M. for my morning deliveries, letters and packages fresh off the train, and again at 5 P.M. A little desk was provided inside the back door, where I sat to log in letters as the two mail sorters standing at their wall of pigeonholes handed them to me. I also inherited my predecessor's bicycle, a vehicle with a large basket in front of the handlebars, over a half-size front wheel.

Only as Christmas approached did the basket, rattling around as I made my deliveries both at dawn and dusk, carry enough parcels to justify its capacity. Most days there were only a few letters—sometimes only one—tucked inside the hinged metal slate I carried for signature receipts. On frosty mornings, my wheels slid on the icy streetcar tracks. I fancied myself a very important official, bearing news of the highest priority—definitely a promotion over my newspaper delivery days.

Every morning I crossed the railroad tracks as well, and made my way through the muddy, unpaved streets of what was called Niggertown where I knocked on the door of my only regular customer. Myrtle Jones was a middle-aged black woman with breasts shimmering out of her pink slip and loose bathrobe. It was a rare day that Myrtle failed to receive a letter addressed with a carpenter's thick pencil. Her admirer sent his letters from New Orleans. As Myrtle signed for them, I imagined men fighting over her, since she had a scar from a knife wound on her neck, and I had always heard that Negroes had a lot of knife fights. I had seen knife fights on the sidewalks and in the alleys of Nowata, but they had always been between white men.

Myrtle's house was a small, unpainted shack much like the one we had lived in on the farm and it was heated by a potbelly stove. After the first few days of my ritualized arrival, her watchful terrier did not bother to get up from his place near the stove. The open door let out a welcome blast of warmth, smelling of wood smoke and Myrtle's breakfast of ham and eggs. She invited me in to get warm and share breakfast.

The town needed me.
It drove me on. Winters

I slid on the iced rails
Of streetcars.
Summer I dished stew
down at the Oasis Grill
and Poolhall, another place
the decent folk
wouldn't want to look
for love or stew or snooker.
The town needed me
desperately.
One June I mowed the whole
cemetery, then swept the stones.
It's a wonder I didn't build that town.
But I return and there's still
no town built there
nor anyone sowing the seeds
of Communitas
on the right side of the tracks.
But I cross over and stare
where chickens peck
at the ruins of black Myrtle's shack.

The town, of course, had no need of me at all, as I was often aware. It was Paul Goodman who said that if we want to solve the pressing problems we should consult the children. As if consulted, I had many jobs during that period, but I doubt if they solved any problems. Standing at Myrtle's open door with a double vision of a woman whose smile and hospitality beckoned me in even as my mind processed the pervasive prohibitions of racism, I did not as yet have words for my dilemma. The racism around me must have soaked through my skin, for it was a mystery to me how anyone could love an ugly old woman like Myrtle enough to write her such thick letters every day. Politely declining her offer of breakfast, I rode my bike past the fenced school for black children and across the tracks. Like that of the Indian school in Sapulpa, the fence suggested a prison.

In the post office, the clerks sorting mail while I logged out my Special Delivery letters kidded me about my trips to see Myrtle. "Are you going out to see that old nigger woman again?" they would taunt. And when I returned they would ask, "What did that old nigger gal have to say to you this time?" I dared not defend Myrtle. They assumed she was a whore, as well she may have been, but the reason I was sure her letters were from a devoted suitor was that one of the mailmen had opened and resealed enough of them to provide a graphic report on their contents, romantic in the extreme.

Because of the noise and smoke in Lee's Place, which triggered my asthma, I preferred to stay away, using the excuse of jobs and homework which I did back at the house. I bicycled out to the highway for meals, usually hamburgers, before returning for the evening checkout at the post office, in case any special deliveries had come in on the late train. Sometimes, morning or evening, I would go down and watch as the mailbags were unloaded.

As my thirteen-year-old stringbean of a sister served meals at the tavern, she had to endure the teasing and flirtations of customers. When Lee thought the kidding had gone too far, he came to Ellen's defense. "Leave her alone," he would say. "She's my girl." Mother urged Ellen not to be so touchy, and made excuses. She did not like it either, she said, but it was not wise to offend customers.

There were other arguments. If business was active, Ellen was not allowed to go roller-skating, or anywhere else, with her friends. Whether she liked it or not, she had to help out. In addition to waitressing, she helped Mother in the kitchen. With watery eyes she sliced onions. She rolled hamburger meat into balls, then flattened the patties on the gritty black griddle with a spatula. She lowered the wire net basket with French fries, lifting it with a dance step, backing away from sputtering grease.

She slapped at Lee's hand when he patted her. Lee called her stuck up.

Once in a while Lee would allow Ellen to go out with her friends, but not without a warning that the boys just wanted to get into her pants.

Lee became more and more obsessed with Ellen. He seemed to follow her everywhere, disregarding her complaints. Since it often seemed inconvenient to drive home after the tavern closed, Mother, Lee, and Ellen often stayed in the streetcar overnight. It had been turned into something of a home. More than once, when Ellen had gone to the streetcar to have a bath in the round galvanized tub, she settled herself cross-legged into the water only to detect an unwanted presence. Lee had slipped in the door and crouched down to peek at her through chinks in the wall of beer cartons. She screamed obscenities and threw a wadded washcloth. Her face came to reflect tension and indignation, while her sulky posture twisted her slight frame into a defensive slouch.

I was never surprised when I woke up to an empty house, but on nights when the three did not stay in the streetcar and returned late, I would get up, awakened by the old DeSoto pulling up on the gravel. Crouching at the small window over the front door, I looked down on the yard. In the shadows an argument in progress often spilled out beside the car. The shoutings and pleadings were familiar.

"You think I don't have the guts to do it, don't you?" Lee taunted, flailing about. "Nobody gives a damn. Just give me one goddamn reason."

"Lee, you know I love you," Mother said.

"That little bitch doesn't."

"Of course she does, don't you, Ellen?"

"I'm going to bed." Ellen avoided the question.

"Dammit, I asked you a goddamn question." Lee grabbed her arm.

"Let go of me."

"I said I asked you a goddamn question."

"Ellen, just tell your stepfather you love him."

"I love him, is that good enough? Now let me go inside. I've got to get up and go to school in the morning."

"That's a good idea. Honey, let's go on in. We're all tired," Mother pleaded.

"I'll go in when I'm goddamn good and ready." Lee was in his familiar sulk.

"Let me have the gun, Lee, please," Mother begged.

Lee stumbled around in a circle, waving the gun about. Eventually he tired and handed it across, dulled at last by the day's steady drinking.

His behavior became habitual. He waved the pistol around and babbled threats to commit suicide, wallowing in self-pity. When Mother's pleas failed, she turned to Ellen, saying "You try to reason with him."

After an exhausting argument the girl managed to get the gun. She became expert at wheedling and shaming, imploring and daring. Sometimes she grabbed the gun away from him after a tussle. My sister had, despite her slight, almost anorexic frame, assumed a formidable power over our stepfather, but she never dared throw away the gun as she threatened. She passed it to Mother, then stood with arms akimbo giving Lee a scornful look which reduced him to whimpering apologies, begging forgiveness. Sometimes he wept. Humbled at last, he would consent to being led in to bed, a model of meek obedience.

Before long, persuading Lee not to kill himself became Ellen's regular chore. She chased after him as he stumbled to wherever he had most recently tucked the weapon—in the glove compartment of the car parked outside the tavern, or in a drawer behind the bar, or in the streetcar.

His babbling was a hodgepodge. It included grief for his long-dead first wife, anger at his son Charlie's behavior, though Charlie was stationed far away in the navy, and complaints about alleged mistreatment by a variety of persecutors, including the law, his boss Iseli, and my mother and sister. Anything could set Lee off when he got morose and paranoid after several hours of tipping his ever-ready bottle of beer to his lips.

If it ever occurred to Mother that there was danger to anyone besides Lee himself when he waved a loaded gun around, she never showed it. Again and again my brave sister returned with the weapon in hand. When Lee sobered up, Mother quietly returned it to him.

"You're the only one he'll listen to," she told Ellen. Our mother had become deferential and appreciative, acknowledging her own power-lessness in dealing with her husband.

I saw Lee more than once put the pistol to his head. And more than once the big lumbering man broke into drunken tears. Deprived of the pistol, he became a sobbing child.

Watching repetitions of this scene through the little bullseye window over the porch, I fought back the urge to run down and intervene, instinctively aware that Lee had not granted me the immunity from harm that Ellen seemed to have. I gasped with asthma and tried to understand why Mother had brought this man into our lives.

Such was the Spring of 1947. By that time I had taken refuge in my after-school jobs and weekly Boy Scout meetings in the Presbyterian church basement. I had copped out on my responsibilities in the peck-ing order of family strife. Uncle Skeet, who slept on the floor of Lee's Place, shared my impotent rage and witnessed some of the scenes I fled, mumbling every excuse I could devise.

Stepfather Lee at The Oasis

12.

WHEN MY FATHER sent a postcard with an unexpected invitation to visit, I grabbed at the opportunity. He and his second wife, Gilda, now the parents of two young boys, had settled in a small town in Kansas. Dad had prospered, first as a barber, then by opening a restaurant that had become popular. I knew my little half-brothers only from snapshots sent on to us by my father's sisters, with whom my mother stayed in touch. In those pictures they wore white sailor suits like my father's Seabees uniform. The oldest had been born eighteen days after the official divorce of my parents.

I took the bus, with a change in Ponca City, where I was alarmed to run into my seventh-grade teacher, Charlotte Whitford. The serendipitous meeting—she greeted me pleasantly enough—evoked a stinging blush of shame because of an incident that had happened back in Nowata.

My friend K. P. Haverfield who, with his divorced mother, lived next door to us in another garage apartment, was sitting with me on the post office steps late one afternoon when Miss Whitford ascended the steps past us, giving us a pleasant smile and greeting. K. P., notorious for his vulgarity and mischievous pranks, made a highly audible remark that the teacher must have heard. I could not believe what he had said. With a whistle through his missing teeth he had said loud and clear, "I sure would like to get me a piece of that."

Miss Whitford paused, her hand on the brass door handle, but did not look back at us as she entered the post office. She delayed her exit, perhaps to give us time to disappear. Those minutes before she came out seemed interminable. I urged K. P. to leave. I was mortified to think that Miss Whitford would associate me with his obscenities, as if I too harbored such forbidden thoughts.

K. P. said, "I want to see the expression on her face when she comes out." My painful strategy then switched to an attempt to pretend I had not heard his remark, or to act as if I had no idea what it meant. I suppressed the urge to flee because that would have been a confession of guilty knowledge. I edged away from K. P. and sat looking up at the sky, studying the clouds, a model of innocence, as rigid as a bronze statue although my face was burning. When she finally came out, she strode halfway down the steps and addressed us sternly. "You boys should not think such things, and even if you do, you should not say them." She looked at our faces in turn, then went on down.

When Charlotte Whitford , my favorite teacher, resigned to get married at the end of the school year, K. P. bragged that he had driven her to quit. That had been his goal every time he sassed her in class, threw erasers, or made grotesque faces and obscene gestures whenever she turned her back.

In the bus station, my behavior may have seemed equally strange to Miss Whitford for, remembering that encounter at the post office, I stuttered and blushed when she approached and asked where I was going. I barely glanced at her face as I explained that I was on my way to Kansas to visit my father. I could not but believe that she too was remembering the afternoon she had remained inside the post office for many extra minutes before dealing with her two students. I was relieved and broke away with a hasty goodbye when the boarding call for my bus came over the loudspeaker.

Dad's restaurant, next to a movie theatre on the town's Main Street, was a great success. He had quit barbering, but he drove me by the shop near the railroad tracks where he had worked after he had come out of the service, when he was new to the town. He had managed to recover and transport to Kansas the barber's chair bought ten years before with the hundred dollars borrowed from Ellen's trust fund.

Just as my father's barber shop customers back in Mounds had pre-
dicted, the war had helped the economy. His luck had changed phe-
nomenally, and he was pleased to share some business secrets. "It's the
mashed potatoes," he told me, explaining that customers in his restaurant were delighted that they could have as many extra helpings of
mashed potatoes as they wished. I made a mental note to employ that
trick if I ever got me a restaurant.

Dad was in his element behind the cash register—charming, genial,
proud to be a respected citizen of the town. Behind him on the wall
were framed licenses for the restaurant and pictures of himself as a
Seabee, barbering inside an open-front Quonset hut set under palm
trees. His left hand cupped a sailor's head, holding it atilt for his scissors.

There were also photographs of his new family, but none of the two
children he had left behind in Oklahoma. It was neither the first nor last
time I would get a sinking feeling in my stomach and chest, with a shattering awareness that Ellen and I barely existed for him. Not once during that weekend did he say anything he might not have shared with a
stranger. And yet I was impressed and pleased, even proud, that he was
so popular and successful. He was, after all, a big man, my father, not
the sharecropper who had given up on a stony acreage. And the evidence of his service on a Pacific island seemed to refute Mother's persistent claim that he had merely malingered through the war to avoid
active service and combat. Were not at least a few of those palm trees
denuded and shredded from fire, or something? Not for years did I learn
that the Marshall Islands were among the most heavily bombarded areas
of the Pacific war.

A can next to the cash register solicited donations to a local Boys'
Home, and the glass display case was full of cigar and candy offerings. A
long counter accommodated the town's pie and coffee customers, and a
number of booths and tables were available for groups eating the
mashed potatoes.

On the Saturday of my visit, I rode along as Dad drove into the country, stopping for purchases of vegetables and melons, which he carefully
inspected before loading into the car. At one farm he bought a full side

of beef, still dripping blood, and managed to cram it into the back seat, protecting the upholstery with padding of an old quilt. He filled up the trunk with hams and a side of bacon as well as baskets of apples and peaches for pies.

On the way back to town I swatted at flies. Dad seemed oblivious to the smell of the bloody beef. "Potatoes is cheap," he went. "It's this here beef that costs a man. But my customers is all good people and they deserve the best."

A double table near the kitchen was reserved for family. For dinner, my four new stepsisters, Gilda's daughters from her previous marriage, came in along with my two little half-brothers. Grudgingly I acknowledged that they were, as their half-sisters asserted, "cute."

That evening we seven scrambled siblings went next door to the movie theatre and saw Walt Disney's *Fantasia*. Animals tumbled pell-mell, their helpless paws and hooves clawing the air, right into a fiery volcano. I have never wanted to see the film again to find out if the scenes were as nightmarish as they seemed. The shrill and dissonant music of Shostakovich still triggers for me a picture of huge animals plunging through the smoky air and into the consuming fires of nature.

Eileen, the oldest of my new stepsisters, reminded me of Charlene Greeley, my foster sister in Mingo. Over the weekend I once opened the bathroom door at the wrong time, just as Eileen, naked to the waist, was leaning over the sink, washing her hair. It was such a precise repeat of a scene back in Mingo when I had walked in on Charlene that Eileen might well have been Charlene's twin. Before she could say anything, I said, "Excuse me," and backed out of the steamy, shampoo- and perfume-scented bathroom.

Eileen seemed more amused than outraged. The odd fact that she was my sister—or stepsister—seemed irrelevant to my churning feelings as the image of those pink-tipped, gently swaying breasts lingered.

But there were more urgent concerns. For years I had had persistent infections. The slightest cut would get infected, and my gangrened hangnail had left a scar on my right thumb. Boils—puss-tipped furun-

cles—cropped up everywhere, swelling into volcanoes of pain on my
arms or legs, buttocks, under my arms, in my nose. When I had boarded
the bus in Nowata the boil on my left wrist, though poulticed and bandaged, had seemed manageable. But over the weekend the condition
worsened by the hour, as if the toxicity fed on disappointments and the
ugly and frightening imagery of *Fantasia*.

On the return journey I watched a dark purplish line snaking slowly
up my arm. In the window seat a few rows back from the driver, I turned
from watching telephone poles and roadside signs flashing by to study
the driver's face in his rear-view mirror, trying to decide whether to ask
him for help. But I knew he could do nothing out in the middle of
nowhere. I sat there frightened and trembling, watching the dark snake
working its way up my arm. I did not know if I would be alive by the
time the bus got back to Nowata, for I had already sensed what I was told
later—that if blood poison reaches your heart it will kill you. I arrived
back home just in time for the boil to be lanced, oozing a white and
blood-streaked mass. The snake was killed, but I was sick for days. The
boils always came back, their virulence well matched against any available medicine.

The trip left me sick in both body and spirit. I brooded with jealousy
over those two half-brothers in sailor suits, taking little comfort in the
news that not long after my visit, Dad abandoned them and their
mother. Just as he had run off with Gilda earlier, he went away with the
blonde waitress who had served me all the extra mashed potatoes that I
wanted. I had watched her as she dumped them on my plate with an ice
cream scoop, and may have sensed even then her power to enchant a man.

My father's restlessness drove him to move on, abandoning successes as
well as failures. From Kansas he traveled on to the western edge of the
continent, where his sister Edris was living, to undertake anew the task
of starting from scratch. Once again he would work up from nothing to
become the proud proprietor of his own barber shop. He would soon

remarry and have a fresh family—a boy and two girls. It was this last son, none of his first three, whom he would refer to later, in my presence, as the apple of his eye.

As if he had an aversion or an allergy to any kind of success, my father always left his gains behind. His dilemma was complicated by an intolerance of failure as well. He was like a boxer determined to throw a fight but always assaulted by second thoughts. He had ways of punishing himself that he had never put into words. Gazing upon his self-doubting eyes in snapshots, I realized that I inherited, as if genetically, many of his ambivalences about personal worth, success, and failure. In his book, *A Blue Fire*, James Hillman writes of such a trap: "The pain of his father's failings teaches him that failing belongs to fathering. The very failure fathers the son's failings. The son does not have to hide his share of darkness . . . . The commonality—and commonness—of shared shadow can bond father and son in dark and silent empathy as deep as any idealized companionship."

Like my father, I have often felt a discomfort with success, as if it were failure; with love, as if it were scorn; and with possessions, as if they were only a burden. The temptation to abandon responsibilities is, perhaps, a variant of the fight or flight response to stress. Like Sisyphus, we often lift stones only to let them fall, let them fall only to lift them anew. I was always moved by, and identified with, tales of vagrancy and the fresh starts men who have failed must undertake with all the disadvantages consequent to their flights or fights. Sherwood Anderson one day took a close look at his prosperous life, his stable family, his good job—and began walking away down the railroad tracks in voluntary exile from a small Ohio town. My father obviously suffered such a compulsion to flee his life, turning his back on the wreckage. He could go no farther west than California, so his flight stopped at ocean's edge. His new barber shop was on Pacific Avenue in Long Beach.

"The terrible traits in the father provide a countereducation," Hillman wrote. "How better bring home a true appreciation of decency, loyalty, generosity, succor, and straightness of heart than by their absence or perversion? How more effectively awaken moral resolve than by provoking moral outrage at the father's bad example?" But when trying to avoid the pattern, we may become even more mired in it. Hillman's uplifting view may overestimate the power of will and underestimate a son's desperation for the father's nurturing at any price. Conscious judgments may be irrelevant compared with the driving pain beneath the surface. Vows not to be like him become a mask for the unfinished business of the hunger within.

An instinctive snob, I felt superior to my father—he was still the "hillbilly" of Mother's denunciations. Had he visited me at some point, I might well have snubbed him—like Pip in *Great Expectations* when his blacksmith brother-in-law and benefactor, Joe Gargery, comes to London.

In fact, I did snub Dad when, as if in fulfillment of my fantasy of his return, he appeared suddenly one late afternoon in Nowata. He found out that I was working at the post office and parked his blue Pontiac coupe nearby. He hailed me as I walked past after leaving my special delivery job. I went over and stood beside the car.

"Come on and get in," he said. "We're heading for California."

His sudden presence was a shock, for in my earlier Kansas visit he had shown no sign of wanting me to live with him.

I hungered to climb into the car, but loyalty to Mother stiffened my pretense at coldness. I rebuffed his invitation, yet longingly took in every detail of the Pontiac and imagined the trip I was refusing. The blue metal of the Pontiac hood was divided by strips of chrome, and the hood ornament was a silver Indian Chief's head, a noble prow jutting into the wind.

The trip was not to be. It would have been unthinkable for me to give in to the temptation. I had fantasized his coming back for me a thousand times, yet now I stood shy and disapproving.

He did not seek out Ellen and make the same offer to her, and I did not mention the encounter at home. It was a hard secret to keep, especially since I soon bragged to my friends K. P. and Johnny Mack about having sent my father on his way. It seemed quite a triumph of will. To have rebuffed my father despite my craving for him was a declaration of loyalty to my mother's heavy judgments.

I kept my father with me in another way, internalizing a self-image all too much like his, or the opinions of others about him. Like a sleepwalker guided by the same forces that had led him, I later wandered through the same precincts he had explored. Even in adolescence I sometimes behaved as if I had determined to earn for myself the same slanders by which he was remembered. Born "hard-wired" with the traits of our fathers, we follow in their footsteps, regardless of warnings. I was willing to work hard to fall in love with alcohol and failure.

The boils came out of hiding, monsters that sapped my energy. A boil in my nose would appear, and I recalled a fear from an old wives' tale—if my nose got blocked, the infection would go directly to my brain and kill me fast, just as the snake up my arm might have inflicted a fatal bite had it reached my heart. Antibiotics came along just in time.

13.

THOUGH I HAD sent the real father on his way, Mother's choice of a replacement was neither mine nor Ellen's. A better candidate, I had thought, was Ernie Spicer, the Scoutmaster, devoted to his boys with a mix of mentoring and jocular camaraderie. On campouts he told loud, obscene jokes as we sat around a crackling and smoking campfire. Some of them we tried to explain to one another later in whispers as we settled like worms in our cocoon-like sleeping bags.

Ernie offered the great outdoors and the twelve- to fifteen-year-olds felt flattered to be treated like woodsmen and as if we knew enough to understand his jokes. On weekend campouts we escaped the puritanical restraints of town, and Ernie had no objection to some of the boys drinking beer and smoking cigarettes. After dark, though, when boys were settling down in their tents, the jocularity took on a new turn as Ernie initiated a game of pursuit he called grease-a-dick. A boy was designated at random and was chased by the others until he fell like a harried rabbit to a gang of yapping dogs. Ernie led the attack, yanking down the victim's pants and gleefully directing the Scouts to smear great gobs of axle grease from a can onto the boy's genitals. Sometimes the victim was chosen while sleeping, awakened rudely. His startled fears fed the fury of the game until he broke into tears and begged relief from the torture. Yet he would join in when Ernie designated another victim.

None of these activities kept Ernie Spicer, a good family man, from being a highly respected member of the community, recognized for his work with adolescent boys. Eventually he was elected and re-elected to the presidency of the board of education. The later ban on homosexuals as Scoutmasters would not have kept Ernie from having his way with us. The public impression was that the Boy Scouts spent all their time working on new merit badges, practicing their cooking skills at the campfire, identifying birds in the trees, and earning glory with treks through the wilderness. My pursuit of merit badges to adorn the olive green sash I wore over my shoulder was voracious. Soon it had a double row of the colorful round icons of achievement, embroidered in silk.

I had earned an engineering badge by constructing a swaying suspension bridge of string and twigs, impressive enough until it was tromped into the dirt by snaggle-toothed K. P. Haverfield. Some of the Scouts had earned sailing badges by rowing a boat across a pond and under a creek bridge.

As in the military, the Boy Scouts of America glamorized rank hierarchy, saluting, and superpatriotism. We were good little soldiers, snapping our two-fingered salutes and squeezing each other with our two-fingered handshake. It took a loner like K. P. to scoff at the honor of joining. Tom Sawyer to his Huck Finn, I was aware of what a good boy I was compared to K. P., who led small children he was charged with baby-sitting through the local stores, teaching them to shoplift. He wrote obscene notes to teachers. He engineered diabolical hoaxes. My sex education was hardly enhanced or clarified when K. P. found a way to sneak us into an army V. D. film that was being shown in a local theatre for adults only. Although titled "Mom and Dad," the documentary footage included grotesquely mutilated genitals of both sexes, a penis looking like a burst frankfurter, and a vagina meant to horrify servicemen away from brothels.

Like the brightest of fishing lures, the most important merit badge was for fingerprinting. Ernie informed me of an arrangement that was common around the country—a Boy Scout could acquire his badge by helping to fingerprint prisoners. After school once or twice a week for a month or so, I headed downtown to the sheriff's office and jail in the courthouse basement. The sheriff and his deputy, like anyone who plays along with a good joke, took me seriously, and prisoners were tugged before me, their handcuffs removed for my ministrations. I would roll their fingers across the inking slab, and was told that the extra copy of the prints would go into the national database for the FBI in Washington.

J. Edgar Hoover's ambition, the sheriff explained, was to have a print of every citizen on file. Helping to achieve that goal was not only an opportunity, but a duty. Rarely have I felt so important, and the sheriff made a pretty good father surrogate that winter. When I needed yet more prints for my badge, he rounded up the courthouse clerks, and I suspect he stepped up his arrest quota for bootleggers, derelicts, and vagrants, for their numbers increased over the weeks.

My knowledge that the prints were going into the national database was justification enough for thinking of myself as a federal law officer. Those prints would follow citizens for life, helpful for the solution of any crime. I looked forward to one day becoming a G-man in Washington. Earlier I had clipped crime tips from the Dick Tracy comic strips—one apprenticeship led to another. With my new expertise I jabbered about the number of whorls and curves of ridges in prints and what made each unique. Hanging around the sheriff's office, being accepted by him and his deputy, serving by rolling fingers across the inking pad, then onto the cards, was a great pleasure, a justification for my existence.

But after one memorable incident on a Saturday afternoon in mid-winter, I lost my enthusiasm. The sheriff and his Cherokee Indian deputy had arrested and dragged in an African-American man. He was moaning in distress and blood was flowing down his face onto his shirt. "There's no way to do a man that-away," he said as I rolled his prints.

"Shut up while that boy takes your damn prints," the deputy ordered. The thin, grizzly-bearded man was having a hard time standing up. Using my cleanup rag, I wiped both blood and ink off his fingers.

When I had finished, the sheriff and his deputy dragged their captive down a cement corridor past the jail cells, shoved him in one, and clanged the door shut. I could hear the prisoner whining, "Why do you-uns do a man that-away, gentlemans?"

"What did he do?" I asked.

"Resisting arrest," the sheriff laughed and rubbed his fist. "You got yourself a good set of prints, dint ya?"

"Yeah," I said, "I just wondered what he did to get arrested."

"Like I said, resisting arrest. That nigger almost broke my fist." The deputy was examining his fist too, kissing it.

"What was he resisting for?"

"Just resisting, that's all." The sheriff and his deputy seemed to think it was all good clean fun. Years later I wondered if they had arrested the poor fellow just to oblige a kid's need to get more prints for his merit badge—and fulfill J. Edgar Hoover's ambition. That vagrant plucked out of an alley, thrown into a cell with a rusty iron-webbed bunk and a stinking hole in the floor, had fielded a question that still haunts me. Why do they have to treat a man that-away?

Our Scoutmaster had his tender side. When I was in the hospital to have my appendix out, Ernie Spicer visited every day. When I was due to be discharged, he arrived to give me a ride home in his pickup, bringing along a dozen roses. He stood in the doorway, waiting for me to change from the hospital gown into my clothes. I reached for the rolling privacy screen and jerked it into place. Mother, who had been bustling around the room, pulled it back. I felt my face flush. "Can't I have some privacy?" I whispered at her, almost hissing.

"You're too little," she said. "It doesn't make any difference."

Ernie laughed as he stood holding the red roses. When I was dressed he handed them to Mother and picked me up in his arms, though I protested that I could walk. Mother followed us out to the pickup and handed me the roses after I climbed in.

He parked in the alley behind our apartment and carried me up the outside stairs and over the threshold like a bride, reminding me that it was still risky for me to walk. He was right about that, since the osteopathic surgeon—one of Mother's two bosses in the Clinic Hospital—

had used the wrong kind of incision for my appendectomy and I had almost died. The so-called McBurney's incision, which severed the abdominal oblique muscles, was an archaic technique. The long wide scar developed adhesions and became a permanent pink ridge on my belly. After the same doctor later used the same technique on Ellen, she had to have follow-up surgery in Tulsa to remove the sclerotic knot her incision had become.

Onto the stage of this soap opera in Nowata—Lee's suicide threats, his trial for shooting the customer at the Oasis, my struggle with after-school and weekend jobs, Ernie's infatuation with me—a new father surrogate appeared. A war veteran, back for a visit to his home town, joined his friend Reverend Hooten and Scoutmaster Ernie in the Presbyterian church basement at one of our meetings. The three men addressed the Scouts as if they were reviewing troops. They heard progress reports on our work for merit badges, and stood sternly while a boy who had broken a rule was put through the belt line. For that ceremony, we lined up in two rows facing each other, took off our belts and swatted at the boy as he ran the gauntlet. The official Scout belt of military webbing was ideal for the purpose, as the metal buckle inflicted considerable pain.

John Kingsbury Warner, the visiting veteran, looked like Glenn Ford the movie star. He wore a Stetson hat and new cowboy boots and had a cigarette in his hand. We learned that he had been an infantry captain, and that he had bought a ranch in Arizona where he was going into the cattle business. It sounded just like a movie. When the meeting broke up and we left the church basement, we gathered around his car, a luxurious Lincoln Continental with a stylish bustle-trunk at its rear. It was Tucson tan, he told us, the color of the Arizona desert.

The Continental was the most impressive car I had ever seen other than the limousine that had once been displayed in the schoolyard—the long black Mercedes that had carried Adolf Hitler through cheering throngs in parades. As war booty, it had been brought back to the States and taken on tour by the G.I. who had claimed it. One by one we children climbed into the back seat and stood for a moment grasping the handle that Hitler had held with his left hand while he heiled himself with his right. Some of the kids threw their arms up, mimicking the dictator.

John Warner's Lincoln had maroon leather seats and a beautifully grained wooden dashboard. He allowed us to climb in and marvel at its luxury, demonstrating the radio that could be operated by foot switches, and the seats that could slide back for comfort.

The boys chattered in whispers about how rich the Warners were. John's father owned a large Hereford ranch and his own oil company. John and his brother Alex were the two surviving of four sons. One, an aviator, had been killed in the war, and another had drowned in a bathtub when he was a child. After that incident, Mrs. Warner had been committed to the insane asylum in Vinita. All this history was widely shared gossip in the town.

A day or two after the church basement meeting, I was walking home in the late afternoon, when a car honked and I looked over. It was Captain Warner. He called out, offering me a ride. In the car he inquired about my cough. I explained that it was asthma and allergies. He said that Reverend Hooten had told him about my health problems.

Warner pulled the Continental into the gravel drive in front of Lee's house and continued talking. Within minutes he made an astounding offer. When he left for Arizona in a few days, he said, I should come along. I could work on his ranch in return for room and board. The dry climate is good for asthma, he said.

"What kind of job would I have?" I asked.

He decided I could be a yardboy or even a cowboy. "You could help out with the cooking and housework, too." I must have looked doubtful. He added that I could have my own horse when I helped the cowboys.

I pictured myself on horseback, rounding up cattle. With an apron I could be like one of those camp cooks in the Western movies—a younger, unbearded version of Gabby Hays. I tried to contain my excitement, and wondered what Mother would say. My father's invitation to go west had not had the benefit of a consultation with her, but this trip, if I took it, would need her permission. But when I raised the issue as soon as I saw her the next morning, she surprised me by saying she had already thought about it. John Warner had called her. She would miss me, she said, but there was no way she could deny her permission. The doctor had been pressing her to find a way to send me to a dry climate.

When Warner headed west three days later, he stopped by the house just after dawn for me and my suitcase. I climbed into the back seat, which I was to share with Marie, the bride of John's older brother, who had recently married. The couple would leave us at Albuquerque to continue their honeymoon before traveling north to Boulder, where Alex was a professor at the University of Colorado. Mother and Ellen stood in the yard and waved goodbye as we pulled away.

Although Highway 66 at that time was a narrow, hazardous road, climbing hills that have since been deeply notched, rounding sharp curves that no longer exist, plunging through the centers of towns now bypassed and forgotten, Warner drove fast, idly grasping the steering wheel, his cigarette ever smoldering away in his right hand. He slowed only when he had to—for a smoke-belching truck directly in front of us or a town that had adopted speed traps for the protection of its pedestrians. Warner thought it unfair to have to slow, and the occasional necessity of stopping nothing short of outrageous. He cursed at anyone with the audacity to cross in front of the Continental as it paused at a stoplight. The car itself seemed anxious to press on. We would leave a town like a racehorse bolting a starting gate.

Late in the evening Warner chose a motel for the night. Alex registered first for himself and his bride, then Warner signed in. When I saw the double bed, I was embarrassed but I accepted the order to take the first shower, while Warner sat on the edge of the bed in his boxer shorts, smoking a cigarette.

Sometime in the night I got up and went to the bathroom, closing the door as quietly as I could. When I slipped back into bed Warner was sitting up again, smoking another cigarette, the acrid aroma filling the room.

"I'll bet you have a hard-on," he said.

I felt my face flush as I settled back under the covers, edging to the far side. "No, I don't," I said.

"I'll bet you a quarter you do," he said.

"No, I don't." I tensed.

"Let me check and see." His hand reached into my pajamas, cupping my genitals. He felt around with a thorough examination, then a kneading and manipulating of my penis. I resisted with a passivity like that of a dog on a vet's table. My genitals shrank up even more limp than before. He hummed disappointment and at last let me escape back to sleep.

We had breakfast at the round table in a corner of the diner, with views of highway traffic. The conversation among the three Warners was breezy, but John looked at me often, as if I might be about to say something. Alex and Marie did not seem very excited about their honeymoon, but assured John that they had slept well. They worked out plans for taking leave of us in downtown Albuquerque, telling me I could switch to the front seat for the rest of the trip to Tucson.

Sorry I could not offer to pay for my own breakfast, I waited for John by the door as he paid the cashier. From the change he was given, he picked out a quarter and handed it to me as we left. I nearly stumbled to the car in my confusion.

"What's that for?" I said.

"Don't you remember?" he reminded me. "You won the bet."

So it had not been just a dream. Mortified, I climbed into the back seat of the Continental and sat hunched as if in a toy car.

We drove Alex and Marie downtown and said goodbye. John seemed pleased with himself, but said nothing more about the incident of the night. Perhaps that was the end of it and we could pretend it never happened.

14.

WHILE THE ADOBE house on John's ranch a few miles northwest of Tucson was being renovated, we settled in a guest cottage at the estate of a wealthy family John knew on Rudasill Road at the north edge of the city. The Catalina Mountains rose above the foothills, and giant saguaro cacti stood like guards in the sun along the walks of the garden. Midsummer heat was like an oven, but there was plenty of shade, as well as air conditioning inside the thick adobe walls of the main house and guest cottages. Only one was occupied by another guest, and John dismissed the host's offer of a separate casita for me.

These days were for me an introduction into a life of luxury—indoor bathrooms, elegant furniture on gleaming Saltillo tile floors cushioned with Navajo rugs, well-dressed and genial people, splendid views from picture windows. As the Catalinas turned lavender, then violet, and the shadow of the Tucson Mountains to the west crept over them, the host and his family presided over cocktails, the ritual of watching the sunset.

The host had become wealthy in the tallow business. His empire of trucks roamed the area, collecting dead animals and waste grease from ranches, restaurants, and hotels. His rendering plant prepared tons of oleaginous goo for soap, cosmetics, munitions, and glue industries. He and his wife often entertained executives from the east, who were visiting in order to bid for this product. The candlelit parties were in sharp contrast to images of dead horses and cattle, barrels of grease, or the stench of the rendering plant.

John and I made frequent trips out to Rillito to check on the progress of the ranch house. Mexican workers were making new adobe bricks to extend the house, repairing walls battered by years of rain and wind. They knocked out openings for larger windows and modernized the plumbing, adding a septic tank and piping from a windmill with a trough like that on the toy pump I had stolen in Mounds.

An olive green Kohler generator, a war surplus item, was wheeled in to provide electricity. A corral was repaired for horses, and an earth mound dike was reinforced all around the house for flood protection during the monsoon season. The dry bed arroyos runneling down from the mountains looked harmless but could become suddenly violent with racing runoff. The ranch was covered with mesquite, sagebrush, palo verde, ironwood, and a thousand forms of cactus. The land reached with sandy tentacles into the quiet canyons.

We had been in the guest cottage only a day or two when, after an afternoon swim, John lay down beside me while I was taking a nap on my twin bed. I woke to feel him fondling me.

This time I objected. "Why are you doing this?" I said, bolting upright.

"Don't get all excited," he said. "You know I'm a psychologist. That's what I studied at the University of Missouri and that's what I did in the army. I'm conducting a psychological experiment. I'll explain it later."

"What kind of experiment?" I asked.

"A psychological experiment, that's all. Just do what I say and I'll explain it later when I've got the data I need. It'll make a lot of sense then."

I stood up and walked away from him.

"It's classified," he said. "It wouldn't work if I told you now."

As if submitting for a medical exam, I reluctantly returned to the bed. No question, he was studying me. There must really be an experiment. He watched my pelvic area as if he were a doctor, intent, fascinated.

He manipulated and stroked until a spasm throbbed through my penis, acting on its own like a disembodied muscle, a frog leg touched by an electrode. I felt strangely detached, anxious that I could not control this phenomenon of both sharp pain and pleasure. Suddenly I was limp and wet. John tossed me a towel. "Finish wiping yourself off," he said in a tone of disgust, "then take a shower."

"There's more to the experiment, of course," he said. "When I ask you questions you have to tell me everything with complete honesty. You can pretend you're a prisoner if you want to. I always managed to get everything out of them, those Germans. Or you can pretend you're a Catholic."

I must have looked puzzled.

"Confession," he said. "Just pretend I'm a priest and you're telling him everything. That's part of the experiment. Don't leave out anything or you'll go to hell."

"I'm not a Catholic."

"Just pretend you are."

"How long will this experiment go on?"

"I'll ask the questions and you just give the answers. When the time comes I'll explain it all, don't worry."

He then asked me if I had ever done anything like that before, and I told him I had not. He asked me if I was lying, and I told him I was not.

"You never came like this before?"

"I got wet after dreaming," I said.

My ignorance was, in retrospect, downright mysterious. Though I had just turned fifteen I was still small for my age. Perhaps asthma and Mother's taboos had suppressed an earlier development. Fondling myself had never resulted in orgasm.

"Wet dreams," he said. "Just you?"

"Yes."

"Nobody else?"

"No."

"Good timing." His smile was mechanical, a twitch.

And then it was over until the next time, another submission to Warner's manipulations. After a few sessions he added another obligation, taking my hand in his and forcing it around his stubby penis. His hand covered mine until he was satisfied that I was obeying.

I still asked questions about the "psychological experiment." He assured me it would not last much longer and then he could explain it. He must have thought I would begin to like the activity. The only safety lay in submitting, letting it get over with.

"Do everything I tell you, and report everything that goes through your head," he would repeat. And as if the entire business were only for good health and even medical treatment, he would look me over with clinical appraisal and say with a sigh of satisfaction, "We've almost cured your asthma. You're breathing better now." Placing his palm on my lower abdomen, he would order me to breathe deeper. It might be five or ten minutes before his hand strayed lower.

"You're lucky I can watch your progress," he said. "You could get in a hell of a lot of trouble on your own."

"What sort of trouble?"

"People could take advantage of you."

"In what way?"

"Never mind. Just count your blessings and be glad you've got a big brother to watch out for you." He huffed out a hefty cloud of smoke. "I want you to write to my mother," he said. "She worries about me, and you too, so you need to write to her once a week and say things are O.K."

"What sort of things?"

"Just gossip. Tell her how the weather is out here, and what the furniture looks like."

"I'll try."

"Tell her you hope she'll get well."

"What's the matter with her?"

As if I didn't know. People in Nowata said she was crazy. But John had no word. Maybe he had become a psychologist in order to understand her, but he flicked his cigarette away and closed his lips firm and prim and gazed off into the distance.

I had trouble picturing myself as a prisoner of war, but I could easily imagine Captain Warner interrogating a prisoner. He had a collection of war loot brought back from the battlefields of Europe, including two

Luger pistols that he took out of his suitcase and kept on the ready. Our host forbade him to use them, though. "Save it for your ranch, John. You can shoot all you want out there."

Our relationship must have been obvious, but the secret and my shame that kept it secret had been born. The so-called experiment kept me edgy. I never knew when John would demand the ritual of mutual masturbation. Wet dreams had been puzzling enough back in Oklahoma. This new experience with its mandate of secrecy was bewildering and unsettling, and I looked forward to its early cessation. But every time I mentioned the subject, he would glower and remind me that it would ruin the experiment to discuss it prematurely. When challenged with unwelcome topics, he reminded me that I had other responsibilities to attend to in order to earn my keep. I pressed him for a clear definition of my duties.

"It depends," he said, the matter never quite clear. I was always on probation. He reminded me repeatedly that it was important to make a good impression on everyone we met.

John Kingsbury Warner was accepted as a charming raconteur in Tucson society. When others at social gatherings expressed curiosity about me, he referred to me as his yard boy or an apprentice cowhand. He would grin, the picture of geniality and bluff good humor, and say that he had brought me out to Arizona for my health and that he was thinking of adopting me.

He would glance my way, throwing a minatory and skeptical look. In private he said he was not yet sure the arrangement would work out, that it depended on a lot of things. The warning was clear. My having a home depended on my behavior, submitting to his orders. Out on a walk he would grab my arm and pull me off the path. In the bed of an arroyo he did his thing, masturbating me to orgasm, making me do the same to him.

He cut off my complaints and questions about the experiment by reminding me that I had undertaken the Boy Scout's oath to be Obedient, Faithful, Kind, Truthful, and Loyal, and that it began with obeying him in all matters. Such virtues were not merely pledges under-

taken for the Scouts. His emphatic pronunciation and later writing
about those sterling qualities were connected in my mind with his
German heritage. Before long, as he drummed Obedience, Loyalty, and
Truth at me, I thought of his ranting references to those nouns as capitalized and in German script.

"Your character isn't formed yet," he observed. "You need all the dis-
cipline you can get. I came along at just the right time."

I sometimes came close to telling someone what was going on, but I
halted as if at a border crossing, a barrier, enforced by taboo. To the most
idle or searching of queries from people we met, I kept up the pretense
that John was my great benefactor and I respected him mightily. To
accuse Warner would have been to accuse myself. Maintaining my own
dignity depended on defending his. Whenever someone suggested that
John had been foolish to take up ranching on such a big scale and with
so little experience, I would point out that his father had a ranch back
in Oklahoma. "Well, it's none of my business," his critic would back off,
as if referring to more than what we were discussing.

But at a cocktail party one afternoon, John's friend Philippe gave me
a perfect opportunity.

"You know," Philippe said, "I've been thinking about you. Do you
know what I think?"

"What?"

"I think John Warner is a very nice fellow, that's what I think."
Philippe pinched a flake of tobacco off his lower lip and studied my
face. After a minute or so he added, "But I think he's not the sort of fellow you should be living with."

It was music to my ears, yet I looked as dumb as I could manage.
"Why not?"—as if I could not possibly imagine. "The doctor told my
mother I had to get out of Oklahoma," I said. "The asthma was real bad
back there."

Philippe did not pursue the matter in that brief kitchen conversation,
but did drop the suggestion that I contact him if and when I should
need help, perhaps to find another job or living situation.

Philippe was a tall debonair Frenchman, who claimed to be

descended from Louis Philippe, and may well have been. It was not unusual to meet celebrities at the parties Warner was invited to—even titled visitors like Lady Astor. The sculptor Jo Davidson, Joseph Wood Krutch who had recently retired to Tucson, the Belgian novelist Georges Simenon—along with his wife and mistress—were among the guests who turned up.

As for Philippe, though he often spent his nights elsewhere, the tallow king had assigned him a casita, too, where he was always welcome.

Philippe was a true Don Juan, with a procession of beautiful women. John was pleasant enough with him, only mildly and with good humor chiding him about his womanizing. Philippe was one of John's closest friends, though that might not have been the case if the Frenchman had known what severe judgments John unloaded on him out of his hearing. Philippe was a gigolo, John said, because he lived with one wealthy widow after another. He was a freeloader, John said, to accept the hospitality of our host. As soon as Philippe left for a jog down the road for a rendezvous at another friend's swimming pool in the grapefruit grove, John would rant about his immorality, citing Philippe as an example of the worst sort of social parasite.

John was delighted when one of Philippe's wealthy patronesses exploded with jealousy about his liaisons with younger women, University of Arizona coeds ten years younger than the Frenchman. The girls could have been precursors of *Playboy* centerfolds. One of them later became a beauty queen. I saw her several times when we went for a swim at a lush estate surrounded by grapefruit and palm trees. In her bikini, Sandy climbed the diving board again, standing in the sun as if to permit its worship, and mine.

From the other end of the pool I watched, keeping my sunglasses on so I could admire her on the sly. I had made another discovery—that my body was mine, at least part of the time, not just a toy of Warner's. Surreptitious self-stimulation was a way of disobeying him, asserting a secret freedom. Underwater, my defiant erection was mine alone, though the beautiful diver might have sensed my devotions as she took her time on the board.

When others left the pool area, I stayed behind. With wordless complicity Sandy seemed aware she was putting on a show for me. When cloudy streaks floated to the surface I broke them up by swirling the water, looking around to make sure Warner was not in sight.

Philippe owned a blue Packard convertible which had survived the thirties, and he often rented it out to Hollywood directors when they filmed in Tucson and in the fake environment of Old Tucson, a permanent mock-up of a Western town. At the conclusion of a movie starring Gene Autry, the guitar-playing cowboy, the car was featured in a parade with much confetti and loud cheers. Back in Oklahoma, the cowboy troubadour had once dated Mother — or so she claimed — when he was a young railway telegraph operator. In the film, with his cowgirl at his side, Autry sat high on the back seat of Philippe's convertible waving at the crowd as confetti rained on his Stetson.

From our host's Catalina foothills estate, and later from Warner's hacienda, Philippe would turn routine trips into town for ice cream into mimicry of the Gene Autry parade. I sat high on the back seat like the cowboy star, but was too bashful to wave my Stetson at mystified bystanders. Such moments were among the few happy scenes in those embattled days. Philippe, despite his scandalous love life, was the only one of John's acquaintances who had shown any concern for me. And he had offered rescue.

Against the backdrop of spectacular sunsets and crisp clear mornings, with the blue mountains off in the distance, Warner and I tensed for a struggle that would bring him close to murder and me close to suicide. And yet, locked into secrets, I had rebuffed Philippe's offer to free me from the captor whose role in my life was so tormenting that I did not even know whether to think of him as John, Warner, or the legalistic John Kingsbury Warner that I saw him sign on documents. John was human, genial, a family member, a friend to many interesting people. Warner was the captain, controlling, angry, sadistic. Kingsbury was a strangely prim-lipped aristocrat from a distinguished family, its terminal generation consisting of the four sons of a schizophrenic mother who mourned two but had not given up on drowning the surviving two in the tears that mottled her letters sent from the Vinita asylum. She addressed me as if recruiting me to be the fifth son, contingent upon my obedience to John Kingsbury Warner.

David and Ellen

David and Ellen

Dowell Adolphus Ray

15.

WE MOVED INTO the refurbished ranch house and I registered at Marana High School, ten miles from the ranch. Although Warner sometimes drove me, I usually hiked across the fields, catching the school bus in front of the Rillito general store. The bus turned off the highway in order to collect the children of farm workers, Mexican immigrants who lived in tarpaper shacks along section roads and irrigation ditches. The poverty and flat boundless cotton fields reminded me of Oklahoma.

Sometimes it seemed that my only friend was Lady, the brown and white cocker spaniel Warner bought for me in a Tucson pet shop. She would follow me over the hump of the levee that protected the ranch house from floods, turning back only when I boarded the bus. She had pups sired by a roving Doberman, the improbable match requiring a bucket of water to part the pair. The first time Lady resumed following me across the fields after she gave birth, she tore her sagging teats on the barbed wire of a fence I crawled through. She was a sorry sight with her belly wrapped in a bandage.

After school I attended to my duties of keeping the house and cooking for what had become a household of three. The northwest corner room of the house was occupied by Chuck, the cowboy. A serious student of ranching, the University of Arizona graduate was amused by Warner's choice of ranching as a rich man's indulgence, and openly wondered how long the undertaking would last. Warner had invested heavily in a herd of Brahman cattle, another experiment, to see if the breed would do well grazing on desert land, surviving by browsing sagebrush and cactus. The cattle ate the quivering cholla and prickly pear, then stood for hours at the watering troughs soaking their jaws until the thorns softened and oozed out.

School was welcome escape from the ranch. I felt uneasy around Chuck, knowing he could not fail to overhear some of the bartering, pressuring, squeaking moves from one twin bed to another. As soon as the lights were out, Warner would either crawl into my bed or order me to come over to his.

"I don't want to," I would say. "I'm sleepy."

"You heard me."

"You said I didn't have to anymore."

"I said to get the hell over here." His heavy whisper was threatening. If I did not obey, he got out of his bed and yanked my covers back, climbing in next to me on the narrow bed.

"Shut up," he would tell me, loud enough for anyone in the echoing house with its adobe walls and tile floors to hear, yet caution me with, "I don't want Chuck to hear."

The door to the living room was thin, as was the door between the living room and the cowboy's corner room. I assumed Chuck could hear us, for we could easily hear him turn over in his bunk. When his voluptuous, red-haired fiancée visited, sometimes sharing dinner with us, Chuck usually drove down the road about a half mile and parked. The distant brake lights pulsed. But sometimes the lovers used Chuck's room. Their moans and whispers resonated. There were few secrets in that house, and yet—as in a dysfunctional family—there was the pretense that nothing unusual ever took place.

My life had become secrets within secrets. There was the secret Warner ordered me to keep, the ongoing experiment that permitted him access to my body. There was my secret within that secret, my effort to steal some privacy and find out if I could achieve a throb of explosive pleasure without the pain provoked by his aggressive hand, for I was still resisting even as I obeyed. In letters both his mother and mine urged obedience, over and over, as if they felt the need to coerce.

Of all the Germanic nouns Truth was the most invasive, the knife Warner used to carve out my confessions. During the interrogations I felt hollowed out as I desperately sought details that might satisfy his lust for information. I was supposed to tell him everything, and his vigilance was ever alert.

The twin beds, heirloom mahogany with pineapple finials, were a sham, a mere stage set. Visitors often strolled through the bedroom. None of them asked if a guardian really had to sleep so close to an asthmatic boy he had rescued from Oklahoma. Perhaps, as tacit subtext, Warner wanted it known by his socialite friends that he could afford a boy from his home town at bargain rates.

Warner conducted his social life like a maharaja, an Indian prince, inviting acquaintances from near and far to visit. There were weekend javelina hunts on horseback through the foothills and canyons, followed by barbecues. More than one acquaintance suggested to John that he turn the place into a dude ranch. He would make the perfect host, they told him, and cowboy Chuck, with a sneer, referred to the guests as dudes anyway.

They leaned on the corral fences and laughed at the castration of protesting calves and the branding of newly arrived cattle. Chuck's fiancée, dressed up like a movie cowgirl in boots, fringed jacket, and white Stetson, was often the star. She could rope a calf, leap off her horse and tie up the calf even faster than Chuck could. The pair sometimes performed in rodeos, and were considering movie careers as stand-ins. They had both grown up in California and numbered famous actors among their friends. Movie stars, they assured me, were real people. One played the piano. Another was writing a book without even employing a ghost.

For the castrations, Warner himself sometimes stepped forward to do the honors. When the animal was hog-tied and helpless, he stooped down and applied the sizzling branding iron or squeezed the emasculators—half pliers and half miniature iron maiden—to crush the testicles. The lesson was not lost on a witness who remembered his father cutting the throats of pigs on the farm.

When at night Warner came from his bed to mine, I hoped he would leave after only a quick visit to accomplish his purpose and wipe up the aftermath with a towel or tee shirt. Though I never screamed out, I was aware that when Chuck was gone—he often made trips to California as well as into Tucson—we were far removed from anyone who could have heard. When we were alone, Warner and I, free to raise our voices, entered a new stage of bargaining. He shouted orders, reminding me that he was still a captain. It occurred to me that in the war he had been fighting his distant cousins.

"Maybe you'd like to go back to Oklahoma?" he said, as threat and reminder that I was dependent on his largesse. He reminded me that my mother was on his side in all matters. "She told me you were a good worker," he would say, as if his disappointment was only an employer's complaint, though he never mentioned such matters except when he was irate and casting about for artillery.

"You know damn well she told you to mind me, or else." His eyes became big globes inside his steel-rimmed glasses when his threats were fired with rage and exasperation.

He could be all kindness, though, with sudden shifts, softening his voice. "All I'm asking is some cooperation," he would say. "If you don't want to go back to that mess in Oklahoma, you'll have to show some Loyalty. I've been looking into the legal situation as far as adopting you is concerned. But frankly, my lawyer tells me to make sure I've found the right person." It was as if I had applied for a promotion he was considering. I did not know if I wanted him to adopt me, but I knew that was what my mother wanted. He had talked Mother into appointing him as my legal guardian, and he reminded me that the guardianship gave him complete authority. To disappoint him, he emphasized, was to disappoint her as well, and to let down everybody back home who had any faith in me, meaning his friend Reverend Hooten, I supposed.

Warner did his best to convince me he was a mind reader. "I can see right through you, don't think I can't," he advised. And in case I had not considered it, he asked what I would tell them if I went back to Nowata. "Nobody would have anything to do with you," he said. "Do you think anybody would believe some brat who couldn't even be trusted to show some gratitude? Who would they believe? You know damn well your mother would be heartbroken. But if that's what you want, go ahead and break her heart. It would kill my mother, too, if you spread some snotty lies, but go ahead, go back to your squalor, if that's what you want."

"It's not what I want."

"Then shape up, Buster."

The glandular explosions of puberty are not easily shared with an aggressive predator. One afternoon, having amazed myself by achieving, in a hasty jerkoff session, a less painful orgasm than those exacted by Warner's ministrations, I heard his car drive up. With anxious haste, I wiped myself with a dirty tee shirt, then stuffed it in the bottom of the clothes hamper. He stormed in, as if alerted by telepathic surveillance. He glared at me as if he really could see right through me, then went straight for the clothes hamper. He pulled out the wet tee shirt and flew into a rage. He began to slap and shove, cursing and denouncing me.

"You just couldn't wait, could you?" he mocked. "I can't trust you as far as I can throw you."

I said I was sorry, but did not really know what I was sorry for.

"You've ruined the experiment," he accused, when his rage had calmed down to exasperation. You might think I had broken a test tube. He looked as if he would break into tears. His hands trembled and his face flushed plum red. "I'm trying to teach you some Honor, for Chrissake. It takes some Loyalty, though. It takes some Truthfulness. You were going to lie your ass off, weren't you?"

"I would have told you," I lied.

"God should strike you dead," he said, and was inspired to drag me to church the following Sunday. The Episcopal church pleased him with its shining brass and purple velvet cushions, its altar and ceremonial panache. He made me kneel and mumble the antiphonal responses.

We were at war, it was just not declared. Warner's threats to send me back to Oklahoma shook me. I dreaded returning to the squalor and melodrama, the poverty and crummy school. I knew the schools in Arizona were superior to those in Oklahoma. I knew my asthma would get worse. And any break with him would mean the withdrawal of the privileges he bestowed.

Another part of me wanted to rush back and escape at any cost, get away from his rage and rhetoric. I would rather be back in the mulberry tree, I thought, locked out by our foster mother. I would rather be back in the Children's Home. But those hellholes had been consigned to the past. The question now was whether I would rather be back in Nowata, with an armed stepfather who was trying to molest my sister. Nevertheless, I planned to stay there when we went back for Thanksgiving.

"You've got it pretty good, Buster," Warner reproached me for my lack of appreciation, reciting a list of what he was providing. He had offered me the sanctuary of a home, room, and board. He taught me to drive. He bought a second car, a Mercury coupe, hinting that it might soon be mine. If I buckled down, shaped up, and showed myself deserving of his generosity, there would be no limit to his support. But! I had to demonstrate some Loyalty first. I would have to quit defying him.

When he had first invited me to Arizona, I had briefly thought my dreams of replacing my lost father had been fulfilled. But the relationship had become like a bad marriage—with a captive and unwilling wife trying to see her way to freedom. The captor, with rifle and shotgun, souvenir Lugers, swastika-adorned S.S. knives in their scabbards lying around on the heirloom furniture, was armed and dangerous.

Comparisons between the ranch hacienda and my stepfather Lee's leaning house back in Nowata were stark. If I went back to Oklahoma I would miss the fine furniture I dusted two or three times a week, polishing the mahogany and cherry wood with lemon oil so I could truthfully write to John's mother that I had followed all of her housekeeping instructions. I would miss the Oriental carpets, the books and records. There would not be a swimming pool back in Nowata. I would miss Philippe and Warner's society friends, the cocktail parties, the dinners at the Club where Warner sometimes gave me a few silver dollars to drop in the slot machines on our way out. It would be hard to leave Lady behind, but I knew that though Warner had given her to me as a gift he would never let me take her to Oklahoma.

"Our Adobe Hacienda" was always an ironic song for me. Mine was both home and torture chamber, but I could often retreat to a quiet corner with a book—with Tchaikovsky or Offenbach on the record player.

Warner promised by day, broke those promises by night. There was no longer talk of an experiment. It was just "Do what I tell you or else!" The question "Why?" had only one answer, "Because I told you to."

We drove back to Oklahoma for the Thanksgiving holiday. I had packed my suitcase and told him I was going to stay there. "Too bad," he said, as he stopped to let me take my turn driving.

He sat in the passenger seat, his ever-present cigarette in his small hand. The only thing he never complained about was my speeding, since he too seldom drove under eighty. Driving the Continental was so much like piloting a plane that I played with the notion that it would, when rounding mountain curves, take to the air like the twin-engined, butterfly-tailed Beechcraft Bonanza one of Warner's friends had taken us up in a few times.

That notion of sailing into the air, the car plunging into a canyon, occurred to me as a solution. There were often no guardrails along the perilous curves. Warner would not know what hit him, I thought. But the distractions of traffic pulled me back to the task of driving, my proudest skill. He could not take that away from me. On second thought, he was about to.

Lee would never let me drive his old DeSoto, and I would have been ashamed to be seen in that rattletrap anyway. Grampa's wooden wagon had been elegant by comparison. And the battered DeSoto was a hell of a contrast with the Lincoln Continental with its leather seats and stereophonic radio. Warner would never know how close he came to sailing off the launching pad of highway over and into one of the most scenic canyons in Arizona.

David with cowboy at Warner's ranch, Tucson

16.

BACK IN OKLAHOMA I stayed in my stepfather's tilted house while John visited his father. Mother and Lee and Ellen were living in the streetcar, more convenient for their late hours at the tavern. Behind Lee's house the geese still quacked and waddled their routes between fence and the weathered privy reached by planks laid through the mud. A black widow clung to a web in the corner over the seat. The source of water was still the angled pipe on the concrete slab that had once aspired to be a back porch. The yellow pine flooring of the house, pale and unpainted, was warped and had become discolored in splotches.

On Thanksgiving Day John picked me up and took me to his home on the hill. The African-American cook, Ruthie, a rotund woman who had been the family servant for years, had cooked a large turkey, which John's father carved while she stood beside him with first one plate, then another.

Though the elder Warner and his son spoke of amusing memories, such as the time the family dog had leapt across the dining room table and sailed away with a roast in his mouth, the tone at table was subdued. The house was old, the woodwork dark, the lighting dim. Photographs on the wall were reminders of ghosts not present—the inmate of the asylum thirty miles away, the brother who had been killed in the war, the toddler who had drowned in the bathtub. John's father moved slowly, always in house slippers. He seldom looked up from his mournful sulk, and seemed to have little interest in anything but the food Ruthie set before him.

The subject of my status in the family came up.

"Dad thinks it's a good idea," John said.

"What is?"

"Adopting you."

"Somebody's got to carry on when we're gone," the old man looked up, a somber and impersonal observation.

"I've been telling him he'll have a lot to live up to," John told his father.

"I suppose so," the old man mused, and forked his turkey.

John threw me a nudging look. Should I not be expressing some gratitude for this endorsement?

"My mother may need me to stay back in Nowata," I said, building my resolve.

"Nonsense," the old man muttered. "I can help her out if she needs." He saw a chance to be needed. "Tell her to come by and have a talk with me."

Ruthie did the dishes and came into the living room to tell John she was ready to go. He had offered her a ride home. We made the trip downhill, over the cobbled streets and across the railroad track to the roads of a muddy ghetto.

I thought of going by to say hello to Myrtle Jones. But I had no gift for her, and John would have made fun of her. He seemed to think that even the sight of the obese woman who had helped raise him was amusing.

"Just look at that old woman," he said, as Ruthie made her way on wobbly planks to her front porch.

"What's funny?"

"Doesn't she remind you of Aunt Jemima?"

"I guess so."

"She always totes something home, I've never known it to fail. I guess it's better than feeding the scraps to the dogs. Of course, she makes sure she has enough to take home, when she shops for Dad. It was always like that."

"It's part of the deal, I guess." Evidently John had forgotten how he had generously urged her to take leftovers as we had moved through the kitchen.

My contract was spelled out as obliquely as Ruthie's. In return for the privilege of removing unwanted food and clothing from her employer's house, she provided the cooking and housecleaning as well as adoring care for the family. She supposedly considered herself a member of the family, and would have been surprised to know that John's racism brooked no exceptions.

John Kingsbury Warner could be generous. He picked up restaurant checks, he dropped money in Salvation Army pots, he slipped friendly notes with cash here and there, saying he just wanted to help. But he was, like Aunt Ruth, a counter. He could have told you to the penny what his charities cost, and what you owed.

He drove on through the muddy roads and turned onto the highway. We passed Lee's Place and I spotted Mother through the restaurant window. The business was closed, but she was serving a Thanksgiving dinner for Lee, Ellen, and Uncle Skeet.

"Maybe you'd rather have had a hamburger and a beer in there than dinner up on the hill," John said, in a sardonic tone.

What a demotion staying in Nowata would be! No more fancy meals, no more Continental or Mercury coupe to drive, no more cigarettes, no more Old Grandad, no more indoor toilet, no more family heirlooms to keep shining. No more horses to ride. No more silver dollars. No more being special.

Twisted as his attentions were, they had conferred a special status. Lolita could hardly have failed to note that she was important to Humbert, no matter how unwelcome his lusts. Like Humbert, John offered a rich array of bribes, and threats when the bribes did not work.

We drove into the country, then he abruptly made a U-turn and returned me to Lee's Place.

"Think it over," he said. We sat in the gravel parking lot, engine running. He promised me that if I returned to Arizona he would let me have my own room and keep his hands off me. "I won't touch you," he said.

That was the new deal when we headed back to Arizona a few days later. For a week or so he honored the promise. Then he fell back to the old arguments. His authoritarian demands escalated. I tried bargaining, then reminded him of my right to leave. We made another trip back to Oklahoma for Christmas. Things were more tense than ever. This time I vowed to stay home, regardless. I would rather put up with the squalor and asthma than his room with a deal.

Christmas afternoon he appeared at Lee's Place with gifts for all. Mine was a wool Pendleton shirt in green plaid. Mother's was perfume. Ellen got a sweater as well as perfume. There were fancy pipes for Lee and Uncle Skeet, along with cans of Bond Street tobacco.

John invited me to go for a drive. He took the same route as a few weeks before, but this time turned onto a dirt road and ordered me out, to open a gate, then waited while I closed it.

"Where are we going?" I asked.

"I just want to have a little talk. We need a private place."

"This is trespassing. There was a sign on the gate."

"Dad owns this farm," he said.

A mile or so up the road he pulled onto a grassy shoulder. He reached over, but I edged away. He unzipped himself and exposed himself.

"Pull down your pants," he said.

"I don't want to."

"You heard me. I'm not asking, I'm telling you."

I stared straight ahead, arms folded. He pushed himself back into his trousers, zipped up, opened his door and stepped out. He came around the front of the car, opened the passenger door, and pulled me out.

"Are you going to do what I say?"

"Come on, John," I said. "You promised . . . ."

He began pummeling me.

"Stand up and fight like a man," he said.

"I can't fight you, John."

"Oh, so you admit you owe me some Loyalty and Obedience. Maybe you still have some Honor left."

"I never said I didn't appreciate all you've done for me."

"Then get in the car."

I got in, and he went back around to the driver's side. I sat still while he masturbated me with his right hand and himself with his left. Then he popped open the glove compartment and took out a Luger pistol.

"I ought to give you this and tell you to take a walk," he said. "I'm disgusted with you."

"I'm pretty disgusted too," I said, feeling nausea.

When he dropped me off again at Lee's Place, I told him I had decided to stay in Nowata regardless. For several days he came by with his arguments, enlisting Mother on his side. After he left, she worked to persuade me.

"He can give you a better home than I can," she said. "And if he adopts you, you'll be rich one of these days."

I kept back the secret that might have helped convince her—or so I thought.

As a battered woman she had faced the dilemma herself—and always gone back to her abuser, each worse than the last. Everything figures into the decision—a lack of options, the illusion that the other might change as promised, the conviction of being the one at fault. Pressures from family are intense. Secrecy and shame protect the abuser. Bribes, pressures, promises, emotional blackmail tantamount to brainwashing—all figure into the equation.

"You want to live like that?" John snarled his contempt, dropping me back at Lee's leaning house or at the tavern.

"I'd rather do that," I told him.

"Don't be stupid."

"I don't give a damn what you say. I won't go back."

He found it hard to believe that I could choose squalor over the luxury he offered, even the Continental that excited me every time I got behind the wheel. How could I give it up, along with Lady and the better school?

"I'll sign off on your adoption," he said repeatedly. "I won't lay a hand on you. You can have your own room. Just do a few chores for your keep and I'll leave you alone."

My mother sat me down in one of the booths at the tavern and told me how disappointed she was in me. Why could I not just obey John and do what he wanted me to? It was a small enough thing to ask. It was a new year, and we should get off to a fresh start. She seemed to think I was disrespectful to John because I was mad at my father. Could I not see how hard John was trying, and how much pain I was causing him? Besides, Arizona had been so good for my health, that was clear. Thanks to him I had gained twenty-five pounds since the first snapshots of the skinny boy standing by the giant saguaro. She thought it was wonderful that John talked of adopting me. Alex and Marie had probably married too late to have children. I would be heir to the oil and ranching fortune.

Like a recaptured runaway I returned to Arizona. Again we drove west in the Lincoln Continental, passed the diners and motels and curio stands along Highway 66. I was well aware that this was the route I would have taken with my father had I accepted his invitation that afternoon when I finished my post office deliveries. Had I climbed into that Pontiac, I would have been free of both Lee Pape and John Kingsbury Warner. At least for those minutes when my father tried to talk me into going with him I was somebody special, even to him, my real father.

One weekend I hitched a ride with Chuck the cowboy and his fiancée to Los Angeles. Chuck and Paula were going to visit family and their movie star friends, with whom they had gone to high school. My father had agreed to meet me at Union Station, as if I were arriving on a train. After a drive across the desert and into the city, Chuck pulled up at the curb and let me out. I went in with my small suitcase and found Dad and his new wife Jane waiting in the cavernous station, sitting on a bench.

"This is your new mother," he told me, presenting a large-boned redhead. We went to lunch in a nearby cafeteria famous for jungle greenery and an indoor waterfall. Hunger was a distraction from this latest disappointment. I was not interested in acquiring a new mother from Arkansas. He had a few years earlier presented his second wife as my new mother, and I wondered what had happened to her and the two little boys back in Kansas, as well as their half-sisters.

Red streetcars still ran out to Long Beach. Not far from the ocean, on Pacific Avenue, Dad led the way to his barber shop with its shoeshine stand in the foyer, three barber chairs, a manicurist's table by the front window, and a rear panel behind which he kept sleeping quarters and a bathroom. He said he and Jane had lived there before he found a house.

A bed was made up for me in the back room, and they left me. Dad said he would see me in the morning, and to make myself at home.

In the night I got up and paced the floor around the barber chairs, noted the many bottles of tonics and lotions, the sinks and the rubber hoses for shampoos. Dad had once more made a success out of a new business. Examining the red leather upholstered chair in front, I wondered if it was the same he had had back in Oklahoma. It looked like the same one, with red leather seat and white enameled arms. I propped the front door open with a hair oil bottle and went out into the moist night air. I walked down the street and through alleys in a thick fog smelling of the sea, and at last tired myself out enough to sleep. Dad woke me when he opened for business, rattling the venetian blinds.

Sensing my boredom as I hung around the barber shop, Dad's manicurist offered to do my nails. I sat across her little table in the front of the shop while she trimmed and filed, pumping me for information. "What do you think of your Dad?" she asked, when he had gone out for a while.

I clammed up, unable to think of an answer. At last I managed a grumpy, "He's okay, I guess."

"Maybe you don't know him very well," she suggested. I looked into her face, astounded at her understanding. She asked if I wanted some clear polish on my fingernails, but I declined. Chuck would not be coming by until Monday to pick me up for our return trip, but I had lost interest in life with my father within hours.

On Saturday afternoon a fat man named Frank came in. Dad gave him a quick trim. While he was in the chair, Frank told me about his hair oil business. He mixed the stuff in a bathtub at home and took it around to barber shops. My Dad's shop was about his best outlet, he said. Most customers could not get away without buying a bottle. He said his recipe was secret, but he could tell me it had a lot of lanolin in it.

Dad unhooked the apron and let Frank up. "I got a favor to ask ya," my father told him. "My boy here could use him a new pair of pants. Maybe you could take him down to J. C. Penney's and pick him out a pair."

He handed Frank a ten dollar bill.

Frank said, "I got a better idea. They've got a sale on, good quality stuff, over at Facett's. Maybe we could whip by there and find something."

"Penney's was always good enough for me," my dad said.

"Come on, kid." Frank gave me a light punch on the arm and I followed him out.

We exchanged a few words with Ben, the African-American shoeshine man, who was all geniality and grins. "I can see your dad's got hisself a good boy," he said. "I know he's gotta be real proud of you."

One hand on the steering wheel, Frank turned out to be quite a gossip. "Your dad is one hell of a make-out artist," he told me. "Where did he take you for lunch?"

I told him we had gone to the corner restaurant a couple of blocks from the barber shop. "Did you see the blonde with the big ones?" he said, and gave me a leer.

"I guess so."

"He's got something going with her," he said.

"You mean he did?" I said.

"Still does," Frank said. "He's something else. The only time I ever saw your dad slip up was that Sunday morning."

I was taking in the sights—palm trees and bright sporty cars, convertibles colored like Easter eggs. I did not want to hear any more, but Frank babbled on, ebullient. "I went over to make my hair oil deliveries one Sunday morning," he said. "I guess your dad forgot I have a key to the shop. Anyway, I let myself in and I reckon he didn't hear me. He didn't look up from what he was doing until I was all the way in the door."

"What was he doing?"

"He was using two of them hand massagers he's got," Frank said. "They feel real good on your scalp after a haircut. He was standing behind that gal that does his manicures. He had him a massager on both hands, and they were buzzing away."

I still did not get it. "What was he doing?"

"I told you," Frank said. "He was giving her a massage."

"What kind of massage?"

Frank looked at me like I was stupid. "I guess we should go buy them pants," he said, pulling up in front of a warehouse-sized store. Inside we examined piles of trousers stacked on tables. Frank helped me pick out a pair of ivory sharkskins and a pair of blue cotton summer pants. He encouraged me to try on both pairs, not bothering to find a dressing room. "Don't get me wrong," he went on, "your dad's a great guy. Tell you what, though, I'm going to give him a ring to make sure it's okay to get both pairs. He can be funny, your dad."

The sales clerk let him use the phone. Right away he and my father got into a heated argument. "This is a real good deal," Frank tried to explain, but winced at what he heard on the line.

We put the two pairs of trousers back on the stack and drove to Penney's, where we bought the first pair that fitted me, khaki work pants. I kept them on and carried my old pair. The clerk dropped them into a paper bag.

Back in the car Frank sighed. "Seven dollars is about all he's good for. He'll be counting the change." His tone toward my father had changed considerably. "He's a real sonofabitch," he said, "and I'm going to tell him so when we get back."

That is exactly what he did. Frank strode past Ben without a word, went into the shop where my father looked up from a customer he was shaving.

"This kid comes half way across the goddamn country to see his dad, and you can't even buy him some decent pants," he said.

"What's he wearing, then?" my father asked, looking at the new ones.

"Them Penney's pants ain't worth a damn, Dow, and you know it."

My father thrust the straight razor in Frank's direction with a backward flick of his wrist. "Get on outta here right now, while the getting's good," he warned, "and don't bring any more of your goddamn hair oil."

"That's fine with me." Frank turned to me. "I'm sorry, kid, but that's the way it is."

"You just lost your best customer," my father called to Frank.

"A titty massage," Frank whispered as he passed me on his way out.

"What did he say?" Dad asked.

"Nothing," I said.

Dad finished shaving his customer. "There ain't a damn thing wrong with them pants," he said. "They'll do just fine for church tomorrow."

"I think you've got a real nice pair of pants on," the manicurist told me.

I had no interest in going along to church, but my father insisted. Lusty for waitresses or not, he had become a fervent member of the Church of the Nazarene. I had not heard such hymns as the congregation lofted to the rafters since going to Pickett Prairie church near Grampa's farm. After a hellfire-and-brimstone sermon, the congregation was called forward to be saved by the preacher. The soupy and plaintive music calling sinners to come home to Jesus reminded me of the recorded music in the churches Ellen and I had sampled back in Nowata. Dad insisted that I accept this assurance of salvation.

It was no big deal, accepting the minister's palm on my forehead and letting him give me a severe push. At least I was able to beg off being dipped in the bathtub behind the altar, as some other members of the congregation were. My sister, who would change churches for a dish of strawberry shortcake, had gone through that several times in Nowata. I wondered if being saved a second time canceled out the first, in which case I only had to find out how many times my sister had been baptized to know if she'd go to heaven or hell—to heaven if an odd number, to hell if an even.

We went to Dad's new house for a chicken dinner. Jane served the same fare Grandma Ada had prepared on the farm—mashed potatoes and gravy, corn on the cob, and peach cobbler. Only the luxury of ice cream had been added to the urban menu. Jane's sorrowful face made it clear that she had no illusions about becoming my new mother, but when I left after breakfast the next morning she gave me a hug and said, "You come back any time, you hear? And you let your daddy hear from you."

On the trip back to the ranch, I sulked as Chuck and Paula regaled me with tales of their weekend pleasures. I paid little attention to their chatter about their movie star friends. I was adding up all the things my father had ever given me. Now I had a pair of pants and a bottle of Frank's hair oil to add to the list. I turned from counting telephone poles along the highway to counting the times I had seen him since he had left on the watermelon truck. There had been the trip he made back to the yellow tenement in Tulsa, a Christmas family reunion at Grampa's farm, my bus journey when he had his restaurant in Kansas, and the time he turned up in Nowata inviting me to climb in and go to California.

The incident with Frank had been a reminder of how radically different perceptions of my father could be. He was a deadbeat and a failure, I had heard dozens of times, but at the same time Mother or Aunt Ruth would sometimes grudgingly acknowledge his cleverness when they gossiped about him. "Dow could paint a coffee can and sell it for an antique vase," Aunt Ruth said, trying to make such an ability into a vice. Although my father spoke of being born again in the Church of the Nazarene in Long Beach, only my mother remembered him as "always talking religion." Frank had added his accounts of Dad's philandering, but Dad himself was harsh in his judgments of the sins of others, and unforgiving in his clashes.

During my visit, I had remarked that I was going to the drug store next door to buy a Hershey bar. "I don't want you setting your foot in that place," he said, "or giving him a penny's worth of business. That old boy and me don't get along." I have believed in the economic boycott ever since. Frank and that druggist had suffered Dad's wrath and I too at times have sentenced various businesses to the same penury by imposing my boycott and depriving them of my custom.

How many homes have I fled
as if the landlord chased after us,
and just because my father
set such a good example.
We take instruction where
we find it, and try to replicate
the perfect gestures we have seen.
It is always raining when I flee.

So it was with Dad. So it is
with me. He outran at least
a dozen landlords, including
one who brought the sheriff
with his shotgun—he chased
us through the night, as in
a movie, black and white.
There was no color, not
in those days. Would Dad
be proud of me at last
if he knew I took the fears
he taught to Wales and Spain
and Greece and fled the way
he did?   Is that not the way
to honor such a father, to be
just like the man you swore
you would not be, yet are?

I fled both fascist landlords
and those who agreed with me,
my small boy's fears
gone global—and always,
almost always, in the rain,
the windshield overwhelmed.

Lee Pape, Mother and Uncle Skeet at Lee's Place

17.

MY WAR WITH John Warner was front and center of my remaining time in high school. As with any war, its battles can be charted. My rebellion was fueled by my guardian's efforts at control. Each time he grilled me, he accused me of being incapable of telling the truth, as if he had a monopoly on the virtue. Truthfulness could have been a power I had over him but I did not realize it.

Ironically, I felt a sense of responsibility for Warner. It was not altogether altruistic. If he could be encouraged to get involved with a woman, he would leave me alone. I could not understand why he was not responsive to the women who flirted with him, although he was described by friends as an eligible bachelor. Since I was having trouble suppressing my own attraction to women we met, I found his indifference mystifying.

One of our acquaintances, Philippe's mistress for a time—one of those wealthy widows Warner disapproved of—took an interest in me. At a dinner party she hosted she led me down a dimly lit hall to a bedroom. She opened a closet door, got down on her hands and knees, and pulled out more than a dozen pairs of her late husband's shoes, explaining that they were handmade in Italy. She invited me to try them on. As she bent to help, I glimpsed her freckled breasts. She looked up and smiled at me.

Warner did not delay following us down the hall. He appeared in the doorway as I laced on a pair of white golfing shoes.

"I'm showing him my husband's shoes. I hate to throw them out."

He regarded us with a suspicious smile. He did not like what he saw.

Bonnie babbled on. "I would like the boy to have them, if he'll take them," she said, and stood up.

"He doesn't need charity," my guardian said in a cold tone. "He's got plenty of shoes."

"I'd love to have the shoes," I said. "I think it would be an honor. They fit real well."

Bonnie threw me a grateful glance. "I'll get you a clothes bag," she said. It was a slim victory, a sharper confrontation with Warner narrowly avoided.

She did not flirt with me after that evening, nor did we see much of Bonnie after that. But for a while I wore a different pair of shoes every day—black and white wingtips, brown and white wingtips, white golfing shoes with red rubber soles and cleats, patent leather dancing shoes, loafers, and blue suede. They rubbed blisters and calluses on my feet, but I thought the discomfort worth it to show off my shoes-of-the-day.

I thought of the widow. If she sensed what was going on, she might have been happy to have intervened with "Tea and Sympathy." She as well as Philippe might have been good choices for me to confide in. But when Philippe had provided an opening and offer of help with that remark about John not being the sort of fellow I should be living with, I had jumped to the defense of my guardian, as if honor bound to do so.

A few weeks later, risking Warner's rage if he found out, I called Philippe at the university where he held a job as an employment counselor. I still did not tell him what was going on, or that I was determined to escape Warner's hold. My desire to move spoke for itself.

"I may have just the job for you," he said.

The job, for after-school hours and weekends, was playground supervisor at Green Fields School for Boys. Room and board came with the job, washing windows and doing yard work when not watching after the younger boys on the playground and seeing that they turned lights off and settled down at night. I slept in an upper bunk in a room shared with three of the younger students, one of whom was heir to a pineapple fortune. After lights out, I had the school library entirely to myself and was undisturbed in my homework and reading. Weekdays I rode into town with a rich teenager in his wood-paneled station wagon to attend Tucson High. I got the impression that this boy was boarded at Green Fields because his parents had no other plan for him.

Warner must have been determined to defeat my efforts at independence. Just before Christmas break he showed up to offer me a trip back to Oklahoma. He disappeared into the headmistress's office for an hour or more. When he came out, he insisted that we take a walk behind the outbuildings to discuss holiday plans. When we were barely out of sight of the playground, he grabbed me. A struggle like the earlier ones took place. He must have known I would be too humiliated to cry out.

While in Oklahoma I received a telegram from my employers— Warner must have given them the address. "NO NEED FOR YOU TO RETURN TO GREEN FIELDS STOP MR WARNER HAS YOUR POSSESSIONS." The second sentence was mysterious until Warner, with a broad smile, explained that he knew the job would never work out, that the headmistress had shared with him many complaints about my work at the school, and he had arranged for my things to be delivered to his place. He had not told me, since he knew I would be disappointed. Like the move from the Children's Home, all had been arranged without consultation.

He was very pleased at this development. The rug had been pulled out from under me. I had no idea where I could live upon our return to Tucson. Conditions at home in Nowata seemed more squalid and repellent than ever. How could I swap air I could breathe without wheezing for a tavern and a house that was about to fall down, and a drunken stepfather who waved a gun around? It did not occur to me that I had a duty to stay and protect my sister. I accepted the ride back to Tucson.

Warner's claim that in his "talk with the ladies at Green Fields" he had discovered their dissatisfaction with my work puzzled me. I had been proud of the way I treated the boys, and had carried out menial chores such as yard work and washing numerous windows in classroom buildings cheerfully and without complaint. It took me years and the assistance of a therapist to construct a more probable scenario than my being fired for just cause. In his visit to the school, Warner must have voiced his possessive concern as my guardian in such a way that the wily ladies sensed the true relationship. From their office window they might have witnessed our disappearing behind the outbuildings, returning in obvious disarray. Had the educators come to those conclusions they would have deemed me an unsuitable resident, unfit to be trusted with the young boys I watched over, sharing a room with three of them. That Warner could orchestrate such a complex set of innuendoes, giving away even his own secret to hurt another, was well within his power.

He managed, I believe, to convey to many of his acquaintances what our relationship was—master and slave, Zeus and his cupbearing Ganymede—while hiding it from others. With such finesse, abusers manage to stay out of prison and even move comfortably within their own social sets while controlling their charges with such skills of brainwashing as they possess—considerable in John Kingsbury Warner's case.

I was mystified and chagrined by the telegram, and grieved the loss of yet another home. But if Warner thought I would be driven back to him, he was mistaken, for upon our return I again consulted Philippe and he found me another job, as a bellhop at a Miracle Mile motel. I rented a basement room at the corner of Speedway and Main. I was determined not to cave in to Warner's pressures again.

The room smelled of gas fumes from the space heater and had a red floor. The single bed and small desk provided a comforting sanctuary and nobody bothered me. I could read in bed as late as I wished. The landlady was a widow who taught piano lessons, and when I went upstairs to use the bathroom she offered me coffee and cookies. One day she volunteered to give me piano lessons in return for help with her housework. With a few lessons I got as far as picking out the melody of Beethoven's Ninth—the "Ode to Joy"—before getting discouraged.

After school I walked the two miles to my job, clocked in and had a meal with the waitresses in the motel restaurant. I spent the evening lugging suitcases and taking buckets of ice to the cottages. On weekends I cleaned out the swimming pool and worked as a busboy in the restaurant. Now and then the staff would chatter about some celebrity who had checked in. Johnny, the bellhop of the Philip Morris commercials, turned up in his uniform of red coat with brass buttons and black pillbox hat with chin strap. I had heard his famous "Call for Phil . . . . .ip Morrr— —issss!" on the radio many times and told him so.

"Don't even ask," he said, as we were on our way to his room.

"What do you mean?" I said, putting down his suitcase at the door and noting that despite his four-foot height he had the pale face of a middle-aged man.

"Everybody asks me to demonstrate it," he said.

"I wasn't going to ask," I said. I was curious as to whether he wore the uniform all the time. He tipped me a dollar for carrying his suitcase, and I suppressed my impulse to ask him for some samples. I no longer had a supply of cigarettes from Warner.

Another evening, approaching a cottage with a tray balanced on my palm, a bucket of ice and two glasses wobbling on it, I almost stumbled when I recognized—through the screen door—Vincent Price, the star of horror movies. I had last seen him with vampire fangs protruding from his mouth, but now, rather than sinking them into the neck of a beautiful woman, he was standing behind one, reaching forward to fasten either the clasp of a necklace or of a brassiere. Hearing me knock, he came to the door while the blonde turned away.

"Come on in, just set it over there," the actor said. Trying not to look toward the woman in her bra and half-slip, I placed the tray gingerly on the credenza.

The actor took a five-dollar bill from his wallet and offered it.

"That's too much," I said. My pride always got in the way. I was supporting myself with a part-time job but turning down a big tip.

"Don't be silly," he said, but I persisted, feeling my face flush. The woman stood watching, and it was hell not to look at her.

"No sir," I put my hand up. I could not be bribed, bought, or seduced with money. In what heaven, I have since wondered, are such grandstanding gestures rewarded? I would hate to think they were all for nothing.

But did not the woman admire my stand? Was not my pride intact and glowing?

Not really. I returned to the office totally dispirited, feeling like a fool. I had, after some urging, accepted a fifty-cent piece. What had I been avoiding, seduction or servitude? Bellhopping was a proud job, like Johnny's. Lugging suitcases was manly work. But tips were hard to accept. I was out to be my own man.

A Bulova watch salesman checked in one night. I helped him with his suitcase, and when we got to his room he opened the sample case he had carried. It was full of watches displayed on velvet boards. He described his territory, how he drove great distances, the entire Southwest for his bailiwick. He was heading for Albuquerque the next day, though he would have to turn right around and return to Tucson.

On impulse I asked if I could ride along, make the trip to Albuquerque with him.

"Don't you have school?" he said.

"It's not important. I can skip classes for a couple of days."

"It's okay with me," he said. "Whose permission you got to get?"

"Nobody's. I'm on my own."

"I guess I could use the company," the genial drummer said.

He arranged to pick me up the next morning as he headed out of town, and I rode along—a pure lark. I paid for my own room for the night in Albuquerque, and the salesman was good company. He supplied a tireless stream of superficial chat. The scenery of desert and mountains was fabulous. I was alive to it as never before. Somehow, I felt very safe with the salesman. He was selling me nothing, just enjoying my company, a welcome change from riding along with Warner, ever alert for a new attack.

Back in Tucson, I lollopped down the steps to my basement room. The landlady ran out the back door, called me up, and embraced me as if I had come back from the dead. "Wherever on earth were you?" she cried. "We've had the police looking all over for you."

And indeed, the police arrived and assured themselves that I had not met with foul play. I could never have been more amazed, unable to comprehend their concern. After all, I had not run away to rob a bank. My employer's anger when I showed up for work at the motel mystified me even more. He had always been easygoing about my schedule. I had assumed that if I did not show up and clock in, I simply would not get paid for those hours. I could think of no reason why I should have let my landlady, employer, or teachers know my plans. As for having the troopers searching for me, the whole idea was absurd.

The possibility had not entered my mind that anyone could care whether I was living or dead, present or absent. So numbed had I become that their anxiety—particularly that of the landlady and the high school counselor, an Hispanic woman—could touch me in only an abstract and distanced acknowledgement that I had failed to be present when the roll was called. That they might really care was beyond me.

Although impaired in my ability to feel love, I had, just a week or so before, stopped just short of the act of making love—with Janet, a young housekeeper at the motel who invited me into one of the cottages to help her replace a ceiling light bulb. I had to stand on the bed to screw the bulb in. When I stepped down she suggested that we use the room to change for a swim. The manager had no objection to his employees enjoying the facilities so long as they were caught up on their duties. Janet and the other female staff did not hurt business as they cavorted in and around the pool. Sometimes I had to bring them as well as the guests drinks and ice buckets on trays from the dining room.

"I've got my suit on under my dress," she said. "How about you?"

She fingered the second button on her yellow uniform. The top one was already undone and I managed a glimpse of her cleavage with little effort. She turned her back to me and let fall the housekeeper's uniform, then took her time to arrange it on a hanger. Her lacy black swimming suit looked like underwear. She turned around and appraised my paralysis. "What are you waiting for?"

"Nothing," I said. "I'll go and change in the bathroom."

"Don't you already have some shorts on?"

"Yeah. I just thought . . . "

"I won't bite you," she said.

I was tortured by her ambiguities of glance and gesture and tried not to look at her breasts, bare almost to the nipples. I could feel my pulse racing, my face stinging. Here was a perfect opportunity for an initiation. Janet could only have been more inviting if she had fallen back on the bed and commanded me to make love to her. She smiled, and I realized this was the moment of truth.

"Maybe you already have a girlfriend," she said.

"Kind of," I said, for I had fallen in love with a classmate, Anne.

"I guess you're pretty serious?"

"Pretty," I acknowledged.

"I guess I'm too old for you."

"No, no you're not."

"I got married when I was your age," she said, pondering her cigarette pack.

"I thought you were divorced."

"I am. It only lasted a year, less than a year. He was a bastard."

I must have looked puzzled, locked into literal meaning.

"He beat me up," she added. "I like gentle men."

The cup of tea was before me and I needed only to raise it to my lips. How to proceed?

"What about you?" she said. "Are you gentle?"

"Maybe we should go for the swim," I said, and gulped as if I were swallowing a big drink of water. "They'll think something happened to us."

"So . . . ?" She reached out a hand, but I opened the door and stepped out into the sun, regretting my cowardice. At least, I reflected, I had been loyal to Anne.

Making love would mean violating all the taboos and injunctions from both Mother and John Warner. To surrender to the moment was a crime. No matter what I did, somebody was bound to be displeased.

We went for the swim, but after a few minutes Janet went back in to the vacant room to change. This time she did not invite me to join her. After that day she ignored me, and I tried not to notice her off-duty flirting with guests by the swimming pool. At those times Janet treated me pointedly as a mere boy, hailing me sarcastically. I might as well have been a servant. When, soon afterwards, I was dismissed from the bellhop job, I thought the real reason was my risky flirtation with Janet.

Anne was a virgin, so far as I knew, but she weighed in on the side of pleasure, not asceticism. Her passion for Latin poetry and stargazing, her enthusiasm for ballet classes, her scholarly immersion in Spanish were no deterrents to her sensuality. She was eager to explore it with me, a natural outpouring of readiness and enthusiasm. She told me she was in love, and I was as close to that feeling as was possible for one who bristled when touched, tense and watchful for whether the next move came from friend or foe, was an attack or a blessing, a caress or a stranglehold or both.

Warner moved into the vacuum again. He seemed to know as soon as I did that I had been fired. Blocking my autonomy was, in truth, not much of a challenge. As if endowed with extrasensory powers, although I had not seen him for weeks, he dropped around within hours of my leaving the motel to rescue me once again, taking me out for T-bones and consoling me for the loss of the job. He offered to take me back, yet again saying I could have my own separate room and that he would leave me alone. His serendipitous timing was impressive, catching me at a nadir of discouragement. Maybe his words had no credibility any more, but I acknowledged the defeat and consoled myself with the thought that I could again have the privilege of driving the Continental.

He had sold the ranch and taken a house in town, a bungalow on Myrtle Street. I could have my own room. Once again the arrangement would be one of employer and employee. I would have my set tasks. The new place was quite near the high school, and I could earn my way by cooking and housekeeping, yard care and weekly polishing of both the Continental and the Mercury coupe.

"You can have your friends over any time you want," he added. But that offer meant nothing since he would only interrogate them about me, affecting genial concern as my guardian. He never failed to explain that he was responsible for me, had to look after me, and appreciated all the help he could get.

With this move he came on with humility in sharp contrast to the bullying tactics he had used in earlier battles, a shift of strategy. Perhaps I could hold him to this new standard. If it is hard for us to forgive ourselves for bargaining for our lives, it is even harder when only room and board and the privilege of showing off in a Lincoln Continental are at stake.

For a while the new deal worked. I moved into the house on Myrtle Street and tried to focus on school work. I joined the school astronomy club and studied Anne's freckles as if they were extra constellations. Warner permitted me to date, so long as he got filled in on the details when I returned. He always waited up to grill me about how we had spent the evening. One night another battle was touched off by my late return.

The interrogation began as soon as I was inside the front door. He was waiting in the hallway, alerted by the car aerial flicking the carport rafters. He grabbed my arm, demanding to know where I had been.

"I told you, we went to a movie."

"What movie? Where?"

"*The Red Shoes*, the one I told you we were going to. You said we could."

"It got out two hours and twenty minutes ago." He held up his wristwatch.

"I guess we lost track of time."

I moved back from his whiskey breath. He was hurting my arm, squeezing it hard.

"You were fucking around with her, weren't you?"

"No, not really. I never did."

"What did you do? Did you get in her pants?"

"No, of course not."

"Did she jerk you off? I'll bet she jerked you off. Did she?"

"Christ, no. She's a nice girl. She's still a virgin."

"How the hell would you know? You got inside her brassiere, didn't you?"

An interrogator always knows when he has hit pay dirt. But I tried to distract him. Lying was the only loyalty to Anne I could employ. "No," I insisted. "You're drunk, John."

"You shut the fuck up," he glowered. "I'll ask the goddamn questions. You sucked her tits, didn't you?" he raged.

"No, honest."

"Are they nice? Does she have nice tits?"

"I told you, I dunno. We just went to the movie."

"What movie?"

"I told you, *The Red Shoes*."

He made me recite the plot, and said he would go see the movie the next day to see if I was lying. "Did you feel her pussy?" he went on.

Anne had been taking ballet classes, and not long before had performed in a recital on the stage of the same theatre where we saw the movie, which we had chosen because it was about ballet. Her ambition was to become a ballerina in the Ballet Russe de Monte Carlo. It did not matter if Margot Fonteyn came to a bad end in the film. Anne was willing to be flung to the seaside rocks if she could just dance ecstatically to the edge of the cliff.

Despite my plot summary of the movie, there were still more than two hours unaccounted for. The Continental's aerial had clicked me in and out as effectively as an employee's time clock.

Dragging me by the wrist, Warner stormed out and checked the odometer of the car with a flashlight.

"You put thirty-eight miles on the speedometer," he said, in a cold fury. "Get in the car, Buster. We're going for a ride."

"That's crazy, John. It's the middle of the night."

"We'll see where you went, won't we? I won't stand for your sneaking around. Now you get in that damn car and drive. And the speedometer better come out thirty-eight miles or you're . . . Never mind, just do it."

I drove to Anne's house and pulled up beside the box hedge, just as I had earlier. I wondered if she was sleeping, or if she might look out her window and think it strange to see us out there, pulling up and then away along the quiet street. We drove downtown, following my earlier route, and around the blocks we had circled before parking opposite the theatre. I even backed and pulled forward as I had for the parallel parking when there had been other cars along the street.

"Then where?" he demanded.

I kept hoping John would get tired of this foolishness. But he became more irate as I headed out of town, then up the road winding around Sentinel Peak, better known as A Mountain. I was desperately trying to think of some other route to fool him, but I knew it was too risky.

A mound of ancient volcanic rocks, the small mountain was famous for the chalked A for "Arizona" on its slopes above the road. Its geology had given Anne and me much to discuss, but we had moved on to identifying constellations—the intellectual prelude to petting and kissing. "It's not a long time by star time," she said before we stopped talking. She meant lava flows, eruptions, tremblings of the earth.

As soon as I parked after this second drive up the mountain, Warner leaned over and read off the odometer evidence and checked his wristwatch. If the mileage failed to convict me, the time frame would. He called me a liar.

Of course I had lied to him. I was Disobedient, Disloyal, Untruthful, and all the rest of it. I was in love. An hour before I had been enjoying love and privacy. The lights of the city below had been jewels in the distance.

"How long did you park here?"

"Not long."

"How long?"

"Not very long. Maybe half an hour."

"Did you stay in the car?"

"Uh, I mean, yes. No, we got out and looked at the stars."

"You're a liar. You don't have any goddamn Loyalty. You don't appreciate a goddamn thing I've done for you."

"Honest, I'm not lying. I am grateful."

"Then what *did* you do?"

The third degree continued. I felt sick to my stomach.

"Get out of the car," he commanded, in the voice he must have used as an infantry captain in the Battle of the Bulge. Maybe he got his bronze star for bossing kids like me around. He had gone through hell and was going to see that I did too.

Even in the darkness I could see the fury on his face, his lips pressed and eyes glowering, reflected in the same moonlight that had seemed so romantic a short time before. When Anne and I had sat looking out over the glittering lights of the city, there had been many parked cars, a long line of shadowy love nests. But now I was alone in the night with a man losing control.

He took his belt off and started hitting me with it, turning it around so that I had to dodge the sharp metal. It was a Nazi "Gott Mitt Uns" buckle—one of his war souvenirs.

The belt was not enough. He began hitting me with his fist and, as with earlier sessions, pushed me down and kicked me as I held my hands up to defend myself.

"You ungrateful little sonofabitch. If you had any guts you'd shoot yourself." It was the first time he had been so explicit.

Even within the wild range of his rage, the interrogation continued. "You did, didn't you? You felt her tits, and her pussy too. Were they nice, those tits? How big are they? Did you suck them? Both of them or just one? I want to know. Don't just stand there, Goddamn you."

Then he hit me again and again. I kept getting up, getting knocked down. At last I just sat down on the cinders, whimpering at his feet. He demanded that I stand up, be a man, fight him.

"I can't do that," I blubbered, as I had in the Oklahoma field. My physical struggles with him had always been defensive, but he wanted to slug it out.

"Why not?"

"I don't know. I can't fight you, John. I'm sorry."

The bottom line was that he was still my guardian. He was still the father figure, the one my mother trusted, the one who had lectured me about Obedience. He was out to convince me that if things had gone terribly wrong, it was all my fault.

He was right, of course. I had felt her breasts. I had bent down and kissed them. She had untied a laced ribbon to give me access. I had never been happier. I was in love. And I had not needed words to tell me what we were doing was moral. Hemingway wrote that morality is what we feel good after, and I had felt very good after the necking with Anne until Warner attacked.

I was paying for love. How could I defend it? What felt natural, inevitable, expansive, fulfilling as nothing before had ever been, was— Warner would have it—criminal, sick, disloyal, disobedient, dishonorable, right on through the list of my perversities. God was looking down at me, Warner yelled as if for the man on the moon to hear him, and God did not like what he saw.

Warner was tiring. His blows got lighter and less lethal. He kicked me with no more passion than it would take to get rid of a cat. If I could just not provoke him more, I would survive this scene. He always brought God in last, when he was about to run out of gas, when he would collapse and let the whiskey numb him to sleep. In his rage he had worn himself out. He stood swaying in the moonlight, panting for breath.

His pause scared me to think what he might do next, and I suddenly obeyed the instinct to flee, climbing over boulders down the mountainside. He stood above, yelling down to me that he would not hurt me. Just at that moment I slipped, and pain shot through my ankle. I tried hobbling, then crawled back up to the roadside and into the passenger seat as Warner held the door open.

The next morning I heard the new conditions. "You're grounded," he said. "No more car for a month. And I want your oath you won't see that girl again while you're on probation."

Otherwise, he said, there were would be some dire consequences. He did not say what they were. He reminded me that he had legal control of me and that the law told me to obey him or else. As for spraining my ankle, that had been my fault, and I was not going to get any sympathy for it.

At this point I had no intention of being honest with him. It was just a matter of how to get my hands on the Continental again and sneak around to see Anne as soon as I could. She was bewildered when I tried to tell why I could not see her. To her, Warner's overreaction did not make sense and I could not tell her the whole story. "He sounds worse than my mother," she said. Now we were conspirators trying to outwit Warner and her alcoholic mother.

David with his first love, Anne Greenleaf Wilson

18.

AT A SUNDAY afternoon cocktail party we met Mr. Simenon, who wore loafers and a tweed sport coat with leather elbow patches. He stood swathed in aromatic smoke from his pipe. With easy smile and eyes arched with amusement, he projected an image of comfort and self-satisfaction.

I did not know he was the most famous novelist in France, only that he seemed a nice guy when he told me the cocktail party was dreadfully boring and how would I like to go along with him to the rodeo. John frowned, but I could see that he could not think up a reason fast enough to withhold his blessings. "Make sure you get back by seven. You've got homework to do."

Warner had a laudable concern for my homework, which was what I was usually doing when he dragged me into his bedroom and beat the hell out of me when I refused to climb into his bed. But sipping his martini and jabbering to Joseph Wood Krutch, he gave his permission to go to the rodeo with Mr. Simenon.

When we left the party I sat in the front seat of Georges Simenon's blue Packard, a convertible with the top down. It was a postwar model—a decade newer than Philippe's elegant vehicle. The seats were leather, and Simenon sank into them with a hedonistic sigh. He suckled and played with his pipe, speeding along with one hand on the wheel without the slightest apprehension of cops. He fielded more questions about rodeos than I could answer. "Tell me about the calf roping," he said.

His bemused ignorance about America gave me a chance to be a big shot. I cast about for explanations that sounded complicated. "It would probably be hard for a foreigner to understand," I suggested.

"We will stop at the house," he said, "and get my friend."

He pulled the car up before a large house and asked me to wait, then went in and emerged with a woman whom he introduced simply as D. She opened the front door, greeted me as if she had known me for years, and motioned for me to slide into the middle. I offered to move to the back seat, but she dismissed the idea as ridiculous.

"You stay right here," she patted my sleeve. "Jo, where did you meet such a nice young man?" she said to Simenon. I was in heaven, sitting between a fatherly man smelling of pipe smoke and a woman perfumed and interested in me. What grade was I in? Had I been to many rodeos? Why had I come to Arizona? What were the things they should see besides the rodeo?

"San Xavier." I mentioned the old Spanish mission a few miles out of town. Simenon decided the rodeo was not so important after all. He followed my directions to San Xavier, floorboarding the Packard.

As we wandered through the historic mission church, I had time for the play of fantasy. If only Anne could have been with us, I thought, to see how wonderful Mr. Simenon and his secretary were. What an interesting fellow he was! Why did I not have a father like that? Was it possible he might want to adopt a kid such as myself and help me get away from Warner? Mr. Simenon had a cool, appraising gaze that seemed to understand everything. I felt as if I could, if given the chance, really talk to him. What he did not know about America seemed to be more than made up for by a kind of warm wisdom about people. He was the perfect person to spill my guts to, let all the pain go tumbling out. But something held me back.

"I hate those cocktail parties and all those affairs," the novelist said more than once. "Everything is such pomposity. We didn't come here for that."

"What did you come here for?" I asked him.

"A place to work," he said, as if that were a funny quest indeed.

"He's always working on a new novel," D. said. I thought she was his secretary, but sensed that she was much more.

"It is a very good place to work," he said. "Tucson is good for us."

But he felt no need to be consistent. Two minutes later he sighed and said, "The ennui, it gets to me." He fanned his pipe smoke as if it were ennui—this new word he taught me. I too suffered from it, I decided.

I saw the way Mr. Simenon looked at the girls we passed in the parking lot of San Xavier Mission. He was a teddy bear of a man, chummy and inquisitive. Even in the cool shadows of the whitewashed mission, he would turn to appraise a woman, as if prepared to follow her. D. strolled away from us, admiring the baroque architecture, the elaborate carvings, the gilded wooden saints. She knelt at the altar rail.

I asked Mr. Simenon what kind of books he wrote.

"They are superficial," he said. "I do not think you would find them interesting."

"They are just French," D. said, catching the comment as she rejoined us. She had been crying.

"They are *feuilletons*," he said, "I write in one week one *feuilleton*."

"They are crimes," D. said.

Simenon laughed. "Crimes, yes! Every time I think I should kill someone I write a novel instead. The new one is *Lettre à mon juge*."

"It's worked out very well so far," D. said, doubtfully. "He is not in prison."

"We will not kill anyone today," he said, with resignation.

"But he should be in prison," D. said, and it was not clear if she was joking.

We headed back to Tucson at high speed. They seemed to have cooled and lost interest in me. I did not know what to say to them. As if to begin would have meant telling everything, I did not even get around to sharing my ambitions to be a writer.

I never saw the couple again, but the scenes of that afternoon come back to me out of the years, as if encased in the hyaline plastic of a lending library volume of Georges Simenon's *Intimate Memoirs*. I tried to locate that spot in his life when he had encountered a troubled kid at a

cocktail party and invited him to come along to the rodeo. It must have
been right after his first day in Tucson when he and D. had had dinner
in the Pioneer Hotel and in squeezing half a lemon into his tomato
juice he had spattered the juice into an elegantly-dressed young
woman's face. He expected recrimination, but was surprised when the
woman said, "Well, let's hope this little accident will bring you luck."
That was all the blessing he needed. He sought out an agent and rented
"a big hacienda."

I could find no recollection of me in his story. But what I found out
about the genial Mr. Simenon's life was shocking. Once again there was
that strange inversion, the topsy-turvy overturning of all our impressions
when we pry beneath the surface and uncover a pit of secrets. D., the
woman who had so charmed me, was newly pregnant when I met her,
and the positive rabbit test had precipitated a major crisis, threatening
his *ménage à trois* with D. and Tigy. Even that was not a complicated
enough arrangement, for they planned a trip to Nogales to help get yet
another of his women, Boule, through immigration. Simenon admired
people who, he affirmed, "got away with as much as they could in life."
He pushed the limits.

The wife who had long been tolerant was threatening divorce. It was
no longer enough for her to be "the titular head of the house," not when
wife number two was to be a mother as well. Simenon would divorce
wife Tigy one day soon and marry D. the next. They could no longer
"co-exist under the same roof." Speed limits were being imposed on the
great Simenon and he did not like it at all.

The *ménage à trois*—or harem—was not enough. Simenon always
took his servant girls to bed, and in Paris when stopping for a drink he
would often go upstairs to a brothel to tup a whore, or perhaps two or
three. Group sex delighted him in a casual, affable way. Boule, waiting
for her visa to be approved so she could be united with the *ménage*, was
obliged to stay beyond the fence that divided Arizona and Mexico.
Simenon would whip down to Nogales to sleep with her every few days.
Sometimes D. would tag along, and after Georges had made a visit to
Boule, he and D.—his "secret sharer" of everything—would head up

the hill for La Calle, the street of whorehouses. D. would wait while Georges headed down the hall with a thirteen year old.

It was a mixed-up period, he wrote of the Tucson year, "and the slightest cloud assumed great importance." Yet he had seemed unruffled, a master in control of his life.

Poor Simenon. Had he ever found the happiness he seemed to own the secret of, with all his wealth and talent? His memoirs do not encourage that conclusion. D. became a hopeless alcoholic and eventually had to be sent, like a Fitzgerald heroine, to an asylum in Switzerland. The baby she was carrying as she stood near me in San Xavier Mission turned out to be a brilliant and talented girl whom the alcoholic mother abused sexually. On the back cover of their father's memoirs, Simenon's son and daughter gaze into the window of a candy store as he stands beside them in his glasses, fedora, and with his pipe in his mouth. They look like a happy family. The daughter would grow up and commit suicide.

Georges was the survivor. Through it all, he remained remarkably untouched, even nonchalant. Instead of committing crimes, he wrote novels and sported with the sexual abandon of a dog or a de Sade, a languorous-eyed stroller of whorehouses and banger of servant girls. Yet he produced a prolific body of work. Perhaps he was the fucked-up one, and the one who fucked up others, but they suffered the consequences while he remained aloof.

Mr. Simenon broke many a life, yet wandered on with unwavering aplomb. I have since seen others who have transferred their craziness to others, perhaps even driving them to suicide, then sitting back amazed and saying, "How did this happen to me? Why do these strange and disturbed people enter my life? How do I get mixed up with so many crazy people?"

In my hunger for father and mother, together if only in fantasy and for an afternoon, I had seen Georges and D. at their best—their very best. But in response to their queries about my life, I had provided the neat little cover-ups I was so used to fielding. "Yes, I work for Mr. Warner. I came out here to cure my asthma, and I guess it's cured." Beyond that, I kept the secrets locked up. I could not speak to Mr.

Simenon, to Philippe, even to those worm-eaten saints at San Xavier. And if it was true that we are only as sick as our secrets, I was sick indeed. But where was I to go with that sickness? Maybe there was help, but it might only lead to more betrayal.

In *Iron John*, Robert Bly describes the Wild Man's abduction or rescue of a boy: "When the Wild Man had reached the dark forest once more, he took the boy from his shoulders, put him down on the earth, and said, 'You will never see your mother and father again, but I will keep you with me, for if you do everything as I tell you, all will go well. I have much gold and treasure, more than anyone else in the world.'"

Such a contract between a boy and his mentor, his rescuer, is a model for multiple variations. Warner arrived at an apogee—my ripeness for puberty—and my nadir, my vulnerability. Like any other predator he took measure and moved in for the capture. I could have been a buffalo calf caught grazing alone. But from all sides came praise of John's generosity, blessed by all who heard of how good it was of him to offer a poor, sick boy a home.

In Iron John's terms, Warner had plenty of "gold and treasure." All I had to do to be his heir was obey him in all matters. But the bed he prepared for me was not the "bed of moss for the boy to sleep on . . . ." Nor was the lifestyle of intimidation and the blue haze of his cigarettes "the golden spring . . . clear as crystal, and full of light." On the ranch, I could not free myself of thorns as easily as those cattle loitering by the water trough. I had kept my mask in place as I prepared meals, fare far superior to the food back in Oklahoma. As guests sat around the kitchen while I worked, I boasted of my more manly chores: yard work, fence riding, helping with round-ups. Amid the martinis and small talk, laughs of amused tolerance reassured me that I was regarded as a hardworking employee, not something else.

At the edge of belated puberty, I never more needed an Iron John, a mentor, a protector, someone to help make sense out of the battle with Lee, and my efforts to save Ellen, and even my mother, from his prurience and violence. Warner offered no help in that regard, but only an opportunity to save myself—to flee, little knowing that even a more treacherous battlefield was ahead. Having entrusted her daughter to one predator, Mother wished her son well, seeing him off with another. My death sentence from asthma—which she knew about but had not told me—was reason enough to rationalize her approval. What could be more providential than a wealthy benefactor? I do not know how she rationalized her condoning of Lee's attentions to her daughter.

Using the metaphors Robert Bly developed in *Iron John*, I could say that just at the time I needed the loan of a four-legged horse, Warner arrived to cripple the one I had. Just when I needed a mentor, an adversarial shamer and brainwashing sophist entered my life with all the power of his society and his wealth ranged behind him. Just when I needed a friend for life, I acquired an enemy of great cleverness and cunning. Already depressed, I was pawed, cajoled, and bullied into submission, to a new and degrading helplessness.

The Iron John allegory for me has a literal meaning. The sun of Arizona was indeed gold, and the air was crystal clear, but my rescuer Wild Man offered a parodic travesty of Bly's myth: "The moment the boy leaves with Iron John is the moment in ancient Greek life when the priest of Dionysus accepted a young man as a student . . . ." The literal John who came into my life carried literal iron—his souvenir Luger pistols and S.S. officers' knives in their blue-gray scabbards, an array of war booty weaponry.

Had he been, like Bly's Iron John, a well-meaning role model, a mentor, a shaman, a benefactor, a guardian (as he was ironically called), my life would have taken a different course. My break from my Oklahoma family, the oppressively humid and pollen-saturated climate, along with the threat of Lee's killing me if I defended my sister, could have been genuinely liberating. When I have run across accounts of men like the actor Richard Burton or Senator Charles Percy, who as teenagers were mentored by generous benefactors, I have always been deeply moved. The altruism that changed their lives was what Warner pretended to offer me, fooling almost everyone except those who were complicit.

19.

NOWATA—Lee Pape, 58, operator of a beer tavern, lay in a
Nowata hospital today critically wounded by a .45 caliber bullet
wound in the chest, which he admitted was self-inflicted, according to
Archie Sequichie, deputy sheriff. Doctors gave little hope of Pape's
recovery. They indicated he was bleeding internally. He had three
blood transfusions this morning.

Sequichie said Pape was wounded twice, once through the chest
and once through the left arm. The chest wound was quite close to the
heart. Te [sic] deputy said Pape blamed family troubles for his act.

The shooting occurred about 5:30 p.m. yesterday at the tavern,
called Lee's Place, at the east edge of Nowata.

Pape's family includes the wife . . . , a son . . . , and a step-daughter . . . , all of the home.

The Coffeyville Daily Journal, April 4, 1950

Newspaper articles tracked the events with inconsistencies about
Lee's age and the number of wounds he had inflicted on himself. Any
street corner gossip could have added a more detailed and accurate
account. The media did not report that Ellen's neglected burgers were
smoking and scorching away on the grill when Lee's entrance into the
kitchen that afternoon interrupted her work.

Years later she described it: "He came in through the back door. I
hadn't followed him out like I had every time before when I'd argued

with him and told him he couldn't do it. He said to me, 'I'm just going to kill myself,' and I said, 'You don't have the guts to shoot yourself, Lee, so put the damn gun down.' This time I didn't care. I was just drained. I didn't care. He lifted the gun and fired too soon, and he missed. He hit himself in the left arm. He cocked the gun and fired again. He missed his heart. He fell down on one knee and I took off screaming. My mother and Uncle Skeet were in the restaurant and they ran in just as Lee was ready to shoot me. Uncle Skeet kicked the gun out of his hand."

"It appears that Pape's suicide attempt was the result of a family misunderstanding," the *Nowata Star* quoted the undersheriff as saying on April 4th when the upbeat headline read: "PAPE IMPROVED AFTER SUICIDE ATTEMPT MONDAY."

Lee's son Charlie had been summoned home from the navy, and had arrived before me. Mother had sent me a telegram: "YOUR STEP-FATHER IN HOSPITAL STOP RETURN IF POSSIBLE STOP." I had called her and found out a few more specifics, though she glossed over much of it and referred to the event as an accident. The gist of it was that she needed me at his bedside.

On the American Airlines plane, my first flight on an airliner, I pondered what had happened. I had hated Lee for his aggressions toward my sister, and now tried and convicted him of nameless crimes. If he was not dead by the time I got there, I vowed, I would kill him.

But by the time I arrived, Lee was dead. Charlie had in effect accomplished the same goal, although unintentionally. Lee had inquired about his ruby Elks ring, which he never took off. It had disappeared on the way to the hospital. In his delirious ravings, Lee accused his son of stealing the ring. When Charlie denied the theft, his father, heavily bandaged and disregarding all medical advice, became enraged and tried to get out of bed. The exertion brought on a fatal hemorrhage.

LEE PAPE DIES THIS MORNING

the *Nowata Star* reported.

Lee Pape, 54-year-old drive-in proprietor who had been hospitalized for the past 10 days, died at 10:40 a.m. today in a local hospital.

Mr. Pape had been in a critical condition from a self-inflicted bullet wound since the afternoon of April 3.

Funeral arrangements, to be announced by the Benjamin Funeral Home, are incomplete.

The highway tavern and restaurant was not a drive-in. Lee did not own it. There was only one local hospital, and the funeral arrangements were as complete as they would ever be. I knew it was my duty to attend the funeral and comfort Mother, but Ellen put up a fight not to go. She said she hated Lee for what he had done and would never forgive him. She was enraged that Mother had made her visit him in the hospital every day and pretend that nothing terrible had happened and that our family was perfectly normal.

Mother practically dragged Ellen to the funeral parlor for the service. After a half-hour of mushy electronic organ music and preaching that had little relevance to the man lying in the open casket, we family members were led from behind the semi-transparent curtain reserved for us. Held by the elbows by attendants, as if we were helpless to walk and might all three collapse at any moment, we had no choice but to file in front of the crowd to pay our last respects to Lee's waxen body. Only Mother was weeping into her hankie.

At the gravesite in the town cemetery, Lee's V.F.W. and American Legion buddies turned up in full uniform. One of them fired a rifle into the air. Charlie lingered to collect some of the flower bouquets and placed them on his mother's grave, next to the fresh one. As for Ellen, the scowl never left her face.

I could not wait to leave Nowata this time, nor could Charlie. Each time I walked through town I overheard fragments of gossip about what had happened. I paused, fighting the impulse to talk back to those little groups who aired so freely their obscene speculations. Unfortunately, the vultures had a great deal to feed upon, including the rumor that Lee had said in the hospital that he had only "married the woman to get to the girl." They also gossiped about his violent background, how he had been a bootlegger, how he had been charged in court more than once for assault, and how he had tried to kill someone. I heard this babble with a mix of rage and shame. The voices fell to whispers when I was noticed.

Some of the other things I learned were just as disturbing. During the ten days Lee lived in the hospital, he managed to convince Mother that all was going to be rosy again, as if it ever had been. He would stop drinking and find another job so he would not be around beer all the time. They would move away, leaving all the ugly memories behind.

Mother was already busy eradicating the truth, and finding out that she did not know it anyway, for she was left with many of Lee's debts, and made the surprising discovery that Lee Pape had not been his real name. When she applied for widow's benefits, the Social Security clerk informed her that her husband's real name had been changed for some reason, courtesy of the U.S. Army. "There's no point trying to find out," the clerk added. "The government regards all that sort of thing as highly confidential, you've got to protect people's rights to privacy." Lee's history was safely hidden behind a stone wall. Privacy seemed a strange value to cite in regard to a man who had been unable to respect his step-daughter's right to take a bath.

As if her unconscious took inspiration from the discovery, Mother later on seemed to forget that she had been married three, not two, times. When filling out official forms, she had to be reminded of her second marriage. She had blocked out her years with Lee Pape.

In the years ahead, I often wished I could tell Ellen how much I admired her for the fight she put up. Wadding up a washcloth and fling-ing it at her peeping Tom stepfather was an act of courage no less than was reaching for the gun he waved around. In a better world, she would have had more courageous defenders. In a better world, Mother might have stood up for her daughter. In a better world, I might have been able to protect both my mother and my sister.

"They should not have borne children," T. E. Lawrence concluded of his parents, just as my sister told me, "Mother should never have been a mother." Lawrence noted that many parents manage quite early to reverse roles with their children, as if at birth they dandle them at their breasts not to nurse but only to demand, "Love me!" I came to feel, too, that I disappointed my mother from the outset. With both her children she gave mixed and ever-shifting signals.

T. E. Lawrence carried a lifelong horror of the body instilled in him by his mother's phobias and what he considered violations of his personal integrity. A biographer, Jeffrey Meyers, links the traumas Lawrence suffered in Arabia with his earlier domination by his mother: "The greatest childhood fear of his mother was realized in the most horrible and degrading moment of Lawrence's life." Lawrence, who fled his adolescent home and his father's alcoholism to join the artillery, expressed his bitterness by citing the Greek epitaph, "Here I lie of Tarsus / Never having married, and would that my father had not." He wrote of the damage done in his home by the "atmosphere of overwhelming sin and guilt," especially at "the vulnerable period of adolescence."

Ellen later told me that in the period right after I left Nowata, her teachers—one in particular—had been very mean to her. Her seventh grade math teacher had stood over her and gloated when Ellen had difficulty with equations.

"She'd say, 'You don't have your smartie brother to help you out any more.' She would rub that in, standing over me and checking every answer. Then she'd slap my hands with her damn ruler and make me cry, the old bitch. I didn't want to give her the satisfaction, but sometimes I just couldn't keep from crying."

Recalling those humiliations was the closest Ellen ever got to accusing me of having abandoned her to face the monsters—maybe more than one, but mostly the one she did not mention. I never knew how she survived those years. Lee had not abused her sexually, she said—"He wouldn't dare. But he wouldn't let any boys come near me. He kept saying they were just trying to get in my pants."

She told me of another incident. While we were living in the garage apartment shortly after Lee first started coming around, he made a comment about Ellen's physical development, asking if it wasn't about time she started filling out, and had she begun to menstruate. The question was so blunt that Mother seemed concerned. Ellen had just turned twelve. But Lee's curiosity persisted. "Let me see," he said, and playfully tried to feel her chest, pulling Ellen onto his lap. Mother told Ellen she should not make such a fuss, Lee was just trying to help. After all, he was a grown man who knew about such things.

When Ellen recalled these scenes I reminded her of psychologist Alice Miller's view that the line between physical, mental, and sexual abuse is blurred, and "a witness to violence is a victim of violence." Lee's voyeurism was abuse, I suggested, as was his prurient interest, whether he acted on it or not. Certainly his threats to kill her, even pointing the gun at her, were abuse. It is terrible that any girl ever has reason to be so bitter.

"It was over and done with long ago," she said, seeming to regret having shared even that much of what still festers.

As for Mother, she simply denies that any of it ever happened, and it is that denial that Ellen cannot forgive. The police and court records detailing Lee's violence must have been in error, and he must have changed his name not to escape his past but simply because he was tired of the name he had been born with, whatever that was. Here was a man nobody knew, she least of all. But she can look back only to a bearable fiction.

*Mamma, un tempo fu ancora—il tuo—che in ogni dottrina
la pieu saggia eri.*

—Umberto Saba

The poet Umberto Saba
believed everything that came out
of his mother's mouth—uttered with
the wisdom of an oracle, the infallibility
of the pope. And best of all, she spoke
from the heart, expressing a pure union

of thought and feeling, always tender
and forgiving.
            For such reasons
men and women think of their mothers
as angels.
            But mother, I confess it was never
that way with you and me. Even as a toddler
looking up at your face full of pain, clasping
your knees, I knew you were a confused,
helpless woman, as childish as I was,
and as frightened.
            On that Christmas day
when you paid a visit to the orphanage
you brought no gifts, but asked what we
had for you, and we felt bad because
we had nothing, nothing but our hunger for you.

The question never came up as to whether
you loved us enough for survival—we knew
the answer. If we emerged from the hell
of childhood, it would not be with your help.
From the beginning it was as if you were trying
to forgive me for crimes I committed
                  in a previous life.

And were we, small breastless children,
not expected to nurse you? You wanted nothing
less. Since my failure with you I've made
a profession out of seeking those who might
outdo you in inflicting pain. But none could come close.
In your own way you were as much
               a marvel as Saba's mother.

All this is true.   Yet here am I, an old man
massaging your feet, as if you, Mother,
                                are the only mistress I ever found.

Years later, when I was going through a period of trying to forgive everybody, I drove through Nowata and stopped at the cemetery. I found Lee's grave, a weedy caved-in declivity in the grass at the far edge of the field. It was unmarked except for the small metal stake and frame the V.F.W. had provided. The metal had rusted and the typescript inside the celluloid was faded, as were some garish plastic flowers that had survived for over two decades. I scraped mud off in order to read Lee's name along with his birth and death dates. I sat on the grass and wondered who the man really had been.

I tried to talk to Lee's presence, in the style some book recommended, but my efforts to forgive did not get very far. I realized that I could only forgive someone on my own behalf, but not for a sister or a mother. There were a lot of things I would like to ask Lee, though, and I tried to get answers there in that hour. But I knew that even if he were alive he would have told me no more than the buzzing insects, whose advice to me seemed clear: walk away and never look back.

After Lee's funeral, it occurred to me that there was one person who might be helpful in my negotiations with John Warner — Reverend Hooten, who had brought Warner and me together by inviting him to the basement Boy Scout meeting. He could be influential.

I found Reverend Hooten in his office. He shook my hand and invited me in, closing the door behind us. It was awkward, trying to avoid telling everything even as I said I needed help. Shame stung my face. The minister pressed for details, and I broke into sobs.

He came around behind my chair and put a hand on my shoulder. But when he finally spoke, his advice was in a chiding tone. "You should have more sympathy for John, and find a way to forgive him. He went through a lot in the war, and I can tell you he did not have a very happy life before that either."

Reverend Hooten described the sad events of John's life—the drowning of a small brother in a bathtub, his mother's commitment to the state asylum in Vinita, another brother's death in the war. "Besides," he concluded, "he went to one of those military schools, and that's the sort of behavior they come out with. It's not all that unusual. I've seen a lot of it."

Maybe there was a difference, I struggled to say, between voluntary acts and those forced on you with threats and browbeating. I told Reverend Hooten about the physical pain, how an involuntary orgasm sent needles of fire through me.

"That's a bit graphic, isn't it?" he complained.

"Well, that's the way it is. That's the way it's been since the first week in Arizona. I've got to tell somebody. If you just tell him to quit bothering me, he'll listen to you."

The minister, in a sharper tone, changed course. "Has it ever occurred to you that you could be more grateful for all John's done for you?" This was the familiar line, the one I heard from Mother and from John himself ad nauseam.

The great diplomat Talleyrand once remarked that there are certain favors for which ingratitude is the only appropriate reaction. I assured Reverend Hooten that I was grateful for most of the things my guardian had done for me. He looked doubtful.

I felt more betrayed than ever. Reverend Hooten was not going to stand up for me. I was the only person in my life, with the possible exception of Philippe, who thought people should not have to perform sexual acts unless they chose to do so and with whom they chose to.

"That's the answer," my hometown minister said as he closed his door. "Gratitude."

20.

BY THE TIME of Lee's death I had yet another job, as a movie usher at a downtown theatre. I was delighted with the musty red and black uniform with white piping down the trousers and a red box hat because it reminded me of the bellhop midget Johnny, who called out for Philip Morris. During those long hours between leading customers down the aisle to my choice of seating for them, I would stand by the velvet curtains in back of the auditorium watching the films. I can still recite some of the dialogue in a movie called *Battleground*, starring Van Johnson. Since the movie involved action in the Normandy campaign, it reminded me of Warner's description of his war experiences.

Lee died when I was in the midst of a new battle with Warner. The guidance counselor at Tucson High School had encouraged me to apply for college scholarships. She had made extraordinary efforts to convince the administration that grades and membership in the National Honor Society should not be the sole criteria to take the national exams that would be shared with university admissions committees. "You could have done a lot better with your grades," she said. "That's clear from your intelligence tests." Her tone seemed to imply an unstated sympathy.

She was very pleased when I scored among the top few in the entire nation as well as Canada and as a consequence was offered scholarships at all three of the places I had applied — Pomona College, the University of Arizona, and the University of Chicago. I was excited about the

University of Chicago, having read a laudatory article in *Time* magazine regarding Chancellor Robert Maynard Hutchins and his educational innovations, including the undergraduate curriculum made up, essentially, of the Great Books. When I showed Warner the letter from the University of Chicago awarding me a Murphy scholarship, he was furious that I was not choosing the University of Arizona, which would keep me near him.

"You're not going," he announced, after buying me a restaurant dinner.

"I am going," I said, and our argument escalated until he lost control. When we got back to the apartment I took another beating.

For weeks I tried to convince both my mother and my guardian that it was an honor to get a scholarship and that the University of Chicago was a prestigious place. I shared with them the article in *Time* magazine. But Warner harangued me and tried to bribe me out of going to Chicago. He described America's second city as a web of dangerous slums and the university as a hotbed of Communism. Mother's agenda for me was still obedience to Warner and acceptance of his willingness to adopt me. My turning eighteen did not alter that hope. She stood more staunchly than ever behind Warner.

He had a new idea. Now that I was the man of my family, should I not try to do more for my newly widowed mother and my sister? If I came to Phoenix, where he was taking a new job with the Arizona Fish and Game Commission, he could help me find a place nearby for them. He wanted to help. Once again, his penetrating understanding of what was going on in me was far superior to mine. Nothing could have appealed to me more than a chance to rescue Mother and Ellen from their pathetic situation in Nowata. Putting up with Warner's continuing campaign to veto my move to Chicago seemed a small price to pay. For the first time I had a chance to be "the man of the family," fulfilling the role Mother had laid down for me.

Warner approved my choice of an apartment in Phoenix for Mother and Ellen—a garage apartment almost identical to the one we had lived in in Nowata. There would not be room for Uncle Skeet. Or me—once

again, with a tour of the larger apartment he had rented, I exacted promises that this time Warner would not touch me.

On the trip west over the mountains Lee's old DeSoto overheated and
broke down several times, reminding Mother that her late husband had
left her an albatross. For once I agreed with Warner. "That car isn't worth
the powder to blow it up with." Yet Lee had used it as collateral for loans
and Mother still had to pay off those bills. Warner was willing to help her.

Proud of my autonomy, I got a job selling shoes in Diamond's
Department Store, earning all of nine cents my first day. It was the commission on a bottle of shoe polish. Mother and Sis settled in at their
apartment, and I paid them occasional visits. Warner at last held to his
promise not to bother me, possibly out of awareness that I would soon
be escaping him.

I began dating a girl named Harlene whom I met in a drugstore coffee shop. She was very impressed when I showed up one evening in the
Lincoln Continental to drive her to the city park where she was starring
in an outdoor production of an operetta, *The Merry Widow*. Dressed in
a flaring red gown and breaking into song and dance at the drop of a
handkerchief, Harlene was not convincing as a merry widow, twirling
around the spotlit stage, her swelling breasts aglow. But she was beautiful enough and encouraging enough on our dates that I began to question my love for Anne. Bubbly, buxom, and vivacious, Harlene must
have been mystified by my tense relationship with Warner. I referred to
him as my guardian and she seemed never to have heard of such an odd
role. "Are you a millionaire?" she said. I let her believe it as we necked
in the shadows of oleanders.

I saved up for a portable radio the size of a milk carton and gave it
to Harlene for her birthday, then asked for it back when I discovered she
had another suitor. Generosity in our family seldom came without second thoughts. The recipient was bound to turn out to be unworthy, to
have taken advantage of generosity, and to have betrayed any hope
attached to the gift. Poor Harlene, I am sure she was quite bewildered—
a big-eyed soulful girl prepared to live life on its own terms.

Although Mother and Ellen were settled only a mile or so away, I begged off visits. Climbing the outside stairs reminded me of Nowata. I could not assuage Mother's grief for a man Ellen and I detested, and I was disappointed that she could not give her blessings to my plans for college. I saw in her glum face not the depression she must have been suffering, but only her disappointment in her son.

What had been intended as a rescue operation had turned into hell for the two persons it was meant to benefit. In the blistering heat of the desert city Mother and Ellen were left alone with no social life other than friendship of the two women who ran the nursing home Mother went to work in. I, the rescuing son and brother, was acting all too much like Pip in *Great Expectations*, embarrassed by his poor relations, and with little desire to spend time with them. I felt I had failed them, and could do nothing but lobby for Warner's charity toward them.

"When the mother is truly the matrix of survival," Erik Erikson wrote, "we can learn to trust the world and to develop the basic ingredient of all vitality: hope. Having tasted our mother's body with mouth and senses, we remain part of it and yet also become strong enough to part with it. Our first firmament is the mother's face, shining above the goodness of nourishment; and only the study of universal mythology and of the deepest mental pathology can give us an inkling of the sinister rages and the confused imagery which that early trust must help us to contain before we can emerge from the maternal matrix." The lack of such nurturing, mirroring, and affirming does not soften the shock of separation. A bond of emptiness and hunger can be as strong as that created by needs met and hungers sated.

Erikson adds: "Those moods and that confusion must often be lived through again in adolescence—and this especially in passionate youths beset with a sense of sin—when the original trauma of separation from the mother's body is repeated in the necessity to leave 'home' . . . . " It was as if I had not only left home, a series of homes in name only, but now it was time to move on again, a reflection interrupted as the car radio announced that Communist-backed forces from North Korea had crossed the thirty-eighth parallel into South Korea.

My attachments were fragmented and troubled. My job in the department store and my preoccupations with Warner, Mother and Ellen, Anne and Harlene kept me from focusing on the trip ahead. As if the options were not confusing enough, I received a postcard from my father: "You ought to come out to Long Beach. They got a real good junior college and a barber school out here. If you want to be a barber, I can give you a good job in the shop." I passed up his offer, leaving it for later acceptance by my half-brother.

After one last battle, in which Warner bemoaned his inability to help me do the right thing and reminded me that as a psychologist he could see that my obstinacy indicated a mental illness, I bought my train ticket for Chicago. Mother and Ellen headed back to Nowata.

David in high school

21.

MY ENTHUSIASM FOR the University of Chicago was soon tempered with new challenges. Students were given, shortly after arrival on campus, a battery of exams and given credit for courses they "passed out of." The accelerated program was famous for attracting many bona fide geniuses, "early entrants," who did not even have high school diplomas. My scores were, in that company, average, but I was soon immersed in the Great Books curriculum, reading Sophocles, Plato, Herodotus, and Thucydides—or, as one of my Brooklyn classmates put it, "Thucydotus and Herodides." Chancellor Robert Maynard Hutchins had become famous not only for the Great Books curriculum but also for his opposition to such distractions as football and fraternities, a policy that was regarded as so heretical and anti-American that he had become a prime target for the House Un-American Activities Committee. His anti-athletics attitude and conviction that a university was primarily for education was infectious. It never occurred to me to get any exercise, and only rarely did I bump into someone who had actually used the swimming pool rumored to be somewhere on or near campus.

My classmates were sophisticated, well prepared, and as arrogant as the undergraduates who had made F. Scott Fitzgerald feel like a hick at Princeton. I groveled to be included as a peer. But I soon saw my new friends the way I had watched Johnny Mack years before in Oklahoma as he downed his breakfast, lovingly served by his Aunt Vesta, while I waited with a hungry dog's silence. Some of my classmates were like the young men Ralph Waldo Emerson described as "ever sure of a dinner, sure of their place in the world, and with no need for such a place just yet." Class and caste were well in place and Warner's warnings about the hazards of Chicago were not easily disregarded.

The stigma of poverty was still upon me. I identified with Thomas Hardy's protagonist in *Jude the Obscure* and his struggles at Oxford, an effect heightened by the University of Chicago's neo-Gothic architecture, the echoing corridors and crenellated towers. Jude's loneliness and alienation, his shame when surrounded by more affluent classmates, and his on and off relationship with Sue seemed familiar. His sense of doom settled on me as winter darkened with its flannel skies and smoking chimneys that could have been those of Victorian London.

Although excited by my classes and the readings, I was intimidated by the tireless intellectual rivalry. Wrangling debates with citation of major authorities from A to Z, starting with Aquinas and Aristotle, lasted long into the night, giving everyone a chance to show off his genius. One classmate, Larry, balding and paunchy at fourteen, his pale blue eyes big with excitement, claimed to have read Proust and Gide in French, Goethe and Kant in German, and Dostoyevsky in Russian. He also boasted, to scoffing disbelievers, that he had carried on a summer love affair with a middle-aged married woman—as accomplished a tutor in the art of love as was the great Jean-Jacques Rousseau's mistress, Maman. He claimed to have been given free admission to Broadway plays in return for his service as a laugher on cue in the audience. Larry had a laugh worthy of a hyena.

For a while Larry's reputation as top genius of our dorm seemed solid. He had "passed out" of several of the required courses, but when I told him I had finished one of the novels he had bragged about, Dostoyevsky's *The Idiot* or Conrad's *Under Western Eyes* or Gide's *Counterfeiters*, neglecting assigned course readings for these greater priorities, he whispered a confession, with many awkward hesitations. He had not really bothered to plow through those books, but had only studied the plot summaries. He begged me not to tell anyone that he cribbed.

"It's perfectly legitimate scholarship," he said with bluff relief, "but you know how it would sound if it got out. Nobody admits they've got a drawer full of Classics Comics."

Disillusioned, I transferred my admiration for pure eccentric genius to Seymour Billings, who claimed to have turned down at age thirteen a full scholarship to Cambridge University in England to study mathematics. Grossly overweight and with a waddling walk, Seymour spent most of his time playing pinball machines. When word got around that he had racked up a perfect score on the mathematics exams and passed out of a number of courses, Larry and others tried hard to deny that possibility. But we had to face it—this improbable and awkward freckled kid was not only the brightest but the youngest of us. Not even pugnacious Earl Shorris could find a suitably derisive remark to shoot Seymour down, although Shorris had earned our outrage by declaring "T. S. Eliot is a shit." That heretical opinion fueled several sessions of argumentative one-upmanship. But Shorris stuck to his guns and fired yet another barrel, declaring in even more truculent certainty, "So is James Joyce. James Joyce is a shit." It took decades and my acknowledgement of the talent and scholarship apparent in his several notable books for me to fully appreciate Shorris' chutzpah. His anti-Eliot and anti-Joyce declaration, as bold as Martin Luther's stand, was a predictor of great things to come.

The mix of eccentricity, genius, and some of the university's unique claims to fame reinforced our conviction that we were both blessed and imperiled. We all knew that the first atomic bomb had been nurtured under the stands of the Stagg Field football stadium, as if our Chancellor's banning of football had been to clear space for the atomic wizards. We would soon find out that there were still several "hot spots" on campus, although none of us was quite sure where they were and we had no Geiger counters.

One of the freshmen on my floor had been a Quiz Kid on the popular radio program of the same name. Timothy was a thin, hollow-cheeked boy with thick glasses who gesticulated with skeletal hands as he regaled us with confessional anecdotes about the program. It had not been rigged, he said. "But they would give us stuff to read the week before. If we were going to be asked a question about *La Bohème*, they would give us a picture book that happened to be about Mimi, the soprano heroine. It was really embarrassing one time when a girl popped out with the answer before she got the question." He described how the girls on the program who were beginning to fill out were forced to braid their hair and act childish and wear clothes that hid their figures. They had to talk baby talk and act silly. Otherwise they got dropped from the show. "How could they get dropped if they knew the answers?" I asked. "Simple," he said, "the question would be about something they had not been tipped off on. That's how they got dropped." One girl, though, had been so brilliant that even without being prepped she kept getting the answers right. She posed a problem, because she was looking more mature every week.

One student had arrived at our dorm with a stethoscope hooked around his neck, ready to practice medicine even before he did pre-med. I too had signed up for pre-med, probably because I thought it was the only way Mother would ever be impressed by her son's achievements. Another student, Richard, announcing that he was going to be a psychiatrist, arrived on campus with the *Collected Papers* of Sigmund Freud in the green Hogarth Press edition.

A scholarship student, an orphan named Derek, had been brought to campus by two women who were introduced to us in the dormitory lounge as his aunts. I was impressed that the women wanted to meet their nephew's new friends. When Derek later told us that they were actually former college roommates, a student from Brooklyn, with the conspiratorial intensity of Iago, went around saying, "They can't fool me. Those two women are dykes." When Derek's roommate passed on that gossip to him, Derek was so upset that Richard, studiously puffing on his pipe, told us that "in his professional opinion" he was afraid Derek was going to crack up and commit suicide. Derek, with tears in his eyes, told a group of us that the rumor was a dirty lie. The incident sharpened my fear that the Brooklyn homophobe would target me for his speculations.

The most dramatic character on my dorm floor was Jorge, a student from Mexico. He had a red bullfighting cape tacked on his wall under crossed picador's spears. Bullfight posters were taped around his room. He claimed to have been in the ring himself on more than one occasion, though we could not find his name or picture on any of the posters—I was learning that there was no limit to what my classmates might confabulate.

Jorge's ambition was nothing less than to become a doctor and go back and save the suffering people of Mexico. Without success he tried to interest us in the glamour and problems of his country. After the Christmas holiday we heard that he had, on a trip home, shot himself and wound up as a paraplegic who would probably be confined to a wheelchair for the rest of his life.

There would eventually be several suicides among my classmates who came to campus that autumn of 1950, including our class president, an impressive scholar of German. He had attended gymnasium in Germany, and even had a nick on his cheek which he claimed was a fencing wound. He wore a pinkie ring, its dark garnet conspicuous on his curved little finger as he held his cup. He spoke with a precise and clipped, rather prissy, accent. I assumed he would become a distinguished professor of German, sharing his passion for Thomas Mann and Goethe. But his brilliant career was wiped out on a moment's impulse when he settled an argument with his father by leaping off a Manhattan balcony. The rumor was that Jorge had shot himself after an argument with his father.

Larry, less dramatically, cut short his academic future by being caught stealing books in the university bookstore and being expelled. The dean of students confiscated so many stolen volumes from his room that a special discounted sale was held to complete his humiliation. When she and a university policeman came to Larry's room across the hall from mine, I heard her say, "I must say, Larry, you have marvelous taste." When his father, a bonds salesman, drove from New York to take him home, Larry's forlorn face peering back at us reminded me of the orphans in the Children's Home.

Perhaps I was fortunate after all not to have a father I could honor as

these sons of privilege could. The fathers with whom my classmates had
their fatal arguments may have been very good parents by conventional
definitions, but their best intentions seem to have been resented beyond
enduring by their sons. Even kindness or wisdom can kill, as Robert
Frost discovered when his son Carol stomped out of the room and put a
bullet through his head after assuring the good gray poet that he always
had the last word.

"There is no good father," Jean-Paul Sartre wrote, "that's the rule.
Don't lay the blame on men but on the bond of paternity, which is rot-
ten." Robert Jay Lifton quotes Sartre's view of his own liberation from
the father-son struggle: "Had my father lived, he would have lain on me
full length, and would have crushed me." Sartre felt himself freed to
"move from shore to shore, alone, and hating those invisible begetters
who bestraddle their sons all their life long."

"Always to have sympathy, always to be accompanied, always to be
understood would be intolerable," Virginia Woolf wrote in her suicide note.

One of my university classmates was the son of child psychologists.
Having heard of some of my childhood experiences, he told me, long
after our Chicago days, that he envied me. "Hell, your background is
downright Dickensian," he said, as if that were admirable. I found his
statement puzzling, nothing short of incredible, for he had had the most
desirable of parents. How could he possibly envy someone with my history? He explained that as a teenager he had once decided to run away
from home. His understanding father had met him at the door and
offered money, saying that he would need it. Dispirited, my friend took
the money, walked around for a while, and returned home. His mind-
reading father had understood too much and been too generous. "You
had permission to hate," he told me. "I could not even stage a minor
rebellion." His father had been the Buddha on the road. I still envied
my friend, of course, and could imagine no greater privilege than to
have grown up the son of such wonderful parents. His seemed to have
understood everything. Mine seemed to have understood nothing.

John Warner had also warned me that the University of Chicago was a hotbed of communism. Sure enough, we studied Freud and Veblen, Marx and Tawney, Weber and Durkheim. Around the oval tables of our classrooms we fielded terms like "conspicuous consumption" and "invidious comparison," reminding ourselves that such practices were features of our own times as well as Thorstein Veblen's.

Communist or not, I saw the phenomena of class and caste everywhere. My classmates could buy all the books and records they wanted, skip the dorm fare food their families had already paid for, and eat out at a different restaurant every night. They owned cars they had to leave at home because Chancellor Hutchins had the good sense not to allow students to have cars on campus.

Comparisons were everywhere, and all were invidious. Students bragged of their fathers' professions—medicine, law, banking, teaching. Not a barber or sharecropper in the lot.

David (right) at University of Chicago with classmates

22.

HECTIC ATTEMPTS TO supplement my tuition scholarship meant a new sequence of jobs as varied as those in high school. I was soon heading west each afternoon, crossing Cottage Grove Avenue and cutting diagonally across Washington Park to emerge deep in the heart of the so-called Black Belt, not a white face to be seen. I pumped gas, fixed flats, and polished windshields at a corner service station. While my friends headed out for midnight pizza and beer, I tried to catch up on homework, the heavy reading assignments. One night I decided to join them but realized at the last minute that I had no money. My two roommates looked back and threw pennies on my desk as they jeered and left me behind.

I began to harbor Warner's doubts about Chicago. One night at the service station an irate customer berated me in an obvious effort to reverse the usual hassles of discrimination. From the driver's seat he ordered me to do a better job on his windshield, then polish the headlights and hubcaps. The ritual was punctuated with threats and "D'ya hear me, White Boy? Maybe I oughta get outta here and show you." He shook his fist at me and opened the car door. A day or two later a fellow worker, who could never use a noun without the adjectival "motherfucking" or an adjective without its nominal "motherfucker," tipped me off that I would be the one blamed whenever tires or tools or cash got stolen from the station. He claimed he knew of a holdup that was being planned. I thanked him and did not return the next day.

I went through a sequence of other jobs, including two in the university hospital—admissions orderly and typist for the pharmacy, preparing prescription labels. After a few weeks I was fired for undercharging a pregnant woman who slid a vitamin prescription under the window bars and lamented that she did not have quite enough money. The woman might well have been one of those hungry Okies captured in Dorothea Lange's photographs of migrants seeking the promised land of California. In other words, she reminded me of my own mother, back when my skinny parents could not have afforded vitamins.

Working in the hospital brought me into proximity with the world Mother had known as a nurse, and soon made it clear that I was unsuited for a career in medicine. One day I discovered the green light over a hallway door and peeked in to see that it led to the observation balcony of the pathology theater. Below me, doctors were conducting an autopsy. They were lifting internal organs out of the corpse, placing each in turn on a scale, as if they were working in a butcher's shop. For this I had no talent for professional detachment and could not imagine ever acquiring any. But as if obliged to see it all before deciding to abandon medicine I remained sitting in the balcony as the only witness to the stitching up of the corpse and the vinegar wash—at least it looked and smelled like vinegar. Later I would accompany a mortician and his assistant as they came for the body. They almost forgot to take the internal organs that had been wrapped in butcher paper after inspection, and I in turn wondered if the pathologists had forgotten to replace these items inside the body before they stitched it back up.

John Warner sent Special Delivery letters to me in Chicago, thick as the ones I had delivered to Myrtle Jones back in Nowata. I dreaded them and was embarrassed by the curiosity they aroused.

"Who's this writing you every day?" the clerk in the dorm office would ask, and I would give an evasive answer.

I am not sure why I even read the letters. They all said the same thing. I had no Decency in me. I had betrayed all his Trust in me. In handwriting that reminded me of old-fashioned German printing, all nouns capitalized—and often underlined—he accused me of not only betraying him but also myself. According to him I no longer had such qualities as Loyalty, Honor, Honesty, and Faith. But the good news, he said repeatedly, was that he would offer me another chance, and forgive my Arrogance, Insolence, and Disobedience.

I did not have the sense not to open the letters. A small check or cash was sometimes tucked in, perhaps to ensure their being opened. At such times Warner signed his name with a large dollar sign in front. All would be forgiven, he said, if I would just get some sense in my head and return. I could go to the University of Arizona for an equally fine education. In that case, he would cover all expenses. He got Mother to write me her own imploring arguments that I should honor my guardian.

Warner also set me up for a major and destructive misunderstanding with my new classmates by sending me several Nazi armbands from his collection of war booty, suggesting that it might make an entertaining prank to offer them to my friends. Some joke! I got a quick and sobering education in the history of the Holocaust from my Jewish classmates. Warner surely knew that to display Nazi armbands even in jest was to risk being perceived as an anti-Semitic lunatic. Thus I added to my rich burden of shame and guilt the abysmal ignorance I had brought from the hinterlands, where young scholars of America had been spared all but the most superficial reference to the Holocaust. In magazines like *Time* it had been characterized as a distant aberration. The link between bright armbands and the horrors Hitler had inflicted, and the still suppurating psychic wounds and sensitivities of my classmates had not even occurred to me.

I suspect Warner knew what he was doing when he sent his little package with his sportive suggestion. Nothing could have been more alienating. I reached a new low. Robert Jay Lifton writes of nihilism that grows out of "a combination of 'psychological depression, personal worthlessness, and social despair.' That despair is a manifestation of a sense of futurelessness, a breakdown of connection to groups or principles larger than the self; and there can be a back-and-forth impoverishment and fragmentation of the self on the other." There is vulnerability to breakdown, even psychosis, "when there is 'deficient centering and grounding.'" It is easy to see, looking back, that my emotional fragility was at a critical point, close to breaking.

Warner suddenly reversed the scathing tone of his letters, offering the hand of peace. In a new approach he appealed to my pride in scholarship. I could help him immensely, he wrote, if I would undertake some research on campus. He was inventing a new air conditioner, employing the Bernoulli effect. If I could get the figures on the behavior of certain alloys under various conditions, he would be able to improve the air conditioner he had invented. He would make me a partner in his new company. We could meet in Kansas City over the midterm break and I could share the results of my research and discuss the invention and the business arrangement.

The role of researcher was distracting, though, a new stressor in a busy schedule of work and classes. There was no reason to trust Warner, but the focus on something impersonal was welcome, as was the relief from his bombarding accusations in the letters. His suggestion sounded like a better way to put myself through college than by working in a gas station or typing pharmacy labels or pushing wheelchairs in a hospital.

I got right to work, researching the Bernoulli effect. At first I was mystified by the irrelevance of air flow over metallic alloy surfaces, as most of the literature I found referred to aeronautical applications. The inverse relationship between pressure and air flow velocity keeps airplanes aloft, but I had difficulty visualizing how it could cool down the air passing through plenum chambers filled with aluminum excelsior. The technology was all either too simple or too complex, and I could not figure out which. I went to Professor Alexander Kolin, who taught our pre-med physics class, and got some helpful suggestions, although he too was mystified by the application. When he described to me one of his own research activities—the measurement of blood flow through monitoring of electrical potentials without bodily invasion—I decided that anything was possible. We were, after all, on the campus where the atomic scientists had demonstrated their inventiveness.

Warner had already lost a fortune with his cockamamie inventions, but there was always the possibility one of them would change the world. He had left his ranch littered with the debris of experiments—not only mock-up air-conditioners on the roof of the hacienda, but also innovative cattle guards consisting of metal strips held above the ground with springs, glittering in the sun and making a deterrent twang when touched.

I agreed to meet Warner with my calculations such as temperature differentials between intake and outtake. He met my train at Kansas City's Union Station and took me to dinner in the Fred Harvey restaurant off the waiting room. But even before dinner was finished, there were indications that Warner's interest in my file of research documents was factitious, less pressing than his old concerns with my behavior. As he reverted to interrogation and accusations, I had several beers and tried not to argue with him. It was as if none of my efforts at independence had been taken seriously. He seemed to think that I should offer him some new confessions.

He had rented a room in a hotel near the station, and we had hardly entered it before he began ranting about my ingratitude for all he had done for me. The double bed in the room rendered the sleeping arrangements indisputable. He began shoving me around, and pushed me back on the bed. I was numbed into compliance and lay like an obedient captive as he tried fellatio for the first time in our relationship.

I lay frozen, my powers of observation strangely intact as if I were watching from the immobilized fan above us.

Suddenly Warner jumped up and ran to the bathroom, retching into the toilet. He returned to vent his fury on me, as if I had asked him to give me pleasure in that way. He got out the Luger he had brought along, saying it would be good time for us both to use it. I knew from his whiskey breath and trembling hands that he was drunk. His threats reminded me of my stepfather Lee's when he would wave a pistol around with his wild threats. In retrospect I believe Warner was seriously considering the same course of action. Like my sister, I talked him into calming down. But he was furious that I would not agree to return to Arizona.

Next morning I took the train back to Chicago, more decentered and confused than ever. The people in my life kept turning into one another and then into animals. John Warner had become Lee Pape, but also my father. This visit, like those to the distant barber, had been pure disappointment. I blamed myself for having made the trip. Returning from a visit with my father I had watched the dark river of blood poison creeping up my arm. Returning to Chicago on the train after the encounter with Warner I felt nauseated and worthless. Why hadn't I let him kill us both?

Even after that terrible scene, it did not occur to me that I could throw out Warner's letters without reading them. Frederick Buechner, in *Telling Secrets*, suggests that we go back not only to remember, but to remedy the past, "so that if we didn't play those roles right the first time round, we can still have another go. We cannot undo our old mistakes or their consequences any more than we can erase old wounds that we have both suffered and inflicted, but through the power that memory gives us of thinking, feeling, imagining our way back through time we can at long last finally finish with the past in the sense of removing its power to hurt us and other people and to stunt our growth as human beings." Ideally, a memoir should allow one to exorcise the past, be free at last.

In a less homophobic atmosphere than the one he grew up in, Warner might have been able to acknowledge rather than deny, accept rather than displace, enjoy rather than rage. He might have found a willing partner, one he did not have to bribe and force. He was his own most tortured victim, the equal of Humbert Humbert in his pathetic obsessions. But Lolita could hardly be expected to sympathize with Humbert's problems. Warner's nausea at indulging fellatio after years of managing to assure himself he was not a homosexual was, perhaps, further evidence that the manipulative abuse he forced on me was less about sex than it was about power over another human being.

Once, when I had come home from Tucson High after overhearing a locker room discussion on the subject and asked Warner if that's what we were — "homosexuals" — I got a beating for my curiosity. Even though he was forcing his attentions on me, he was outraged at the suggestion. Like schizoids and politicians, Warner evaded unpalatable realities with abstractions—Loyalty, Trust, Honor, etc., though it was hard for me to understand how those qualities enforced submission to unwelcome masturbation. The one abstraction he never used was Love.

John was not the first homophobe to indulge in homosexual activities—the Nazis are famous for that contradiction. Recent studies probing self-destructive, risk-taking behavior of gay men who have grown up in a homophobic environment include speculation that they have introjected punishing and disapproving authority figures, thereby inflicting sadistic violence on themselves even as they seek pleasure. They are unable to approve of their own lifestyles. John's meanness and duplicity with me may have only echoed his scorn for himself. Within him lived his mother whose physical body could be found in the Vinita asylum, a woman murderous enough to have drowned one of her sons in a bathtub. Within John lived his distant father and an abusive military system he had grown up with, both in a military academy and the army. And perhaps his mind still harbored the Nazis he had browbeaten in interrogations, reducing some of them to whimpering prisoners.

Warner used words such as "fairies" and "cocksuckers" like the most seasoned of homophobes, pointing out gay people with the same scorn he directed toward Mexicans. When we lived on the ranch the slightest of noises in the night provoked him to check with flashlight and pistol to see if "those damn Mexicans are out there." He was haunted by the possibilities of invasion, vandalism, and thievery. When some of his cattle were rustled, however, the ringleader turned out to be not a Mexican but the sheriff of Pima County, to whom Warner had taken his complaints as I sat beside him, confirming that I too had seen the broken-down fence and tire tracks of the truck.

"If you had any Decency left, you'd do it," Warner wrote after my return to Chicago, as if making a constructive suggestion. He offered to send me one of the Lugers.

I saw no connection between the verbal abuse in the letters and my suicide attempts. At first I made tentative scratches on my wrists with a razor blade, then covered up the superficial cuts with Band-Aids. Soon the incisions were deep enough to require bandages. One morning the couple employed as resident dorm counselors came to my room, alerted by a concerned roommate. They stood over me as I lay in bed, so depressed I could not get up to go to class or work. They looked at the bandages on my wrists, but left with no further inquiry or suggestion.

With semester's end I sought cheaper digs, and found a four-dollar-a-week garret in the Homestead Hotel. I thought of this sanctuary, up a creaky back stairway, as Raskolnikov's room, for I was very much in that troubled student's state of mind. I walked the streets for hours, and alternately contemplated suicide and random murder to vent my rage at the world. My anxieties were expansive enough to include fear that Chicago might disappear in a nuclear flash at any moment. An airliner crashing through fog and exploding near the Midway airport a few miles away precipitated an anxiety attack which sent me rushing to the Woodlawn Tavern for glass after glass of draft beer.

My suicide attempts escalated and before long I made a near-fatal slash on my right arm. A fountain of arterial blood spurted across the room, splashing everything in sight. The desire to live returned with the same lightning speed with which the impulse to die had taken over. I had just time to yell for help before I sank to the floor, nearly passing out. By the time two police officers arrived with medics at their heels, my ambivalence had returned. In truth, I did not know if I wanted to live or die. As the medics tried to place me on the stretcher, I struggled.

"We don't have to save your life, you sonofabitch," one of the policemen said. I started to sob, and surrendered.

They took me to an emergency room where, under klieg lights, the wound was sutured and bandaged. The policemen discussed their obligation to take me to Cook County Hospital for ten days of observation, but chose to express their contempt by driving me part-way there, then telling me to get out of the car.

At dawn I wandered into a corner restaurant with dark wainscoting and booths, but chose to sit on a stool at the long counter where a waitress in a yellow uniform handed me a breakfast menu and slid a cup of coffee in front of me. I felt so faint that balancing on the seat was a challenge, and I was about to retreat to one of the booths when I became aware, even as the waitress did, of the blood soaking my clothes.

She reacted with a startled glance, then took my order as if she saw such sights every day. Perhaps killers of the night routinely stopped in for breakfast. She encountered people with blood on their clothes pretty much every time she came to work—that was the impression she gave. But I was grateful for her indifference, her tolerance.

"I tried to kill myself," I blurted out. She looked at me as if I had made a casual comment about the weather, then brought my plate of bacon and eggs with hash browns.

"How long you got to keep them bandages on?" she asked, when she gave me change at the cash register.

23.

IT HAD TAKEN a great effort to turn the rage inward, not wanting to follow in the footsteps of William Heirens, the notorious University of Chicago schizophrenic who had murdered many times, leaving behind a plea scrawled in lipstick on the walls of his victims, "STOP ME BEFORE I KILL MORE." Though Heirens preceded me by a few years, we had some of the same instructors, including the one who—having noticed Heirens' absences and other behavior—was instrumental in his capture.

How close I came to being another William Heirens or Raskolnikov still haunts me. Both those young men suffered what Robert Jay Lifton terms "doubling . . . a form of dissociation [which] entails the formation of a functional second self that is, psychologically and morally, at odds with the prior self." In short, a splitting, a dissociation, a psychotic break. I wandered much of the night in an alcoholic daze, harboring murderous fantasies.

As I prowled alleys, it seemed entirely logical that I should inflict vengeance on random victims, to follow not my bliss but the dictates of hate. "*La haine, c'est la colère des faibles!*" wrote Alphonse Daudet in one of my favorite books, *Lettres de mon moulin*. Carl Sandburg put it another way: "The slums take their revenge," truly the revenge of the weak. But had those nameless benefactors who had sponsored my scholarship plucked me out of poverty that I might compete with monsters? Control was the issue, and I lived on the brink of loss of it.

Why did William Heirens cross over that line and I did not? The answer may have less to do with ethics than with brain chemistry—very subtle differences in brain chemistry. Assaulted with a few more self-administered toxins and with a minutely weaker genetic constitution I might well have wound up on death row or at least skid row. That insight is not only my own. "Why isn't he in here with us?" a man on death row asked a visitor after reading one of my articles in the *New York Times Magazine*. "He has the same kind of history." That reader in his cell understood how close I had come, and I felt more affirmed than insulted, for he had acknowledged the depth of my pain. "There but for the grace of God" is far more than a smug sentiment. In my life it has been a reality, and my opposition to the death penalty is based partly on my awareness of how thin a membrane separates us from our potential for violence. So long as we call the criminal a monster and satisfy ourselves by exterminating him, we will have no vested interest in prevention.

"I saw someone through an open door," Heirens said. "There was a light shining through. I don't know why. I just did it."

A powerful symbol—a forbidden door with light coming through. William Heirens had been looking in windows in what may have been an unconscious attempt to find the family constellation which had been the scene of his original dissociations. Returning to the scene, confronting it again, is always an attempt to master forces that once left us powerless and humiliated.

My own voyeurism could easily have gotten me killed, and unconsciously I may have been tempting that possibility. Chicago police—the same who dumped me like a discarded corpse after my suicide attempt—were well known to shoot first and ask questions later.

The voyeur is like a playgoer who cannot afford the price of admission to a regular theatre. He is willing to pay out all he owns—his reputation, his life—to glimpse the mini-stage of a small room, a basement flat, an apartment beheld from an awkward angle. He will be lucky if on strained tiptoe he can discern the back of a head. Certain colors, lights, shadows strike him as lures, bait for his fishing. He never completely believes that he has not been somehow invited into, as well as forbidden to enter, the taboo territory. If there is a performance, it is surely meant to have an audience.

His boundaries are loose indeed. Being dared and forbidden are sides of the same coin. He knows not where he leaves off and others begin. He looks to everyone he sees as a possible reflection of himself, a lover, an alter ego. He feels odd that he is in no way involved in the loves of others.

He seeks evidence that someone somewhere has found the love he hungers for and envies. Most likely he will settle for a shadow show, as with Indonesian puppets. He is there to pose the proposition that he belongs at the outskirts of life as a bitter observer, or conversely that he belongs at the passionate center, even in the fiery furnace of life. Like one obliged to advance onto a battlefield in tenebrous fog, he accepts the risks to life and limb. He, I say, because to the best of my knowledge women are rarely voyeurs, at least the kind who prowl alleys and spaces between apartment buildings as I did, and as William Heirens had done.

If what one finds when peeking in a window, often through a slit between window and golden shade, or even the tiny hole in a venetian blind's slat for the cord, functions as a stage setting, it may be—and often is—an empty stage. The voyeur waits, freezing or soaking with rain, for the action to begin. He is a culture vulture: he attends as many plays as he can. Some nights falling snow has already piled up a crust in which his footprints lead directly from the public sidewalk along the brick wall of an apartment building and around to the back, under the wooden stairway. As if to review the current play, he is back to compare tonight's performance with that of the nights before.

A woman is propped in bed, the covers over her knees and up to her neck. She reads a book. Perhaps it is *Crime and Punishment*, in which case she is reading about me. I have left my garret to be with her in the night, arriving on schedule.

The woman in bed beyond that windowpane is a slow reader, and I can hear the turning of pages and the occasional squeaking of bed-springs as she shifts about. Now and then she pushes the covers back and gets out of bed. She wears a commonplace pink flannel nighty like the one my mother used to wear. She disappears into another room. I am shivering with cold, my muscles tortured from the tense crouch. Glasses misted, freezing to frost, make the entire effort to see even more of a futility. One finger of a woolen glove clears enough to allow a glimpse like that through a windshield wiper slapping back and forth in a snowstorm. The room is still empty.

After a few minutes she returns. I can almost speak to her through that glass, that window shade. On the other hand, she may well be a mind reader, aware of my presence. Perhaps we understand and respond to each other in some telepathic, nonverbal intimacy, for her unawareness seems to go far beyond tolerance. It seems to be as much a charade, a performance, as mine. She must welcome my feverish attention. If I can hear through the chill glass the sounds of her padding footsteps or the squeak of bedsprings as she resettles herself, surely she can hear my breathing.

Of course she heard my footsteps crunching on the snow as I slipped in under the stairs. Those footsteps must have betrayed me. But has she? Has she left the room of her performance—pretending to read a book, innocent on her two propped pillows—only to call the police? I must trust her. And how I would like to tell her that such an awkward position is not at all good for her back. She is far too nice a person to get a vulturish stance from such habits.

The police might be approaching. It would be impossible to offer an innocent explanation for footprints leading around the building, or why I was crouching under a rear stairway, my face aglow in golden light. But no more than an addict would spit out the pellet just entering his mouth, trying to hide it as the drug squad batters his door, can my transfixed gaze leave off my quarry, my beloved prey.

Looking back on the dark night of the soul, we can see that Dostoyevsky was right—"the greatest tragedy is the inability to love," for without love we care neither for ourselves nor the rest of the world. When lost, anomic, deranged, we are blind to all goodness. Found, we respond to an infinite largesse of wonders, a wider universe.

"How about murder?" the poet C. K. Williams asks in a journal entry. "Reading about the Manson family, it was as though they were involved in the same sort of quest, to try to find the larger experience, but reading about the actual murders, there's the feeling of small tasks, small decisions . . . Arendt on Eichmann . . . Raskolnikov: his tragedy, the moment the murder happens, is that he realizes it was still the most normal, untransfiguring experience. He's doomed then to the everyday, to the investigator, and he knows it: he's only playing out his life then, aesthetically, but tragically. Where is any grand ethical experience then?"

Williams wonders whether "the humblest ethical experience" might be suicide, in that suicide spares the world one's future crimes. "I don't know why I did it, I thought you were supposed to tell me," a death row killer interviewed by Tony Parker for his book, *The Violence of Our Lives*, told a psychiatrist.

"I know nothing about my father, not one thing: not where he came from or where he went," the prisoner told Parker. "My guess is that I'm the result of what's called a one-night stand . . . it's possible he doesn't even know I exist." His mother had given him to his grandmother to raise, and of his mother he said, "I don't know anything about her either, since I've never heard from her or seen her from that day onwards."

After the first abandonment there is no other. Although Mother always returned, sometimes unadvisedly, Ellen and I felt we had lost her. We were each left with a great hollow hole in the aching chest. Longing is learned as one's first addiction.

A prison doctor told me that he has never talked to an inmate who does not have a history of abuse or one who had even one affirming adult in his life. That view is confirmed in *The Racist Mind*, Rafael Ezekiel's study of young men who have joined paramilitary hate cults. Ezekiel found that not one cult member had had the benefit of a concerned older male. Not one teacher, coach, mentor, guru, concerned uncle, benevolent scoutmaster (as opposed to the other kind), counseling minister—quite simply, not one friendly role model—had been in sight or come forward to help these boys. Out of their hunger for belonging grew their vulnerability.

Out of such nihilism came the Raskolnikov who was sent to Siberia and the others tucked out of sight in our prisons. We spare ourselves the disquieting insight that we ourselves, given their circumstances, could have committed their crimes. Plato, in the *Laws*, states that "we should be gentle with remediable criminals and try to see how, in their case too, there was a sense in which they did not err willingly." So long as we see crimes as acts committed by beings fundamentally different from ourselves, we will never solve the problems posed by "the banality of evil." It may horrify us, but we tolerate, empower, and perpetuate it. And with our passion for the death penalty we already have become cold-blooded killers ourselves, gleeful in our murders.

24.

REACHING OUT FOR help should, as in movies, be accompanied by inspiring sound tracks and technicolor illuminations of icons of salvation. However, my long journey through therapies and psychoanalysis began by my boarding a Cottage Grove streetcar which traveled through miles of storefront slums now long since demolished. I got off near Michael Reese Hospital, and found myself in a large waiting room in an area reserved for welfare cases.

I was hung over, unshaven, wearing the olive-green war-surplus fatigue jacket in which, someone remarked, I had fatigued for weeks. My stomach was hurting, my head was throbbing. I thought I was dying. I registered as an indigent patient and after a time in the waiting room was called for an interview with a resident, a young man who must have thought that bluntness was the equivalent of effective surgery.

"How do you get sex?" he asked, after a cursory look at the healing scars on my arm and wrists.

Like a Victorian maiden, I felt myself blush.

"Well, answer the question," he demanded, his tone reminding me of Warner. "Women? Men? Animals? Do you jerk off? How often?"

If this was psychiatry, I did not want it. I froze up to the point that he might well have diagnosed me as aphasic.

I was soon assigned to Dr. Alvin Suslick for therapy in a small room with only a table and two chairs. With a crown of thin dark hair and a benign face, this doctor after many hours became an understanding witness, a concerned and reassuring presence. As the room filled up with my cigarette smoke, he put up with it without complaint, though I later realized he had seen my smoking despite asthma as symptomatic of my skid row complex.

Despite my alternation of long silences and frenetic outpourings, somatizing was still the main language I spoke, having learned it well from my family of world-class hypochondriacs. It was the grammar of pain, the rhetoric of anxiety. Wanting to be sure I was not as close to death as I feared, Dr. Suslick referred me for barium cocktails. I stood still for x-rays as I had for Mother's fluoroscopy. I was probed and all but dissected. When half my face became paralyzed with Bell's palsy, medical students were called in to observe the rare disorder. They poked my face with needles, right side, then left. "Watch closely," a green-gowned doctor told the note-taking students, "there's no feeling at all on his right side." He again poked my numb cheek, then the one that made me wince.

Not all my symptoms were hysterical. I was hospitalized with a recurrence of my old plague—boils. The worse of them attacked under my arms, and I was given dosages of radiation for "axillary furuncles," radiation that was so ill-advised—although "the state of the art" at the time—that my cancer risk was greatly enhanced and decades later I became part of a massive study of victims of such irradiation.

Between coughs as I chain-smoked, I shifted around on my chair, and tried to entertain Dr. Suslick with my barroom brawls and amatory adventures, which he called "acting out." He now and then departed from his nondirective poise in order to ask a constructive question. Did I plan to wind up on skid row? he asked, as if merely curious. He introduced the notion of my taking "executive charge" of my own life rather than passively taking the beating it seemed to be giving me. However, I was too lost in the fog of my sickness to do much beyond putting those questions on hold for a few years, years I could not believe in.

My script was death, doom, and sudden dismemberment. I faced the world in a daze of fear and trembling, a term which may be a cliché but a condition I found overwhelmingly applicable to my state of mind when I picked up a paperback copy of Kierkegaard's *Fear and*

Trembling. I would have to ravage a thesaurus to avoid using the term. Angst does not quite do it. "The dark night of the soul" comes closer to what I was suffering.

For several years Dr. Suslick was both mother and father. When my first teaching job took me to DeKalb, then to Cornell University in Ithaca, I would use holiday breaks to travel back to Chicago to consult him. He saved my life so many times that in later years, when he ironically turned to me for help with his own profound depression, I felt as helpless as I had been with my mother and sister. There was no way I could repay my debt to him, his infinite patience when I was a dime-a-time charity case at Michael Reese or later when I saw him in his Michigan Avenue office.

On the telephone he spoke in a mournful voice. "I was so busy talking you down off the ledge," he said, "that I didn't realize I was about to crawl out on it myself." As he spoke I imagined him sitting in his pleasant twelfth floor consulting room after his patients had departed for the day or when he had a spare fifty minutes if one failed to show up. I pictured him crawling out on that ledge and plunging down the white marble façade of the bank building onto Michigan Avenue. Diagnosing this gentle man who had diagnosed me, I attributed his depression partly to the Reichian reality that a doctor heals by taking on the sickness of the patient. Dr. Suslick's concern, I still feel, was sacrificial. In later years I have dreamed of him as a revenant who can still care for me and I have found his face in a Paul Klee portrait that I see seomtimes as one who understands, and at other times as one who conceals mysterious wisdom. His eyes are penetrating but unhurtful.

> Back from the dead comes Al
> for this important consultation.
>
> He appears as if climbing out
> of the subway, his briefcase

in hand, homburg on head.
He still has a busy schedule,

he tells me as we stand
ignoring the passing pedestrians.

I need to ask you one question,
he says, but almost falls back

into the stairwell of the subway.
He grabs an iron rail, stumbles

down a step, gazes back at me
out of suffering eyes, dark rings

under them. "Who is the center
of your life now? Have you found

anyone other than me?" I knew
what answer he wanted the way

a minister wants one to say God.
But I still could not give an answer,

name the least living ghost found.

Waking from this dream as if I were still back in the Children's
Home, I wept for my incurable afflictions of doubt, my inability to trust
or to love—never giving enough or being grateful enough for what I was
given. Why should it all—the love given, the love taken—be so conditional? Why must we measure out everything? Was my first session with
the doctor worth only a dime? Should I have paid thousands for the later
ones? What are we worth—to ourselves, to others?

It took years of work with other therapists and a psychoanalyst to repair my soul enough to allow me to soldier on. It is humiliating to admit to a lifetime of such need, and doubly humiliating to admit that Warner was right when he accused me of having a mental illness when I was at war with him. He exploited it though my life was at stake, and as a trained clinical psychologist he knew what I needed, and knew it was not what he was dishing out.

Helpful as Dr. Suslick was, my academic career came to a sudden halt with my graduation. The University of Chicago was in transition, the Hutchins program imperiled by attacks from conservatives. I had earned my B.A. degree in two years, having "passed out" of half the required courses, but was unsuccessful in competing for one of the few graduate fellowships. It would have been wiser to have chosen Pomona College, which had offered a full four-year scholarship.

My mother and sister turned up at my University of Chicago graduation. Ellen had my high school classmate Oliver in tow. She had met him during the summer she and Mother had spent in Arizona after Lee's death, and she was wearing his engagement ring. Mother posed for pictures on campus and in front of the Homestead Hotel. I showed the group my attic garret and told them about some of the characters who lived there.

"What a firetrap!" Mother commented with prophetic accuracy. The place later burned down, though by that time I had cleared out, forgetfully leaving in the storage cubbyhole a suitcase containing many of my Tucson mementos including the green wool Pendleton shirt Warner had given me on a Christmas in Nowata and my baseball signed by Bob Feller after a practice game in Arizona.

Since I was a legal resident of Arizona, it seemed to make sense to return and attend the University of Arizona. Had it occurred to me, I would have asked if I could somehow reclaim the last two years of the scholarship they had offered earlier. John Warner was no longer in Tucson, having moved to Colorado, so I would not have to deal with him.

Someone in Jimmy's Woodlawn Tap had told me about an agency

that paid expenses for drivers willing to chauffeur a car to another city. One summer afternoon I picked up a gigantic Oldsmobile and was told I could take several days to make the trip. I decided to stop in Lawton, Oklahoma, where Mother was living.

But first I would make a round to say goodbyes. My first stop was Jimmy's, where I had a farewell chat with Jimmy and his Aristotle-quoting bartender Freddy. I dropped by Stineways for a final cup of coffee and by its umpteenth refill it was time to head back to Jimmy's for Happiness Hour, but I bravely remarked that I had to get on the road. Deciding to drive through the night, I had only three other people to see first.

Vahakn, the Armenian graduate student I had got to know at the Homestead Hotel, was out. I would not get the halva and tea he would have offered me. But Mrs. Kutuzov, who lived halfway down the hall, had just got back from her job as a cancer researcher at a hospital. A widow who had been married to a descendant of General Kutuzov of the Napoleonic War, immortalized by Tolstoy in *War and Peace*, she had often invited me in for tea. She was a constant reader and rereader of Dostoyevsky and had the many green volumes of a Russian edition of his work. Had she sensed that I was living a Raskolnikov existence? Did she know that her motherly comfort had helped me as Sonya's had helped that poor fellow? I wanted to thank her, properly say goodbye. I was half in love, but the twenty or even thirty years between us ruled passion out. And yet, as she pinched her kimono closed over her generous breasts, remarking that she was about to head down the hall for a bath, I sensed more. She invited me in and offered tea.

She was surprised and saddened by my announcement that I was leaving, and before we had emptied the cups we both seemed to sense that much more was possible. Departure opens up intimacy. Perhaps she too had nurtured an attraction. It was hard, but I got up to leave. At the door she looked helpless, years younger. I knew she would fall into my arms if I opened them.

Remembering that I had called a professor I was also going to visit, I gave her a tense hug and kiss on the cheek and left, aware that the door was still open as I rounded the landing on the stairway. Waves of yearning ripped through me. Outside, I left the Oldsmobile parked in front of the Homestead and walked the two blocks to Professor Sitterly's yellow brick building. He had been my favorite humanities instructor and had invited me by his apartment for chats on several occasions.

He greeted me with a more cordial friendliness than ever, as if we were equals now that I had graduated. I had shared some details about my life in Tucson but had not told him the whole story. After a few drinks he gave me many arguments for not setting out in the middle of the night.

"You've had a few beers," he said, "You're tired, you'll be a lot better off if you get a good night's sleep." He pulled down a Murphy bed, all made up. "I'll sleep on the couch," he said. "Go ahead and take the first bath."

Sitterly turned up the volume of a recording of a Beethoven Quartet. I was always impressed by his taste, his reading of Trollope novels, his citations of Greek and Latin classics.

In a borrowed pair of pajamas I fell asleep like a maiden and woke to a slight variation of my first night with John Warner. My professor was lying beside me on the Murphy bed, pressing his erection against me. The scene had already been written by J. D. Salinger in *The Catcher In the Rye* and I had read it. Like Holden Caulfield I got up and departed, ignoring Sitterly's embarrassed offer of a contribution toward my road expenses.

I drove the Oldsmobile straight through to Lawton, Oklahoma, arriving at Mother's rental—a remodeled garage—late the next evening. "You can just flop down here beside me," she said, offering her double bed. But with a thought of Oedipus and of my drinking companion Hall Taylor, who had spoken in alcoholic candor of his experience of having slept with his mother, I was horrified. Hall had spent several months in a psychiatric facility and I regarded him as one of the most tragic characters I knew.

"No, I'll go to a hotel. Isn't there one downtown?"

"Don't be silly," Mother said. "You're my son."

That was precisely my concern, though I did not speak of it to her. I was recalling how, when I slept next to her in the Nowata boarding house, she pressed against me in her flannel gown. As I left, she gave me ten dollars toward the hotel room.

I wound up in a seedy hotel, and was accompanied in the elevator to a third floor room. The bellhop clearly expected to be tipped, though he had carried no suitcase, and as he handed me the key he said, "I can send a girl up if you want."

Suddenly it seemed appropriate to spend the ten dollars that way. "Fine," I said, and soon heard a knock on the door. The encounter was absurd. The peroxide gum-chewer asked me if I was from Fort Sill, stepped out of her skirt, took off her blouse, and left her bra on as she pulled back the sheets and climbed into the bed. The five-minute embrace, my only experience then or since as a prostitute's customer, was not a romantic occasion. It left me nauseated and ashamed, for her seeming indifference was not contagious.

The next day Mother took me to see Uncle Charles, now a prosperous local lawyer. He mentioned that he was the administrator of a scholarship fund, the Laura Fields Trust, and thought I might quality. I filled out an application, and he wrote me a check for five hundred dollars to help with my University of Arizona expenses. The generous arrangement was completed in my uncle's favorite bar, where Oklahoma's prohibition laws were honored. My corpulent uncle brought his bottle along in a paper sack and the waitress brought Cokes and ice for mixers.

His rescue seemed nothing short of a corrective in my view of the family. They were, after all, supportive, even to the point of endorsing my educational ambitions. Uncle Charles and his wife had loved me all along. Surely Mother would not have suggested his help unless she also cared. I recalled that when we were living in Mounds when I was in the second grade, a parcel had arrived for my birthday and it turned out to be chocolate chip cookies. Uncle Charles and Aunt Marge! They had remembered me. I thought that meant I would be remembered every time I had a birthday—but that single remembrance had stood by itself.

And now my uncle had thought of me again!

Before leaving Lawton, I visited a tavern very different from the place Uncle Charles had taken me. Uncle Skeet now lived in a sleazy fleabag, even more tawdry than the hotel where I had spent the night. I found Uncle Skeet waiting in the lobby, gazing out the window that had probably last been washed in about 1920. We went next door to his favorite tavern.

When Mother found a clerical job at Fort Sill, she had brought Uncle Skeet to town and he had got a job with the city public works department. Frail and with trembling hands, my turtle-faced uncle was surely the oldest man on the street crew assigned to outdoor work regardless of weather.

Over a pitcher of beer, my treat, Uncle Skeet asked, "Whatever happened to that fellow Warner you used to live with?"

I told him that we had had a falling out. "I don't have anything to do with him anymore."

"That's good," he said, surprising me. "I didn't like him much." He gave me a long look, then added, "He was always trying to own you. I didn't think that was right. I'm glad you aren't with him any more."

> From an angelic height—
> best place from which
> to gaze upon your birthplace.
>
> If no angel wings
> are on you, a silver plane
> will do—peek out
>
> the window and get
> a glimpse of what
> was surely once or twice
>
> beheld by some god's eye.

Uncle Skeet was the first to take my side, implying a world of under-standing in his brief comment. I bought us a refill of the pitcher, and decided that Uncle Skeet had always been vastly underrated. This dis-reputable old man, with his hand-rolled cigarettes and nicotine-stained fingers, his hacking cough and his liver-spotted hands, had quit high school and gone to work in the oil fields to put his two younger broth-ers, George and Charles, through law school. But now they had no use for him.

I was on the University of Arizona campus only a few weeks when my view of Uncle Charles was challenged anew. Well before the end of the semester I was called into the Dean's office and confronted with a letter in which Uncle Charles had complained, on Laura Fields Trust letter-head, that I was not making the required regular payments on my loan. He no longer referred to it as a scholarship.

The bushy-browed dean would have been a good bill collector. "We don't allow dead beats on our campus," he growled, and I agreed to begin payments on the loan. Interest was already mounting. I felt betrayed by Uncle Charles, just as Ellen had been betrayed by Uncle George. Both lawyers had exploited opportunities to help us for their own profit, with no more mercy extended to family than to others. The five hundred dollar scholarship loan had been secured, without my knowledge, with an insurance policy on my life. Before long I was being dunned for quickly mounting indebtedness.

Mother too turned into a bill collector, writing me letters to say that if I loved her I should pay back Uncle Charles for his generosity. I was stung with this turn of the triangle—the Rescuer turning overnight into the Persecutor of the Victim.

I had broken up with Anne and Tucson seemed empty without her. In Chicago, I had shared an apartment with three roommates for the summer. Anne had arrived by bus for a visit, but finding privacy for our reunion was a problem. A classmate named Kay, who had taken a job at Cook County Hospital, lived nearby in a basement apartment with an entry off the alley. She lent me the key to her apartment, and offered to put Anne up for the weekend. She was eager to meet the freckled and gifted redhead I talked so much about.

Eager lovers, Anne and I went straight away to the basement apartment as soon as Kay had left for work. We were making love on the king-sized bed when we looked up to find our hostess staring at us from the doorway, more curious than indignant. She had returned for some forgotten item and had walked right in. Anne stood up completely naked and strode forward, offering her right hand, and introducing herself with a smile while brushing back her Titian hair with her left.

Kay, living up to her reputation, was as cool as Anne. She promised to knock next time, then casually went over to the closet and found the item she had forgotten. With such casual candor, Kay had made a pronouncement in class that would become a famous University of Chicago anecdote, implanted in history with the anonymous specificity of nursery rhymes and schoolyard chants. I have seen it misattributed in several accounts.

I had been present on the day when our social sciences professor noticed that Kay was knitting. "Are you aware, Miss Boyer," he asked, "that knitting is symbolic masturbation?"

Without dropping a stitch, Kay replied, "Professor, when I knit, I knit. When I masturbate, I masturbate."

At that time, in that class, little notice was taken. Nothing was off limits in the brainstorming approach to understanding culture.

At the end of that weekend, I saw Anne off on the Greyhound bus. Near the station, over a final cup of coffee, she informed me that she had at last made up her mind. For some time she had been pursued by a wealthy Ivy League med student. She was not in love with him, she assured me, but like Zelda Fitzgerald in her first go-round with Scott, had decided that money was more important in the long run than love.

As if to recommend a replacement for herself, Anne had told one of her classmates from Smith to look me up. Lora was working as a society columnist for a Tucson newspaper. Her father had bought a dude ranch in the foothills, and Lora was living in one of the guest cottages. The family's Boston background and society connections qualified her perfectly for her job. She was putting her writing talents to work with a breezy flair for gossip and news of celebrity visitors to Tucson. As a teenager, before moving west with her family, Lora had been a close friend of Sylvia Plath. Long before Plath became famous, Lora carried around with her a newspaper clipping about Sylvia's disappearance, when she was found burrowing in the dirt under the porch of her home.

During the brief period I attended the University of Arizona, Lora and another student from one of my graduate classes, Martin Tucker, became my regular cronies. At first I had no romantic interest in Lora. Small and shy, watchful and supportive, she was no rival for Anne's provocative sexiness. At Smith, as Anne's confidante, Lora had followed the melodramatic reports of our star-crossed romance. The opposition of Anne's mother and the sabotage strategies of my guardian had laid a curse on us from which we had not been able to recover. Lora was fascinated with our story. If she admired anyone more than Sylvia Plath, it was the dramatic and haughty Anne.

In Tucson, Lora and I often had coffee after classes. She strolled back with me one afternoon along University Avenue, and when we found ourselves at my rooming house, I invited her in. My basement room was one of two created with plank floors and plywood walls. The other room was occupied by a winter transient who called himself Buffalo Bill. His Stetson, cowboy boots, fringed jacket, and kerchief should have qualified him as a movie extra, at least, but he made his living by walking around the city with a bucket full of soap and a bundle of rags, washing cars for a dollar.

Fortunately, Buffalo Bill was not at home, or he might have objected to my having a girl in the room next to his. He had already complained to the landlady about my late night typing. Lora was amused to see my pile of clothes, kept on the one chair available. I moved them onto the head of the bed so she could have the chair, then reclined against them and began reading to her. First I read a few stanzas of Byron's "Don Juan," then Arnold's "Dover Beach." I was most of the way through Marvell's "To His Coy Mistress"—"Let us roll all our strength and all /

Our sweetness up into one ball, / And tear our pleasures with rough strife . . ."—before falling asleep on my odoriferous clothing. My mistress-to-be tiptoed out, leaving me to wake up alone, startled to find her gone.

Ingenuous and unintended as my nodding off had been, nothing could have been more effective as a method of seduction. Anyone who could fall asleep reading a seduction poem could be trusted. After that, Lora took the initiative, often inviting me out to the family dude ranch. Now and then I stayed overnight in a guest cottage with a view of saguaros on the mountain slopes.

She took me along to events she covered for the newspaper. For a formal dance at the Country Club, she dressed up like a prom date. Her father, with his strong resemblance to Mr. Pickwick in the Cruikshank illustrations, threw a temper tantrum when we arrived back at the ranch near midnight. His Bostonian morals had been greatly offended, he let me know, with a choler almost as uncontrolled as Warner's.

He strutted around in moonlight by the gate where he had been waiting. "When I was a young man I courted . . . " he began and did not break off his sputtery moralizing until he began to weep. He forbade me to see his daughter again, but she reminded him in the silver moonlight that she was twenty-two, a college graduate, and free to leave home if he insisted on trying to run her life. Mr. Pickwick walked back to the main house, humbled and weepy.

Anne

25.

NOVELIST JAMES JONES, whose bestseller, *From Here to Eternity*, was all the rage, was spending the winter in Tucson in his portable studio, a long aluminum Airstream moored in a trailer park. Armed with a copy of *Life* magazine, where he and his guru Lowney Handy were written up, Martin and Lora were both planning to interview him for local publications, and they invited me to go along.

James Jones was genial, colorful, waggish, jocular, accessible. Like Buffalo Bill, the car wash man, he dressed Western, not afraid to overdo it. He wore a fringed jacket, bright embroidered shirt, cowboy boots — but also turquoise bracelets, bola pendant at his neck, and huge turquoise-bedizened belt buckle. He invited us into his trailer and showed us around, pointing out his row of small Viking Portable Library volumes. "Those are my influences," he said, sitting down at his table with the mountains as backdrop, and pecked at his portable typewriter for a moment, looking at us with a grin. "I should have brought a photographer," Lora remarked.

When I showed him a copy of a local little magazine with one of my short stories in it, Jones said, "You've got to come out and meet Lowney. She's the best writing teacher in the world. She taught me everything I know." We already knew from the *Life* article that her writing colony was based in Illinois, but he revealed that she was in Tucson for the winter. What we knew from the magazine feature was inspiring. This wonderful woman was the answer to every young writer's dream, a mentor and driving disciplinarian who could overcome even the laziest slob's reluctance to fulfill that ambition Scott Fitzgerald voiced: "I want to be the greatest writer in the world, don't you?"

I was eager to meet Mrs. Handy, this dynamic, charismatic forty-nine-year-old woman whom Jones and *Life* had described. When Martin and I made a trip out to the east side house she was renting, she turned out to be a Renoiresque woman who dressed in hip-hugging jeans and a sweatshirt, no bra. She had devoted her life, she reminded us within minutes of our arrival, to discovering and empowering the talents of others. In fact three of those others were present, budding novelists standing like soldiers at the ready. "These are my apprentice writers," she said. "I've brought the best of them out here and another one's showing up next week. He's driving the jeep out."

Captured by Lowney's charisma, I returned almost daily, sitting at her feet with the others. She perceived that my writing had, like Magritte's "apple that fills the room," become an obsession, perhaps my only positive one, for my gloom guaranteed angst-ridden days and nights. Everything I read, except for textbooks, seemed to recommend flight. The protagonist in a Paul Bowles novel, *The Sheltering Sky*, found himself wandering through the North African desert. Raskolnikov redeemed himself only by exile to Siberia. Even Adam and Eve had to flee the garden in *Paradise Lost*.

For Lowney to focus attention on me was a flattery of embarrassing bliss. Each pronouncement signaled a lesson in life and letters. As she would have it, her colony provided sanctuary, a retreat from the madness, where writers followed their divine leadings. She cited *The Razor's Edge*. We need not go to India to seek enlightenment. Her version of redskins and palefaces to represent the bipolar condition of American literature was stark. As she saw it, the Civil War was still being fought, every novel a new battle between "sissy" writers like Henry James and the heirs of Jack London, Theodore Dreiser, and Ernest Hemingway. "Jim's the best of them," she said, denouncing several other claimants to the heavyweight crown of naturalism, reserving her most venomous scorn for Norman Mailer.

Until Jones, Lowney lamented, her efforts had been wasted, but after their meeting in 1943, when he was just back from the service, she had locked him in his room and prescribed a daily page quota far in excess of Hemingway's. She insisted that she was at least as responsible for *From Here to Eternity* as Jones. Whenever he heard this boast, he patiently accepted the judgment with a shrug and a smile. In her version there was no room for the claim he sometimes made out of Lowney's hearing, that he had been working hard all through his army days to become a novelist in the tradition of his idol, Thomas Wolfe. Lowney pointed to the others, her apprentices sitting around the living room, always watching and listening. If they had "the faith of a grain of mustard seed," they too might become great writers like Jones. Between her outpourings, we would break for a lunch of peanut butter and jelly sandwiches and hot liquid Jell-O rather than coffee.

Even before she repeated the myth, we knew she had arranged her life around Jones, who had returned to their hometown of Robinson, Illinois, after some unpleasant experiences in the army. In telling this tale Lowney was not about to give Jim credit—she developed him from scratch. From the moment I met her she was quoting Madame Blavatsky, Nietzsche, the Bible, and a variety of novels, citing authority with every breath. "Morality is what we feel good after" was one of her favorites, though I doubt if Hemingway meant it as a justification for being "beyond good and evil," the context she provided.

Jones was just the sort of sow's ear, Lowney would tell us, that she could turn into a silk purse. As she told it, Jones had been sick, needing a miracle cure. He had been a hopeless alcoholic, at risk of drinking himself to death. He was destitute with no resources. His dentist father had shot himself and Jim seemed on the same road to suicide. Each day I learned more: with the approval of her easy-going husband Harry, Lowney had made a place for young Jim Jones in their home in Robinson, then later developed a property in nearby Marshall for her utopian writers' colony, which she now urged me to join.

Before creating the colony, the pair had traveled together, setting up housekeeping in trailer parks like the Florida scene described in Jim's story "None Sing So Wildly," published in *New World Writing* just before their trip to Tucson. At the end of that story Jones wrote of his hunger for the West: "It was on one of these walks that it suddenly came to Sylvanus that maybe he should try living in the Far West, when this novel was done. He had never lived in the West. But he had read that it was the Western women who had first forked a horse, when the side saddle was still a God-given law of propriety. Surely, with mountains and deep woods all around them, they ought to be different out there, Sylvanus Merrick decided. All you had to do was get out of the great Middle West."

Lowney would assign me a buddyseat on one of the motorcycles as we roared into the foothills to study flora and fauna in order to work local color into our stories. "Don't leave out those big cactuses and all the flowers," she said, inspiring us to make lists of things we had seen. "Then stop somewhere and study some oddballs you can characterize." She also told us to observe one another ceaselessly, analyzing, comparing, describing. Now I knew why the boys had gazed at me with such close scrutiny, practicing how to make a fictional character out of me.

As we roared about and around Tucson, we could have passed for a roving band of Hell's Angels. Only the obligatory notebooks we carried in our jacket pockets gave away the literary obsession. But Lowney's colony involved more than writing. She was worshipped by these young men who sat around her and who were now preparing to make a place for me in their circle. "If Lowney told me to eat shit, I would, and like it," one of the boys told me.

Lowney insisted that I would never be any good as a writer unless I dropped out of the university and joined the colony when they returned to Illinois, like snowbirds, in the spring. When she stared into my eyes as if I were the only person in the world worth sharing her secrets with, I was putty in her hands, just like the others. She had a number of miracle cures to offer, but her main success story was Jones. She had cured him of alcohol and lust, she bragged. What she could promise in return for my faith was the same success Jim was enjoying. All that was necessary was to obey her without question.

Vows of "poverty, chastity, and obedience," were required, just as in a monastery. Far from deterring me, such a challenge intrigued. Lowney demanded a total break with families, lovers, friends. Though she was a woman, she would reflect apologetically, Lowney had nothing but scorn for the world of women, and was determined that none be allowed to corrupt her colonists. Only once had she made an exception and allowed a woman into the colony, and that had been a terrible mistake, she said. In the living room of the Tucson house, leading discussions with her boys seated on the floor around her, Lowney mercilessly attacked my relationship with Lora and made fun of her ambitions, adding that Lora had entrapped me. Giving up Lora was the first sacrifice she demanded. She pointed out that the others had survived similar renunciations of worldly contacts. That poverty, chastity, and obedience were surefire ways to achieve fame and fortune made a lot of sense to me, especially since—as Jones's playboy life made clear—the rules would at some point be relaxed, a life of indulgence being the eventual payoff for the deserving.

Lowney decided that Jones had become attracted to Lora. She taunted him as well as me about the infatuation. With the obscenity of a top sergeant Lowney demanded that Jim admit that he "wanted a piece" from "that flat-chested little bitch." If her purpose was to degrade all of us, it succeeded. Amazed, I felt helpless to come to my girlfriend's defense. Besides, I was sure Lowney was wrong in accusing Jones. After all, he moved in a more exalted world, bragging about his love affairs and brothel adventures. With all those opportunities, why would he be interested in a shy, petite intellectual like Lora? But perhaps green-eyed Lowney had been accurate in sensing a threat, seeing that Lora was far more authentic than the women Jim met in Hollywood or at publishers' parties in New York, or in whorehouses and bars.

Jones seemed to be taking a big brotherly interest in me. I still have a scrawled note he left at my rooming house one Friday, along with a ten-dollar bill. "You weren't in. I won't leave T. until Thurs. or Fri. 16th or 17th. Must go to Hollywood for a week. Here's ten, in case you run short. Will contact you when I return." This was heady stuff. A mention of Hollywood always impressed. He was going there for big business, conferring with producers and movie stars about the making of *From Here to Eternity*.

Lowney escalated her attacks on Lora, saying I would never be worth a damn until I had the courage to set myself free of such a "castrating bitch." There are householders and artists, Lowney harangued, and Lora was luring me into the slavery of being a householder. Lowney would turn to Jim. "She's out to cut your balls off, too," she warned. Obsessed with castration, Lowney often threatened. "I'll cut your balls off and hang them on the wall." She accused Lora of having the same design on Jim and me both. But there was hope—we would escape to the monastic Handy Colony in Marshall, Illinois.

Lowney swung her arms, doubled her fists, danced around like a slowed-down prizefighter as she gave us pep talks, always enriched with quotations. "You must be the hammer or the anvil," she quoted Bismarck, though ascribing the saying to Hemingway. "If you want to lower your standards, get the hell out of here. I demand the best or nothing out of you worthless sonofabitches." To me she still held Jones up as an example. "If *he* could give up his worldly attachments, you can too."

"Lowney, I'm not that bad," Jim would grin.

About that time I got a letter from the draft board ordering me to appear in Phoenix for a physical. Lora drove me, and we stopped midway between Tucson and Phoenix and made love on the sands of a desert arroyo. Little cactus wrens chittered about us. Lora said she hoped this would not be the last time, since maybe the army would take me directly from the induction station. For once, orgasm was not the painful throbbing it had been with and since Warner.

When my turn with the doctor came up, he quickly dismissed me as an asthmatic, and I was designated 4-F. There was entertainment too, for several draftees were unsuccessfully trying to evade capture by the army—they discussed the schemes as we waited naked in the queue, each holding a basket containing his clothes. They groaned as they were given their A-l status, their pleas that they were homosexuals or pacifists or victims of trick knees or bad backs falling on deaf ears. But with no effort whatsoever or act on my part, I was spared my fate in Korea. I would not wind up as one of those soldiers dead in the mud and snow, hands tied behind them—execution-style warfare.

On the trip back to Tucson in Lora's pickup, I told her I was considering going into the Illinois colony. Her first reaction was to ask if she could go along, and when I told her of Lowney's policy against women, she tromped the accelerator and we flew along the highway, the pickup seeming to take flight.

Lowney's haranguing kept me off balance. When her mood shifted, I dodged her wrath like physical blows, trying to survive the verbal assaults. Yet, painful as it was, her attentions were welcome. But my suppressed doubts resurfaced one afternoon when she subjected me to a humiliating rant familiar to survivors of cults. She accused me of not having enough faith or courage to break loose and follow her. She charged me with every kind of weakness she could think of, and her technique might have worked had she not attacked Lora again. Having been charged from infancy with taking care of Ellen, no matter what, such an attack—her most vicious yet—brought out my protective instincts.

Lowney had told us almost everything it took to be a great writer, but she had left out Hemingway's idea of the chief requirement—"a built-in shit-detector." It was as if mine, like a hearing aid, had suddenly been turned on again. I told Lowney to go to hell, and stalked out of her house, ignoring the reproach of her baleful eyes. My choice was Lora and the university, not Lowney's extravagant promises. If I just did not have the faith of a mustard seed, it was just too damn bad.

Even that moment of independence was inspiriting. I returned to my basement room at Third and University, relieved to have made the decision, but I was not back long before my landlady knocked on my door and told me I had visitors upstairs. I followed the waddling woman up the rickety wooden stairs, surprised as ever that they did not collapse under her weight.

Like Mrs. Spessard at the Children's Home conducting a child to a waiting visitor, she led me into the living room. Before the stone fireplace sat Jim and Lowney, looking as they had in the full-page *Life* magazine portrait.

"We want you to come along with us," Lowney said.

Jim added his challenge. "Don't chicken out. Lowney knows better than you do what's good for you. Take my word for it."

"Don't disappoint me," Lowney said, prepared to grieve.

"You'll never get a chance like this again," Jim warned. Here was a man with the authority of Hollywood and the Book-of-the-Month Club. How could I doubt it?

"We want you with us," Lowney said. "You'll never amount to anything if you stay around here."

"You listen to Lowney," Jim said.

"I don't give second chances," Lowney reminded me.

"You can ride back with me," Jim said.

There it was—the same offer my father had made from the driver's seat of his blue Pontiac coupe with the chrome Indian chief on its hood. "Hop in and come along," he had urged. And there it was, echo of the invitation John Kingsbury Warner had made from the driver's seat of his Tucson-tan Lincoln Continental. But this time the offer came from the glamorous, the famous, both the mother and the father—the sorceress and her apprentice—offering me the Holy Grail. Their adoration was embarrassing, and we could all be spared it only by my surrender. They had a place for me. They were rescuing me from poverty and failure. I was wanted, bathed in the warmth of their gaze, respected. Were they here to make up for all those visiting days when no one had turned up? In their long absence, mother and father had become a far more attractive and glamorous couple.

"Like I said," Jim reiterated, "Lowney knows what's best for us. Look at all she's done for me."

Visions of sugarplums! Glory, Hallelujah! But I demurred, hesitant to give up my high ground. "Think about it," Jim added. "Lowney's giving you another chance."

The certainty with which, an hour earlier, I had known Lowney's invitation to join her colony meant disaster vanished in an instant. I was overcome as if by the hypnotic eyes of a regal couple, dictators of a benign kingdom. The shit-detector clicked off.

As soon as I agreed to go, Lowney handed across an olive green war surplus duffel bag. "That's for your worldly possessions, whatever fits in it, not a rag more," she said. "If you cling to things of this world, you won't be worth a damn." The way Warner had put it, whether of Lee's car or me, was, "Not worth the powder to blow it—or you—up."

"I started out with a hell of a lot less than that," Jim said.

"I should make you get rid of all that shit in your head, too," Lowney said, and got up. "That'll take a while. You're too damned intellectual as it is. He reads books with his gloves on, doesn't he, Jim?" For years I would puzzle over what she meant by that comment, but perhaps it was meant to puzzle me.

John Bowers, one of the colonists I spent time with that winter of discontent, later published a memoir entitled *The Colony*, and in it provided an accurate account of my situation.

> A new face was blushing in the house when we returned. This was Arnold, a student at the University of Arizona, who had come originally with vigor and high confidence some weeks back to interview Jim for the student newspaper and had stayed to be worked by degrees into the Colony status. He wore this night a bright yellow sport shirt that someone had starched and carefully ironed. The rest of us were in Levi's and T-shirts, Lowney in her usual sweat shirt, sans bra, with the sleeves pushed up.

Bowers goes on to describe the scene just as I recall it:

We sat in a circle on the floor. Arnold peered through shiny horn-rims, and his black curly hair shot up from his scalp past Colony limits. He had a way of speaking, and then ducking his head as if expecting a blow. His voice was deep, tentative. "Wallace Stevens I've always thought was our best poet," Arnold is saying, then ducking. "Are you familiar with him, Lowney?"

"Wallace Stevens. I know him. He's the biggest horse's ass in the country. Look at that one"—she points to Sidney, leaning back on elbows. "When he came in with us, he was spouting T. S. Eliot. I once caught him and Jim mouthing that crap at each other in Jim's trailer. If I hadn't clipped it in the bud they'd be la-de-da-ing at one another right this minute. *Forget literature!* But I don't think you've got what it takes anyhow. Tell me. If I gave you three wishes, what would you wish for? Tell me."

At this remove, Lowney's ranting sounds like nothing stronger than harsh humor and the shock tactics of a strongly individualistic teacher, but her virulent scorn was biting. Bowers quotes my response:

"I—I—" face scarlet. All of us, except Lowney and Arnold, are back on our elbows. "I'd like to write a book as good as . . . The Naked and the Dead. Also, Eternity.'"

I had added *Eternity*, which I had not read, only because Lowney was taken aback by my mention of Mailer's book, not Jim's. I had caught her instant frown of reproof. Bowers touched on the ensuing inquisition.

"You got a girl friend, ain't you?" Jim says. We're all getting cracks at Arnold. There's a delirious strangeness in being considered now a Colony Vet. The sadistic pleasure of a fraternity man looking over a new pledge.

"Yes—I—uh—have a girl friend. She was the one with me when I first came to interview you."

"A mousy little thing," Lowney says. "Not a peep out of her. But

I could tell she was looking down her nose at us. What does she do?"

"She's on the school paper. We work together."

Bowers had that wrong. Lora was the society reporter for the Tucson newspaper. But he goes on:

Image now of Arnold strolling on campus with a quiet, pretty girl, her fingers stained with ink. There were no oaks that I knew of in Tucson, but I saw Arnold and this blackhaired girl beneath the lush green foliage of that tree.

"Are you fucking her?" Jim wants to know. Here we go.

The inquisition was no less embarrassing than the one at Michael Reese Hospital had been, when the resident asked me how I got sex.

Arnold looks all around, stunned. "Yeah."

"Well, you're never going to write," Lowney says. "You think you're hot shit because some dumb little dame has been making eyes over you. What you want to do is spout this intellectual crap and have people go ooh-la-la. I'm not going to have you coming into my Colony and fucking things up. *You* want to write. Look at this boy— "pointing to me, causing my chest to rise—"he's writing a hell of a book. He's telling painful things. He's holding nothing back and he's giving up everything. Listen, you'll never be an artist till you hit bottom."

Bowers describes his own wrestling with Lowney's tirades, his own attempts to digest her formulas. Then he quotes me as saying, "'I do want to write.'" Lowney retorts,

"Then quit that fucking college. If you're ready to write by next spring, then I'll take you back with us to the Colony. But I doubt most sincerely if you've got the guts to give up worldly things. You'll probably knock up that mousy little girl is what you'll do. They all want to fill their wombs!"

The Colony Vets go to the refrigerator for cans of beer, a decided and daring privilege. Arnold sits, cross-legged, no beer offered, his socks drooping and looking somehow pathetic against his white skin. Intellectual socks, a non-member-of-the-Colony's socks. I was so proud to be a Vet. But I couldn't articulate to myself the beginnings of another terrible feeling: Don't let them take charge of you. They have no right. It's your life, your privacy. Stay with the girl!

Bowers did not give me that advice, nor does he say if it occurred to him to save himself from the same invasion of his soul. He went on to describe his motorcycle trip back to Marshall. He and Bob, whom he calls Bayard, had been left behind there as winter caretakers for the Colony, but had been summoned to Tucson in order to drive the motorcycles back, saving the expense of shipping them.

Lowney opened a large Rand-McNally atlas and marked with Crayolas the different routes we would take to Illinois. Jim and I, in his blue Chrysler convertible, tugging the Airstream, were to take the southern route through Las Cruces and El Paso, missing the mountains. Lowney and Bob would drive the Jeep back, and the others would follow on motorcycles.

The first night out, Jim and I hooked the trailer up at an overnight park. We got in early enough to have a few beers after dinner. Disregarding my coughs, I matched Jim cigarette by cigarette. He was generous with them, and he bought me one beer after another. When we turned in about midnight I was still aglow from being treated like a pal. He pulled a sleeping bag out of a drawer under the bunk bed and I settled down beneath the shelf of his Viking Portable "influences" while he disappeared into the stern. I had a friend now, a purpose, and a future.

The next day a Texas trooper stopped us for speeding. When Jim offered his driver's license and mentioned that he was the author of *From Here to Eternity*, the trooper asked for his autograph, shook his hand, and sent us on our way. It was not the only time I overheard someone exclaim, "Not *the* James Jones," consigning thousands of others to oblivion. One of the most common of names had been turned into a catchword, recognizable all across the country.

As we sailed along the vast Texas landscape, endless plains, endless rolling hills, most of our chat was small talk carried away by the wind, but some was of literary alloy. Jim was not just the bluff tough guy, I realized, as he revealed his thoughtful side. By the time we pulled into the colony grounds I could have done a doctoral thesis on the sources of *From Here to Eternity*. Protagonist Prewitt was Fabrizio, hero of *The Red and the Black*, a tortured half-soldier half-priest. Battlefields, as in Stendhal's book, were never even comprehensible by the poor foot soldier who runs here, there, glimpsing only a little piece of the action. Life is experienced in fragments. Waterloo, Pearl Harbor, what difference? "Pearl," as Jim called it, could have been on a Sunday morning in December of 1941 a battlefield of the Napoleonic War like the one Fabrizio found himself in—or a disputed bridge in the Spanish Civil War, like the one Hemingway gave us in *For Whom the Bell Tolls*, which Jim had studied until he had practically memorized it and the dialogue of his characters would sound like theirs. And was poor Prewitt in the brig the condemned hero of *An American Tragedy* or was he Gatsby? Or was he Jim Jones?

But there was more. The top sergeant in *Eternity* was really Lowney, who had locked Jim in his room and shouted at him if his typewriter went silent. Life was literature, inextricably enmeshed. Jim had soaked up his influences until he had become them—Thomas Wolfe, Ernest Hemingway. And here I was, all excited to be sitting by Jim, another inspiring role model. And Lowney's taking me into the colony was like receiving the best of fellowships, with room and board guaranteed. And with no strings attached.

Jim was a syncretist and lived in the world of Lowney's books. He had been the Robinson boy with steel-rimmed specs who went into the army to escape small town hell—the boy whose father had committed suicide, whose mother could have smothered him. He had typed and drunk his way through the army—though not nearly as much as Lowney claimed, he clarified—and then he had come back and fallen under her spell. "Lowney taught me everything I know about writing" was not altogether a lie. He lived in fear of disappointing her.

Much of this I could not see from the passenger seat of a blue Chrysler convertible moving at eighty miles an hour. But Lowney had him tied up in so many knots, some silken, some with legal contracts, that he might never escape alive, or would he? He had been in love with her with the intensity of Oedipus's love for Jocasta. But that passion had faded. She had tried, or pretended to try, to turn him loose but still clung to him and, like Warner, demanded to know everything that happened, every graphic detail. And she had to make sure he put it all into his writing. As top sergeant, she still saw to it that he was driven into his cage daily.

Literature was riding along in the sun with Mr. Simenon or with Jones the celebrity. Literature was absorbing Hemingway until you wrote like him—or Dreiser until your hero went to the electric chair the way his did. Literature was being roped and led into the corral where Lowney cracked her bullwhip as you took notes on the dust and smells of the manure and manliness. And books were built of debris, the leavings and borrowings of the masters. They were jerryrigged, pasted together, a pastiche. I was soaking up Lowney's way of looking at it.

26.

THE COLONY WAS a fenced acreage at the edge of Marshall, Illinois. I was assigned one of five plywood rooms in a row called the barracks. The compound included a central screened ramada, Jim's Airstream and a weathered house trailer next to it. Around the circular drive were Lowney's small white cottage set up on cinder blocks and another house used as Jim's studio. A pond had been bulldozed behind it for a swimming hole.

For my first conference with Lowney in her cottage, I took along the stories I had written for Robert Ramsey's creative writing class at the university. But she was more interested in grilling me about our trip. "Did anything unusual happen?" she asked, as big-eyed as Warner. I could not think of anything. Had she sent me along with Jim just so I could spy on him and later, with unwitting candor, satisfy her interrogation?

The ramada, equipped with stove, refrigerator, sink, and long redwood picnic table as well as bookshelves, provided dining and library facilities—our only living room. The colony grounds, with the cement-floored outhouse with toilet and shower for communal use, reminded me of a trailer park, though there were only the two trailers—Jim's aluminum cocoon and the one next to it, always referred to as Mary Ann's.

Several rumors were circulating among the colonists about Jim's late sister Mary Ann. She had been the only woman who had braved Lowney's misogyny to become a member of the colony. She had survived there for a very short time. Whenever Lowney mentioned her, it was to emphasize the foolishness of a female's aspirations to be a writer. "She might be alive today," Lowney speculated, "if she hadn't got so worked up about everything. A woman should be a householder and doesn't belong in a writing colony. Mary Ann should have known better." Lowney's message included the warning that stress could kill, adding that it *had* killed Mary Ann.

Our daily routine was rigid, built around enforced hours at work in the plywood rooms furnished with a narrow bunk, desk, chair and typewriter. Up at 6 A.M., wakened by a jangling outdoor bell, breakfast in the ramada, instant coffee and toast (no more food because "you think better that way"), no talking by colony members in the mornings, writing steadily until noon. Lowney patrolled the grounds to insure the constant clattering of a typewriter from each room, even if we were doing nothing but following her assignments of retyping her favorite books, an exercise which she credited with Jim's success. Soon, like a convict, I was typing out letters to Lora and trying to form a plan to smuggle them out of the grounds. Jim's secretary, a local minister's wife, showed up almost every day to take dictation and have a swim in the pond. I thought she might be willing to slip letters into the mail.

Lowney would knock on our doors, demanding to know why a typewriter had gone silent. Her interrogation could be obscene, since she often assumed that one of her apprentices might have quit typing only to masturbate. There was no privacy, and I soon learned that there might as well have been bars on the window, for word got around that two of the colonists, as "trustees," were armed and had orders to shoot any of us if we tried to escape. At first I thought this threat was a joke, or fiction in the making.

A new inmate working next to me on the rock pile confided that Lowney had already given him a rifle. I was amazed that he had so quickly become a trustee, yet another example of the capriciousness with which Lowney kept us guessing. "She said to shoot to kill," he said, seeming to find the prospect appealing, and adding, "You don't think she really meant that, do you?" He offered me a cigarette from a pack of Benson & Hedges, then put two in his own mouth and lit them, an

impressive display of conspicuous consumption. I had never seen anyone smoking two cigarettes at a time. I was not so sure how to answer
him, for I had heard Lowney make threats that sounded very convincing, and she had more than once repeated her most familiar one to me.
"If you ever cross me," she said, with little provocation, "I'll kill you, you
can be sure of it. I can get you killed for two hundred dollars. Most people don't do it because they don't have the guts."

There were only two ways out of the grounds at the edge of
Marshall—the gate next to Lowney's cottage, always locked at night, and
a plank footbridge over a ravine beyond the barracks. When we were not
in our cells, we had orders never to be alone. "Otherwise you'll get
funny ideas," Lowney said. "I don't want you talking. Scott Fitzgerald
said the only way to be a good writer was to keep your mouth shut for at
least three days at a time."

At lunch in the ramada we could talk so long as we avoided forbidden subjects such as family or girlfriends. We sipped from our cups of
the mandatory sticky red Jell-O, a sugary drink I had known only in its
gelid condition. Lowney sang its benefits ceaselessly, but I never learned
to love it any more than I loved the cooked turnips served every Tuesday
in the Children's Home. Colony meals usually consisted of macaroni
and cheese—the same Kraft Dinner I had hated as a child—or peanut
butter and jelly sandwiches, along with the hot liquid Jell-O blessed by
Lowney. Occasionally she would bring over a Mason jar of beef stew
and heat it up, a show of maternal concern, as if not to overdo the aus-
terity. Now and then Jim brought over extra steaks or hamburgers from
his outdoor grill if expected guests had not shown up to consume them.
We welcomed leftovers.

Except for occasional crossovers, a strict caste system was maintained—Lowney and Jim, privileged and boisterously indulgent on one
side of the circular drive, and their humble apprentices on the other.
We usually ate sulkily, stealing resentful glances through the screen.
Aromatic smoke drifted over from the outdoor cooking. Laughter and
loud cavorting of Lowney and Jim and their guests became ever more
obnoxious. What we saw did not look like "poverty, chastity, and obedi-

ence." Yet the most loyal of the colonists made excuses to newcomers, justifying everything Lowney did. They would have it that deprivations were for our own good, a part of her divine plan for us.

Even when we heard Jones tear off in his roadster, headed for the bars and brothels of Terre Haute, tires crunching and hurling gravel, we would tell one another that we would have such privileges as well when we reached his status. Trips to whorehouses were part of Lowney's reward system. When out of Lowney's hearing, Jim regaled us with his adventures, reviewing the sexual prowess of his favorite prostitutes, but never failing to mention Hollywood and "that damn movie starlet that gave me a dose."

Lowney stressed us at every turn with her bellowed orders, whether up close or yelled from her stance in her doorway. She never tired of designing chores to humiliate us and tighten security. Like Doctor Zhivago we could have said that we made our own prison, surrounding ourselves with watchtowers—we did it all by ourselves. We hammered away for hours atop a huge pile of mortar-encrusted bricks, salvaging stacks of them for sidewalks we were to lay around the grounds. We followed her orders to dig a deep hole, then she turned up like a top sergeant to command us. "Now move it over," she said. We filled in the hole and started another. The message included her indignant and shaming conclusion that we could not do anything right. Her rare praise was all the more precious—gold we inmates seemed willing to kill for.

Though I had gone along to town with the trustees, shopping for groceries, I had been unable to steal away to check general delivery for letters from Lora. I missed her and began indulging fantasies of escape, and I soon discovered that I had a fellow conspirator in Carl Pontell, the oldest member of the colony, a World War II vet. On the rock pile we conferred about making a run for it. Carl had a long list of grievances— the monotonous schedule and drudgery, the humiliations reminiscent of the military, and the rules against outside contacts.

Lowney often added new rules and taboos. Her literary pantheon had no room for Walt Whitman or Hart Crane or such "sissy, limp-wristed fairies" as Marcel Proust, which she pronounced "Prowst." "He was a queer," she said. "No wonder he had such a sissy style. If I catch any of you reading him, out you go." You would have thought we were all dying to get our hands on a copy of *Remembrance of Things Past* and thus be corrupted forever. She confiscated my eyeglasses and gave me a paperback of Aldous Huxley's *Sight Without Glasses*, with orders to do the exercises that would strengthen my eyes.

Three of my Chicago classmates found out that I had entered the Handy Colony, which they too had read about in *Life* magazine. Without an invitation, they turned up one afternoon in Marshall and telephoned to ask directions from the bus station. At first Lowney invoked her "no visitors" policy. She called me to her office and accused me of having invited them, thereby violating the rule of isolation. She told me I was lucky she did not kick me right out for the offense. However, she reflected as she calmed down, University of Chicago types should be good material. She called her father, a local lawman, and told him to collect the three and bring them to the colony. Then she rang the bell on her porch and called all the colonists to her cottage. She told them that she would deal with these three intruders, but that when I brought them around for a tour of the grounds they should observe carefully since these people could probably be characters for novels. She expected us to write up a full report of everything they did and said during the visit.

When my three friends turned up, Lowney invited them into her cottage, sat down at her desk and wheeled around, challenging them. She was outraged by what she saw. A beard on the tall one, a black beret on the stocky one, and eyeglasses on two out of the three. Collectively, the students represented horrific unconventionality. I would not have been surprised had she ripped off their glasses and stomped them, and ordered my bearded friend to shave.

Although I was glad to see my friends, it was clear that they were getting me into trouble with Lowney. I wondered if, like visitors to the Children's Home, they had come out of curiosity or to meet the famous novelist. Perhaps she was right—they were indeed characters, as diverse as the three stooges. Larry was the boy genius who had looked elderly at fourteen and would later make a fortune as a popular contestant on a TV quiz show. Earl was a budding novelist, short, curly-haired, and inquisitive about every detail of colony life, as if he might be interested in joining. Daniel, who would become a California guru, was a chain-smoking addict of Saki stories. He spoke with an affected nasal twang. All in all, my three visitors had plenty of qualities that Lowney was bound to find offensive—odd clothes, unmanly gestures, impertinent questions.

She convicted them on sight of nameless crimes and intolerable offenses. After a few minutes she told me to give them a tour of the grounds, then followed us out onto the porch. But then she changed her mind. "Come back in here, young men. I have more to say to you." Again, they edged through her French doors and sat down like naughty students.

"Why are you wearing that silly beret?" she asked.

Larry had no answer. He took the beret off and lay it on his knee. He had worn it to cover his baldness, she suggested, and he acknowledged with a wry smile the truth of her insight.

"So who are the great writers, in your opinions?" she demanded.

"Maybe D. H. Lawrence," Daniel ventured.

"D. H. Lawrence was a queer," Lowney snapped. "That's why he died of T. B."

"Lady, you've got it all wrong," Earl took her on.

She turned on him with fiery eyes. "You stay out of it," she said. "I didn't ask you."

"Hey, Lady, don't pick on me," Earl frowned, puzzled.

She turned back to Larry. "You're the ringleader, aren't you?"

He gave her a wide smile, flattered.

"Do you know why people wear glasses?" she asked.

The three answered in unison that they did not. Lowney stood up and reached for a book, another copy of *Sight Without Glasses*. In doing so, she also lifted her own glasses, on a ribbon, and put them on. Such a stock vaudeville improbability elicited involuntary chuckles. Trying to restrain her temper, Lowney sat down and gave us a disgusted look.

"Don't think you can rattle me," she said. "As far as I'm concerned you're just a bunch of brats. You're not the first University of Chicago queers and commies I've met. And when you hightail your asses out of here, that one can go right with you." She pointed to me.

I assumed I was expected to plead for forgiveness, but I kept silent. Maybe it would be better to leave with them.

"Jesus said throw away your crutches and walk," Lowney announced, removing her glasses and letting them fall on her gray sweatshirt. "Get rid of those goddamn glasses right now. Weak eyes mean you're latent queers, no doubt about it, but if you do the exercises in this book, you can still recover. Look at Jim, he wore those stupid glasses and it ruined him. Even his grade school classmates called him four-eyes. If it wasn't for me, he'd still be wearing them."

My friends began to snicker, and that was the last straw for Lowney. She flew into a rage. "Get the hell out of here, you goddamn queers," she yelled.

For a moment they froze, stunned, disbelieving. She rose up, pushing the visitors out the door and kicked them as they fled, leaping off her porch. I stepped aside as she jumped down onto the grass. She yelled for Jim. He came running over from his trailer, begging her to calm down. She picked up a brick, prepared to throw it.

"Lady," Earl implored, looking back, "I've got a sore foot. I can't run." She threw the brick. He cursed her and ran toward the gate, hobbling with pain.

As my friends approached the gate, out of her range, Lowney ran to her black Buick, and started it up. Jim was trying to reason with her, to no avail. The car spun around, the wheels spewing gravel, and roared down the road. There was little doubt about her intention as she accelerated toward the fleeing trio—vehicular homicide. They threw themselves into the ditch.

She screeched to a halt. "Get in here," she yelled. "I'll take you sonsofbitches to town."

"That's okay, Lady," Earl assured her. "We'll walk. There's plenty of time."

"I'm more of a man than any of you!" she screamed, leaving them in a cloud of dust, as she zoomed through the gate. Within seconds the Buick circled around like an angry bull, floorboarded, heading back through the gate, its grill gleaming like long silver teeth. Again the incredulous three leapt out of the way. Lowney braked again and even as the dust settled called out to them.

"You three cocksuckers better be on the first bus out of here," she warned. "If the three of you ever show your faces around here again, I can't be responsible for what happens."

She slammed the car door and stalked back into her cottage. She telephoned her father again, ordering him to arrest my three crazy class-mates and guard them until the bus to Chicago left. If they did anything funny he was to throw them in jail and she would handle the rest. When I heard her end of that conversation I lost my desire to join them.

Back in Chicago, I would learn later, my friends recounted the day's events with comedic glee, but the fact was that they had been scared out of their wits. Lowney really had tried to kill them, not with a couple of hundred dollars paid to a hit man, as she bragged she could, but with the crude blunt instruments within easy reach—bricks and a Buick. "A brickbat," Earl recalls.

We sometimes crossed a plank bridge over a shrub and willow bordered gully to work chain gang fashion in a large potato and bean garden owned by Lowney's mother-in-law, who lived in the adjacent white house along Highway 40. The garden provided food for the colony as well as for Mrs. Handy, but there was yet a higher priority. As another colonist and I pulled weeds along the bean rows, he told me, "Lowney's afraid we'll jerk off too much if we don't get plenty worn out. That's why she puts salt-peter in the Jell-O." After hearing about the saltpeter I avoided drinking the Jell-O and suggested to Carl that we speed up the escape plan. But he took seriously the threat of being shot, and urged caution.

We dug holes, then moved them over. On the pyramid of salvaged bricks we sat and chipped away. Dostoyevsky, in *The House of the Dead*, writes of the power of such techniques, applied to prisoners. "If it were desired to reduce a man to nothing—to punish him atrociously, to crush him in such a manner that the most hardened murderer would tremble before such punishment—it would be necessary only to give his work a character of complete uselessness . . . . Let him be constrained to pour water from one vessel to another, or to carry earth from one place to another and back again, then I am persuaded that at the end of a few days the prisoner would strangle himself or commit a thousand crimes punishable with death, rather than live in such an abject condition and endure such torments."

Lowney understood that the way to turn young men into slaves was to deny them the feeling that their work was important. It was only as important as she made it, she emphasized again and again, saying things like, "I can make you or break you, don't forget it." George Hendrick in his editorial notes in *To Reach Eternity: The Letters of James Jones* observed: "Lowney constantly subjected Jones to psychological warfare. 'Before I could learn,' he wrote his brother, Jeff, 'I had to be broken. And boy, I mean *broken*. Lowney cut the ground out from under me until I had absolutely no place to stand. I was completely lost. Every way I turned for aid or escape, Lowney was there and cut me off.'" In a letter he begged her: "Don't hurt me, Lowney. Don't hurt me."

Her surgical criticism of our writings, Jim's not exempted, was excoriating, whether delivered in private during conference in her cottage or with shaming scorn in front of the others. She was sometimes inspired to rip a manuscript out of a colonist's hands and rip it up, scattering the pages or marking it up with such slashes and obscenities that the original typescript could not be made out. Yet she could alternate this sort of treatment with cooing praise, as if she alone had unconditional love to bestow. Then she imposed conditions.

Sentencing us to the rock pile and to chores like "moving the hole over" were proof of her powers, though we were not—as in the Gulag—digging our own graves. As for the Jello-O, I only years later connected it with brainwashing when I came across William Sargant's *Battle for the Mind*, a classic study by a British psychiatrist. High glucose levels radically enhance suggestibility, making subjects more receptive to brain-washing harangues. I never again heard of Jell-O as a drink until the Jonesville mass suicide many years later. As the cult leader preacher, the later James Jones, was from Indianapolis, not far from Lowney's colony, he could have read about Lowney's methods, for her colony had a plethora of media attention in the Indianapolis area and beyond.

One afternoon, in one of Lowney's sudden reversals of polarities—from forbidding sex to mandating it—an order was proclaimed by her current messenger that Lowney had decided we could drop our hammers and hatchets and get ready. We were going "to Terre Haute, to the whorehouse." At last I would see what Jones had been talking about. There was no explanation for this sudden largesse. How does one prepare for such an adventure? Forming a quick queue, we took showers and donned clean clothes. We were ready within a few minutes, when the same messenger emerged again from Lowney's cabin. "Lowney's changed her mind," he announced. "Get back to work, you guys. We're not going to the whorehouse after all." With such emotional roller coaster rides we were kept literally at Lowney's beck and call. She gave no reason for changing her mind. Even so, brainwashers and tyrants alternately indulge and withhold with seeming whimsy, reducing their victims to the condition of slaves.

I suspected from the beginning that Lowney's preachings were to some extent irrational, her mystical notions, gathered from Blavatsky and Swedenborg, dubious. Yet when she and Jones had appeared together and sat in that rooming house in Tucson and beamed their smiles upon me and told me they really *wanted* me to join the colony, it was as if Mother and Dad were back together. I was wanted at last, and not just as a poster thumbtacked on a post office bulletin board.

But after a few months in the colony, wearied by Lowney's harangues and threats and even her far from helpful surgery on my manuscripts, escape seemed the only answer that made sense. Carl had a plan all worked out. Montgomery Clift and Burt Lancaster, stars of the forth-coming movie of *From Here to Eternity*, were scheduled to visit the colony, and Frank Sinatra might be with them. Lowney was getting hyper about preparations. There would predictably be a mob of towns-people and friends of Lowney present, distracting enough for us to slip away through the crowd. Carl had the bus schedule—we could get the late afternoon Greyhound to Chicago.

There were hostages, however, that I would find difficult to abandon. Lowney had many of my manuscripts, claiming that she was about to show them to an editor friend in New York, and somehow she had got hold of Lora's unclaimed letters from general delivery. She taunted me with them. "Maybe you ought to go join that little bitch," she snarled, but I did not look at her as my humiliation hardened my vow to escape. Everything was Lowney's property. "I own this town," she boasted, pointing out that her father was sheriff of the County, just one of her network of sycophants.

Lowney showed me manuscripts left behind by others, including a near-completed novel by Tom Chamales, a colonist who broke with her only to die in a mysterious fire a few years later. His official cause of death was asphyxiation due to a cigarette-caused fire in his apartment. Tom had published two novels, *Never So Few* and *Go Naked in the World*, and no writer could have been more appropriate as a colleague of James Jones. They mined the same materials, and Chamales had survived an even more dramatic war record than Jones. *The New York Times* for March 21, 1960, would cite part of it: "Serving in the entire Burma campaign, Mr. Chamales spent a year and a half behind the Japanese lines. He commanded the third battalion of American Kachin Rangers and was tactical commander when the main Kachin forces, numbering about 2,000 guerilla troops, were joined. He became a captain at the age of 21." He was "one whale of a story teller about war," wrote a reviewer quoted in the obituary.

According to a news article in the *Los Angeles Times*, "Police said that Chamales' handprints on the smoke-blackened walls indicated that he made a desperate attempt to grope his way to the door of the fourth floor unit at 1441 S. Beverly Glen Blvd."

Jones had been best man at Chamales' wedding to singer Helen O'Connell, a marriage that turned out to be disastrous—Chamales battered his wife. But the two writers had much in common. Their friend Frank Sinatra starred not only in *From Here to Eternity*, but also in the movie of Chamales' *Never So Few*. Invited to write an article about Chamales, Jones begged off, saying, "There are so many bad things about Tom which would have to be said, and which I would not like to say but which must be said to get anything like a true picture, that I think the thing is better left untouched."

Well before his death, Lowney bragged that Tom's manuscripts were "up for grabs." She felt justified in confiscating the property of those who crossed her. Evidently thinking it was superior to the novel I was writing, she offered me a manuscript left behind by another writer. I had no interest. My racing thoughts produced so many ideas within an hour that I was doing well if I could focus on a project for a week or two.

A few years after I fled the colony, one of the colonists published a novel with a plot suspiciously similar to a manuscript of mine that Lowney still had when I left. A magazine editor who knew I had been at the colony sent me the book for review. I tried to give the author, who had arrived at the colony shortly before my departure, the benefit of the doubt and not think of him as a plagiarist, but his story had remarkable parallels with the material I had shared with Lowney. Still, I remembered her policy, "up for grabs."

Jones and Handy became ever more bewildering with their contradictory behavior and violent quarreling. Like children with warring parents, we speculated on what was going on. Lowney's tirades always accused Jones of being unappreciative and ungrateful for all she had done for him. We would hear fragments. "If it hadn't been for me, you'd have . . ." "Goddamn it, Lowney . . ." Sometimes I was wakened late by the roar of Jim's car on the gravel. He was back from the Terre Haute whorehouses, or so he would say the next day. John Bowers claims that he went with him a time or two. "God's angry man," Lowney sometimes called Jim in an admiring tone, but threw violent tantrums whenever he stood up to her.

Lowney went even further with her technique of control by degrading and accusing: "There is no more than a hair's breadth between the artist and the criminal," she wrote in a letter of March 15, 1950. "When Jim first took the test here—when he first came—he registered criminal. That didn't surprise me at all—for I had already told him that was what he was. The army (especially the enlisted men—or most of them) are of criminal tendencies. Don't let that worry you—the artist graduates out of the criminal class and looks into his heart and writes—or else he watches those around him with a cold clinical eye and writes about himself as he sees them."

In addition to the wondrous relationship described in "None Sing So Wildly," Jim would base two novels—radically different—on Lowney. *Some Came Running* was a total whitewash, with a saintly protagonist named Gwen who gathers young men around her, a fiction that Jim may have once believed in. But the later book, *Go to the Widow-Maker*, was accurate enough that it partly divulged the truth about Lowney's violence. Carol, the character based on her, was more like the Lowney I knew, who had no tolerance for other women in the lives of her young men, who threatened to kill you if you crossed her, and who claimed she had had people eliminated by paid assassins. Earlier, in *From Here to Eternity*, Jim had characterized his mistress as a saintly whore, adulterous but with a heart of gold. I suspect that over time Jim saw in her all these mythic versions. But the rosy one was overcome by disillusionment, the glasses shattered.

Lowney hated all women who had anything to do with her disciples—and James Jones was first and foremost. But Mary Ann desperately wanted to be a novelist like her brother. She was persistent enough, with Jim's advocacy, that Lowney reluctantly agreed to accept her as a resident, the first and only woman at the colony, ever. Mary Ann moved into the trailer next to Jim's aluminum Airstream, but soon died mysteriously at the age of twenty-six. I say "mysteriously" because I heard several different and very specific versions of her death, and the last was the

most disturbing, though I would never have believed it had I not experienced Lowney's murderous tirades and heard her many scornful references to Mary Ann.

As hurtful as Lowney's strident rants were to males—nothing more dangerous in plain daylight than thrown bricks and attempts to run disrespectful visitors over with her bullish black Buick—her hate of women must
have been devastating to those who interfered in any way with her control
of her colonists. The preface to *James Jones in Illinois* (Sangamon State
University Archives) cites Lowney's conviction that "women could not
make good writers because they were egotistical and tended to shift the
blame for their problems onto others." Again and again she lamented:
"Even I don't seem to write, but teach, so I guess women haven't got what
it takes. I will stop trying to find a female writer and give up and go back to
the people I can work with."

"Part of the problem was that Lowney had extremely negative
views regarding women," the Sangamon archivist points out, citing
Lowney's musings: "'Nature says to a woman you are here to breed—
she looks around and hunts for what will make the best mate to help her
watch over the nest and take care of and fight for the young. Certainly
she isn't looking for some young buck who has a roving eye and is out
catting around when she needs him.' This attitude toward 'women the
parasites' was reflected in most of the books produced at the colony. Few
had any believable female characters." A *Chicago Tribune* critic,
Richard Gehman, referred to "that strange circle in Marshall, Ill., den
mothered by Mrs. Lowney Handy, which gave us James Jones, Tom T.
Chamales, and other members of the masculinity-is-meaning school."

Lowney's diatribes about the dangers of women—the enemy of a
man's creativity, as if they are only out to steal sperm for their babies—
were powerful attacks, curses on relationships. True to her doctrine that
women are out to castrate men and keep them from becoming artists,
Lowney even included herself. Her frequent threats to "cut off your balls
and hang them on the wall!" reinforced her dual role as castrator and
castrated. If ever a female believed in "penis envy," it was Lowney.

Jim's sister, in clear view as a target, the sole representative of her sex, was not spared Lowney's misogyny. Trying to become a writer she had to contend with constant reminders that her efforts would prove futile. The titles of the young woman's uncompleted manuscripts may reflect a profound depression and preoccupation with violence aimed at her: "Avatars of the Bitch (Love and Death)" and "Flame for Tears" and "The Third Time You Killed Me." The last title is particularly ironic, since I heard and read of three different versions of her death, not counting suicide. Even without assuming prescience, a reader can be disturbed by Mary Ann's anxieties.

An African proverb says "Cross the river in a crowd and the crocodile won't eat you." Just before the arrival of the celebrities, when a crowd was already gathering at the colony, Carl and I slipped across the plank bridge over the gully and headed through the bean field like runaway slaves, then made our way into Marshall where we boarded the late afternoon Greyhound. Whispering as we sat next to each other on the bus heading for Chicago, stars over cornfields blurring the window, Carl told me why he had taken Lowney's capacity for violence with the utmost seriousness and planned the escape as carefully as convicts would have. Seemingly a rational person, Carl was either hallucinating or carrying a burden of knowledge that could get him killed. He claimed to have discovered—just before my arrival at the colony—the body of Jim's sister in her trailer. He had gone there to awaken Mary Ann—his assignment when the wake-up bell was ignored. He knocked on the door, then opened it when he got no answer. He told me he saw Mary Ann's battered and bloody body on the floor. His description was graphic and frightening.

But Lowney had spoken in my presence of Mary Ann's having fallen off her bunk, breaking her neck. On another occasion I heard her say that a brain tumor had killed Jim's sister. Various printed accounts refer to "a kind of convulsion" and "some kind of seizure." Carl's version was yet another. He said that Mary Ann had been quickly buried in a closed casket and that Lowney's uncle, said to be the local coroner, had signed the death certificate. There had been no autopsy. Though I was skeptical of Carl's gothic version, Lowney's threats were stunning, and she sometimes blurted out strange references to Mary Ann. While helping Jim edit a manuscript he was having trouble with, a session I witnessed since she had broken off her conference with me when he came into her cottage, she became enraged when he resisted her order to scrap major passages. "If you don't shape up," she warned him, "God will punish you the same way he punished Mary Ann." Jim was about to reply, then looked at me and kept his silence, jerking the manuscript out of her hands and storming out, slamming the screen door.

The statement that left Jones speechless and pale bewildered me too, for Lowney had succeeded in making it clear that as far as she was concerned she was God, her power omnipotent at least within the territory of the colony. Her cooperative relatives and friends in public office were minions to enforce her absolute control. As if suffering were a positive, Lowney, in various comments, seemed to see value in the loss of Jim's sister. "Hell," she would say, "a novelist has to suffer or he wouldn't be worth a goddamn."

As the bus neared Chicago, Carl told me he was sure Lowney would try to have him killed because of what he had witnessed. In a cult, an exile or escapee is consigned to the dustbin of history or wiped out altogether, is declared a nonperson or is destroyed. Although Carl had left Lowney a note claiming that he was leaving to get an old war wound treated at the V.A. hospital, he was sure she could not be deceived. She would be after him within hours. Furthermore, she would assume he had told me. He planned to get a bus from Chicago to Toronto, he said as he gave me an address. As for me, in Jones's novel *Some Came Running*, I was dismissed as Mac Pierce, who "ran away to Chicago and was never heard of again."

Carl was visibly frightened and suspicious, looking around the Chicago bus station as we said goodbye. I took the Illinois Central train south to 55th Street and again stumbled into my Chicago headquarters, Jimmy's Woodlawn Tap, as if I had spent months in the desert. For a while I too was secretive about my address, and stayed with a girlfriend in Chicago. But after a few weeks and immense quantities of beer, I began to think life at the colony had all been a dream. Running across journal entries would remind me of how it had been: "It's impossible to leave here openly, because once you tell her you want to leave she starts a tirade and in two minutes proves to you with sheer violence that one can't possibly become a writer any place in the world but here. Lowney's forte is this ability to control people and all of her devotees share a belief that she has the power of God. Her husband, a quiet, easy-going chap, tells her, 'I wouldn't bet against you that the sun would come up tomorrow.'

"She is a firm believer in the theory of 'Beyond Good and Evil,' and she frequently reminded us that 'There are those outside the law. And today there are some of us outside the social and man-made laws. A criminal is the next stage to an artist—and the artist becomes a criminal first.' These beliefs have produced in her a tremendous tension, a high-pitched incessant reminding you of her freedom from guilt, despite her capacity to do things others wouldn't dare."

In his detective novel, A *Touch of Danger*, 1973, James Jones wrote sentences that could easily have been inspired by colony life. "Where's all this peace and human kindness stuff I've been hearing so much about? . . . The atmosphere was as charged as an electrical storm cloud bank that hadn't flashed yet."

James Jones and Lowney Handy

27.

I TOOK A job as a night clerk in a Lake Shore Drive hotel and lasted three days for lack of a recommendation that might have guaranteed permanence. I had telephoned the genial classicist, Professor Sitterly, to ask for one, leaving a message. He did not get back to me, and when I passed him on the sidewalk one day he walked right past, pretending not to see me. When I saw a notice posted on a tree offering a ride to New York, I grabbed the opportunity. The timing seemed propitious, for I heard that my classmate Paul Finkelstein was vacationing and would let me housesit for his apartment on East 33rd Street, almost in the shadow of the Empire State Building.

In New York I got busy looking for a job, applying everywhere possible, including the U.N., where there were openings for typists. And then I heard from Lora. She desperately wanted to join me. In a telephone booth I tried hard to talk her out of coming, telling her I was no good for her, but she insisted. I met her at Penn Station when she got off the bus after a ride across the continent.

Women of the apartment building often sat on the front stoop of Paul's apartment, gossiping in Italian. They greeted me each time I stepped around them. Several times they told me of a man who had turned up asking about me, telling them he would be back later. I assumed it was some friend of Paul's. With no air conditioning, the borrowed apartment on the first floor of the brick building was sweltering in the heat, and my friend Paul was due to return soon to reclaim his place. My efforts to find employment had been frustrating and unpromising. If I could just sell a novel, I thought, I would solve our financial problems. But I made a misstep that only later occurred to me as significant.

At the colony I had met a Doubleday editor, such a close friend of Lowney that they talked regularly on the telephone. On her colony visit, at lunch in the ramada, Clare had taken an interest in my novel-in-progress and even suggested a contract. But Lowney had interrupted, saying, "He's not ready. I'll tell you when he's ready." Now, I unwisely concluded, I could pick up the pieces.

Clare may well have mentioned to Lowney that one of her colonists had come in to see her. In Chicago I had been careful, but the sense of threat had faded. Lowney was not at all on my mind after I returned from the inconclusive conference with the editor. Since Lowney still had my manuscript, I could only promise the editor a new version—I glossed over the manner of my departure from the colony. There was not a lot to talk about. Still, Clare was friendly—we would stay in touch, and all that. I gave her my address, and it did not occur to me to ask her not to share it with her friend Lowney.

Our living conditions were not what Lora was accustomed to. She was no more enamored of New York than I was after nearly starving there. By the time she arrived I was living on canned beans and sardines and had endured torture from the pungent aromas drifting from Joe's Seafood Restaurant around the corner on Third Avenue. Unemployed and hungry, I was grateful to Larry, who had turned up just in time to treat me to a meal in Joe's and lend me some money. Lora declared that she could think of no better use for her savings than to subsidize a retreat in the country. Her offer was welcome, though I felt uneasy about her supporting me. But all that would change as soon as I sold a novel. Hadn't Jim gone in a flash from struggling writer living off his mistress and her cuckolded husband to a best-selling celebrity with heavy tax problems? Utopia might yet be found in bucolic surroundings, though thankfully without Lowney's tyranny or enforced chastity.

We studied a map and arbitrarily chose Williamsport, Pennsylvania, as a destination. We quickly packed our few belongings, including my duffel bag from the colony, walked to the corner and hailed a taxi, taking it to Penn Station. Inside, we joined a queue at the ticket counter. A short, bouncy man in a black leather jacket, in his mid-thirties, approached us just as we reached the ticket queue and grabbed my arm. "Where are you going?" he asked in an anxious tone, as if he knew me. He was breathing hard. His accent was foreign, maybe Irish.

"Williamsport, Pennsylvania," I replied.

"Why?" he demanded.

"We've heard we can find a place to rent around there," I said. "We're writers and . . ."

"Williamsport!" he exclaimed. "That's a coincidence! I'm heading that way myself, actually Buffalo, but I wouldn't mind dropping you at Williamsport. I thought if I could find somebody to share expenses, maybe buy some gas, I could save us all some money. I'm short of cash myself. It'd be a lot cheaper for you than the bus." I had the cash in my hand for our tickets, and I did not like his pushy manner. Lora seemed interested in his proposal, though. "Not only that," the pushy man jabbered on, "I know some people around there that may want a couple of housesitters. They travel a lot. It would be a perfect situation for a couple of writers."

He babbled on frenetically, as he tugged at my arm. There was the "rescue thing" again, the hand too much like that of providence. He had our bags in hand even before we consented to go with him. He was persuading us as the queue advanced toward the ticket counter. Was I going to wait a few more minutes and hand that money across or accept this offer? He led us out to a black four-door sedan, double-parked, motor running, right where the cab had pulled up. He opened the trunk and tossed my duffel bag and Lora's suitcase in. The trunk of the car was completely empty, even missing a spare tire. The interior was also empty, front and back, despite his plan for a long trip.

He headed over the George Washington Bridge, and gave us his name as Ray Maynard. Just west of the bridge, he pulled up next to a phone booth and said he had to make an important call, then returned to tell us he had to wait for a return call. As he stood by the phone booth, smoking, for the better part of an hour he kept his eye on us. At last he gave up waiting and returned to the car. As he drove west, Ray told bizarre anecdotes involving mercenaries who had been his drinking buddies in the bars around Piccadilly Square in London. One of them, just back from Africa, had a collection of human ears he liked to show off. Ray also told jokes involving castration and decapitation. Some of his feverishly related tales concerned his sexual adventures. He had once picked up a beautiful woman in a pub, only to discover she was a transvestite. He had beaten the man up, he said, leaving him for dead.

Lora was appalled at these obscenities. It was odd, too, how often Ray's answers to our curiosity related to billboards. If we had just passed a big sign advertising Hoover vacuum cleaners, the name Hoover would soon come up. Ray mentioned that he lived on Hoover Street in Buffalo. When I asked him about his job, he said he worked in a Buick factory. Coincidentally, we had just passed a Buick billboard. It was uncanny, the counterpoint between his frenetic rap and the highway signs. There was another odd response. In making small talk, Lora and I chattered about the colorful colony—Jones and Handy—an indulgence of namedropping. But Ray Maynard, fanatically interested in every other subject that came up was markedly silent only on this one. His cold, steely silence was pointed, extreme, as if he had withdrawn into an isolate corner or we had mentioned something more offensive than his own vulgarities. I recalled the Texas trooper's excitement at confronting the author of *From Here to Eternity*, a reaction which until then had seemed universal, for Jim's fans were everywhere. Ray's reaction was at another, polar remove.

When we stopped at a diner Ray Maynard did not sit near us. He sat at the end of the counter, watching us as a bus driver might at a rest stop. Despite the earlier jocularity, he now seemed to want to keep contact with us impersonal and at a minimum. By that time, Lora and I had become disturbed by his behavior and his willingness to accommodate us. When we made a gas stop, he turned down my offer to pay.

By the time we arrived in Williamsport in the evening, Lora and I were anxious to part with Ray Maynard, and resisted his pressure to undertake an immediate trip into the country to see that mansion he had told us about. We had a meal in a streetcar diner, and I insisted that we were too tired to go anywhere. Only after much effort I finally convinced him that Lora and I needed to get a hotel room. He left, but only after accompanying us to a corner hotel, watching us check in, and promising to pick us up early the next morning. Lora and I breathed sighs of relief to be rid of this man.

Yet after about two hours Ray turned up again at our second-floor room, babbling a tale. Next to him was a frowsy blonde, a heavy, muscular woman with thick makeup. He blurted out an absurd story about having met this lovely woman in a bar. Lo and behold, she was a friend of the wealthy people he had told us about, with a mansion on a hill with a beautiful view. Though it was now late at night, she was sure they wouldn't mind showing us the house. Moonlight would be fine for viewing it. We would see how wonderful it was, what an opportunity. He was tugging at my sleeve, and the woman craned to look around the open door at Lora, already in bed and pretending to be asleep. "We would love to," I said, working hard to sound casual, "and we will—first thing in the morning, okay?" It took much persuading, but finally he agreed to turn up at nine in the morning. He and the woman stomped down the wooden stairs, their disappointment obvious.

There was one thing they did not know. After checking into the hotel and waiting an hour, Lora and I agreed that we were in danger. I phoned a rental agency, then walked several blocks and returned in a car, parking it on a side street around the corner from the hotel.

"He knew that woman," Lora said. "No way were they strangers. And what an absurd story!"

I still did not connect him with Lowney and her threats, but suddenly Lora did. Everything then made sense, down to every seemingly trivial fragment of conversation. Now we kept the lights off and conferred in whispers. Now and then I got up and checked the streets and sidewalks, a shadowy Hopperesque reality of red brick storefronts and lampposts. Hand in hand we slipped down the hotel stairs and around the corner. If we just could make it to that rental car.

I drove south out of town like a madman, checking the rear view mirror, expecting pursuit. In the first town large enough I called the police from a pay phone and was told that we should go to the FBI, since our situation sounded like an attempted interstate abduction. At that time I was too rattled to follow through on the advice and instead chose to wait until we could assume our pursuers had left Williamsport, then return the car. The area had lost its glamor overnight, and Lora and I headed back to Chicago.

When I did get around to discussing the experience in an FBI office, blurting out details of our strange journey, I mentioned that at one point Ray Maynard had given me a contact address and phone number in Buffalo. One of the agents handed me a phone and invited me to try the number. An operator came on the line, saying, "There is no Cherry exchange in Buffalo." The agents connected the dots, suggesting that the man had followed us to Penn Station, made a phone call from the George Washington Bridge location to his female accomplice, then waited for her to meet and follow us in a second car. Just as FBI agents used case names, so might "Ray" Maynard. Then I recalled the description the 33rd Street ladies had given of our mysterious inquiring visitor. It all fit. Ray Maynard must have turned up again just as we headed out with our suitcases. Another few minutes and we would have been free of him.

But who would want to harm us, the agent wanted to know. Every threat Lowney had made came back verbatim. "I didn't really believe the gossip about Mary Ann's murder," I told the agent.

"But maybe it was true," he said. "At least you made it." He suggested that our escape had earned us a kind of immunity. I was puzzled, and asked how that could be. "Clearly you figured out the game plan," the agent said, "or you would not be here. Your friend Lowney Handy would draw the conclusion that you've left whatever evidence you have about that murder. That's about what it would take to get that body exhumed, and she could never let that happen." Even Lowney's coroner uncle could not have blocked an FBI investigation.

"So we should put it all in writing?"

"Yes, the sooner the better," he said and advised me to send out some certified copies. He also made inquiries on the telephone and established that the address Carl Pontell had given me was also fictitious. He had vanished.

Actually, had Lora and I not escaped, our disappearance would have left no trace, for even the FBI had no idea where we had gone from New York, although I was hardly an unknown person to the agency. They had had me under close surveillance for some time, suspecting that I was a Communist and possibly even a spy "in contact with so called Communist front groups or so called Communists at the University of Chicago." They suspected, it is reported in my dossier which I acquired under the Freedom of Information Act, that I had tried "to organize a 'cell' group at the University of Arizona . . ." and was interested in the "geographical layout of the Davis Monthan Air Force Base, Tucson, Arizona," as well as the White Sands Proving Grounds, New Mexico.

I got a chance to deny those allegations only because Chicago agents approached Lora at her workplace for information and she told me of this. I assumed they were trying to contact me about the Ray Maynard episode. Actually, they had no desire to talk with me, and since they had used case names it took several insistent phone calls to get an appointment. When the interview turned out to be not about Ray Maynard at all, but about me, and the charge that I was a Communist and a spy (with the usual invitation to wriggle out of such a hot spot by turning in the names of others), I explained that my interest in such scenes as White Sands and air bases was purely literary, so-called local color for my fiction. What they described as basement cell meetings had just been student parties, and my purpose in a trip to Los Angeles, which they assumed was to make contact with a cell of Communist spies, was only to visit my father. All the accusations were absurd, but by no means amusing.

Not much after my interview, according to my dossier, Lora, concerned with the extreme mental strain I was suffering, "voluntarily appeared at the Chicago office" and tried to get assurance that I was no longer the subject of their suspicions. According to the dossier she was advised that "such information could not be given to her." As for Ray Maynard, there had been no efforts to follow up, unless they are described in documents unavailable to me. My dossier is full of blacked-out names and passages and references to other still classified documents in other agencies. The FBI agenda was, at least in that McCarthy period, smoking out Communists.

Lowney herself would have been happy to know the conclusions of the "Internal Security" investigation for my time at the colony. According to the report from the Springfield, Illinois, office on August 5, 1953, an Informant (name blacked out) "advised that writers' colony attended by 16 young men is operated by Mrs. Lowney Handy and that he knows of no subversive activity in connection with this writers' colony." The report noted other details, including James Jones's post office box number 186 and that "Mrs. HANDY is the daughter of J. M. TURNER, Police Chief, Marshall, Illinois, former Clark County, Illinois, sheriff and former Illinois State Legislator from the 34th District of Illinois. The informant advised that he has known Mrs. HANDY for many years and that during this period he has never noted any indication of subversive or communistic activity on her part. The informant advised that the only thing of a suspicious nature he has ever noted concerning the colony is the fact that strict secrecy is maintained and no strangers are permitted to enter the premises of the colony." It was noted that I had headed for Chicago and was not expected to return. The report "advised that a large number of out-of-town people visit the Handy's Colony and that in the past these visitors have included singer FRANK SINATRA and his wife AVA GARDNER."

For me, the surveillance was another form of abuse, with consequences that are still beyond understanding. But in my lighter moments I reflect that some of the blacked-out pages are works of art and I try to find something positive. The busy agents could be viewed as research assistants, reminding me of the many places I resided, e.g.:

"DAVID EUGENE RAY as of 7-8-53 was residing care of the
Handy Writing Colony, Box 186, Marshall, Illinois. DAVID
EUGENE RAY HAS RESIDED AT THE FOLLOWING residences:

342 W. Moreland Street as of 7-5-50

1005 E. 60th Street, University of Chicago

5441 Kimbark Street, Chicago, as of 7-28-51

5610 Dorchester Avenue, Chicago, as of 2-25-52

1161 N. Columbus, as of Nov—1952

874 E. 3rd Avenue, Tucson, Arizona, June—1953"

The last place is where Jones and Handy came for me. As I sit having coffee at an outdoor table across the street at Time Market in
Tucson, I look at that house (more accurately the address, at least today,
is on University Avenue), admiring the outside of the stone fireplace
before which Jim and Lowney sat, convincing me that they had come to
rescue me and lead me on to fame and fortune. An FBI dossier is an
effective stimulant of memories. But some of them I would rather not
have stirred up. It is an effort to remember Moreland Street, which must
have been Warner's apartment in Phoenix. In truth, an FBI dossier is
not a desirable possession.

Inquiring agents aroused suspicion and hostility by visiting friends,
family, and employers. Since I did not know that the agents had come
calling, I experienced the distrust and rejection they provoked with
inevitable paranoia. I entered a Kafkaesque world familiar to those who
are accused but not allowed to confront their accusers or informers,
inspired to indulge malice and imaginative speculation, and wild gossip.
I felt betrayed each time I discovered that an acquaintance, colleague,
or family member had participated in this misguided patriotism and not
informed me. Lora was the only one who ever told me of the FBI
approach before I obtained the shocking dossier.

Once you are under surveillance, information will be put together to
make the worst seem true. Jokes and remarks are taken out of context.
Everything is exaggerated. All facts are assumed to be relevant to a probable conspiracy. The agents, far from neutral, are soon out to prove the

worst possible conclusions. In my case they were dangerous. Within a year of the Rosenberg executions, had I been unable to convince the FBI of my innocence, I might have been arrested and charged. With a swing of the pendulum even now, I could have a problem with my activist record. And the pendulum has indeed been swinging far to the right.

There have been times of crisis when writing has saved my life, but writing could also have got me killed. Another African proverb says, "Only when you have crossed the river can you say the crocodile has a lump on his snout."

Back in Chicago, disregarding what Lora and I had gone through, I wrote a satiric article about the Handy Colony for *Chicago* magazine. "A refugee tells of his experiences with this remarkable retreat, and its totally outlandish sponsor," is how George Garrett described my essay in his book about Jones. The piece triggered two responses from southern Illinois. One, Jim's inquiries to his lawyer as to whether he could sue, I did not learn of at the time. Jim was offended that I identified several of the literary sources and parallels that could be found between *From Here to Eternity* and the works of Thomas Wolfe, Norman Mailer, John Dos Passos, F. Scott Fitzgerald, and Ernest Hemingway, basically the works Lowney had had him copy.

The other reaction was a series of impassioned, indignant, pleading letters from Jim's uncle, Charles Jones, a well-known lawyer in Robinson. He wrote of his bitterness about Lowney. "Mrs. Handy has apparently thoroughly instilled in Jim her 'commandment' that he give up all members of his family." The attorney tried to enlist my help in forcing an investigation into Mary Ann's death with the considerable evidence he claimed to have, but I was in no mood to play detective. I felt I had been lucky enough to escape with my own life. Then, not long after making those accusations, on December 4, 1956, Charles Jones died in an automobile accident. The mystery of Mary Ann Jones's death was never cleared up.

I caught up later on events in Jim's life that included, on a trip to

New York, his meeting and falling in love with Gloria Mosolino, a woman who fulfilled his requisites for a bride. "I'd like someone who looks something like Marilyn Monroe for openers, but who is intelligent, knows writers, who's interested in writing, with a great sense of humor," he told his friend, the novelist Budd Schulberg, who arranged a date with "a beautiful blonde who had been a stand-in for Marilyn Monroe, had written an unpublished novel, and knew many writers." Jim was driven not only by desire to find a beautiful and brilliant bride, but to be sure to avoid the wrong kind of love. "Did you ever see real love between a man and a woman that did not end up as anger and resentment and fury that the other party could make one need him or her so much?" he wrote in a 1955 letter. After a whirlwind courtship, Jim soon made the mistake of thinking Lowney could tolerate the new relationship, and even bless his marriage. He took Gloria back to Marshall to meet Lowney Handy.

George Hendrick, in his notes to *To Reach Eternity: The Letters of James Jones*, wrote: "Gloria had no idea that Lowney was not her fiancé's foster mother . . . Jones had stuck to that story . . . Jones was left to break the news to Lowney of his impending marriage. Lowney battled to keep her young, now famous protégé. She suggested a marriage contract which would protect his assets should there be a divorce . . . Gloria still had no idea that Jones and Lowney had been lovers."

After a three-month honeymoon in Haiti, following their marriage by a voodoo master, the couple moved into Jim's new house in Marshall, adjacent to the colony. "Lowney was friendly the first times they met . . ." Hendrick went on. "Nothing unusual happened until the Fourth of July holiday . . . an agitated Lowney came crashing through the screen door, screaming at Gloria . . . then attacked Gloria with a Bowie knife. The two women fought until Jones came in and separated them. Neither was injured, but it was to affect all the participants traumatically: Lowney had lost Jones to a young and glamorous woman, Jones at long last was going to be forced to speak openly and truthfully about his relationship with Lowney . . . James and Gloria Jones packed up and left Illinois, never to return . . . . Finally, they decided they would never again talk about Lowney, and they did not."

Jim, his departure as precipitous as mine, had abandoned all his possessions. I was in Jimmy's Woodlawn Tavern when a friend mentioned a newspaper advertisement announcing that all the property of author James Jones would be sold in Marshall, Illinois. I was surprised because I thought Jim had built the house to live in for the rest of his life. Nevertheless he had left abruptly, authorizing a friend to sell everything.

"Boozing does not necessarily have to go hand in hand with being a writer," James Jones later wrote. "I therefore solemnly declare to all young men trying to be writers that they do not actually have to become drunkards first." But no more than he had I yet learned that lesson. I was in Jimmy's again when my friend returned from the auction with word that the sale had been a surreal scene. The house and its contents looked as if they had been abandoned by someone fleeing an earthquake. There were clothes stepped out of, an unfinished chess game, letters lying around. Whatever had happened, Jim had not taken time to pack. He had fled. My friend walked through the house, amazed at the collections of knives, guns, stuffed animal heads, stamps, jewelry, china, rare coins, Havana cigars—all sold for a fraction of their value. In the bathroom, a robe and a bikini lay on the floor next to the bidet said to be the only one in southern Illinois. Outside were the cars and the trailer. All the precious things that Jim had so lovingly collected with his royalties were soon gone, as if plundered by the milling mob.

It was obvious that Jim and Gloria had fled Lowney's wrath. But scattered through Jim's later writings are scenes, images, and lines of dialogue that sound like echoes of colony life. In his 1973 potboiler, *A Touch of Danger*, there is a scene in which Jim's detective, Lobo, asks the sort of questions that haunt me about Mary Ann. Investigating the murder of a young woman named Marie, Lobo says, "There wasn't anything, not anything, not a damn thing I could do for her. My stomach seemed to have fallen completely away out from under me . . .She hadn't been killed by any accident. She'd been murdered." Then comes a paragraph that could have referred to Mary Ann, not a fictional Marie:

"Everybody had used her in her life. She had been used, and cheated, by just about everybody she had ever come in contact with. Now, somebody else had used and cheated her in the final, worst way possible."

Repeatedly Lobo asks if individuals he suspects "are capable of it." The character Countess Chantal, who has resemblances to Lowney, is in contact with Chicago mobsters and drug lords, for whom she had been a courier. As Lobo pursues the mystery of Marie's murder, a few lines remind me of my conversation with Carl Pontell. Lobo says:

> "I heard you declared the girl's death accidental."
> "That is correct . . . Does that case interest you, too?"
> "No. But I happened to be there when they found her. And I got a chance to look her over pretty closely. It looked to me like she was murdered."
> "Oh? The medical examiner and I did not think so. Nor did any of the other officers who examined her. What made you think that?"

I cannot but believe that James Jones's lingering suspicions could have been, like mine, too close to the surface not to emerge, sublimated in fiction. Lobo at one point says, "I cut and ran," which was also about the only thing one could do to break from Lowney. In addition to exile and shame, possibly even death, punishment for escaping a cult is banishment from memory.

In 1963, Lowney wrote to Bowers: "Your trouble as ALWAYS is still living in the past—CHRIST SAID, 'Let the dead past bury its dead.'..." And if Lowney could bestow fame, she could bestow obscurity along with her curses. "Do you think I recall anyone who was even in the camp...not a soul. If I had to give a remembered picture of James Jones to the cops—I sure as hell couldn't do it. That was another life. THE HANDY COLONY IS NO MORE. I DIED."

According to John Bowers, Lowney not only perplexed her charges while they were in the colony, but cast a long shadow over their later lives: "And one must remember that this writers' colony took charge of one's life totally; it in no way at all resembled MacDowell, Yaddo, or the Iowa Workshop. Come to the Handy Colony and Lowney told you how to get your hair cut, what to eat and drink, how to consider your parents (particularly your mother), how to treat your body, and who to vote for — everything."

He mentions a feature of Lowney's imposed regimen that I was spared. "We ate cottage cheese every day and were encouraged to hook ourselves up to enemas, something that had a curious Victorian twist to it. ('You need to get that shit out of your systems,' she said, 'or you'll never write a damn line.')." It was bad enough to remember Mother's enemas forced upon Ellen and me, so I am glad Lowney never got around to me on that score.

Lowney is as pitiable as anyone I have known and survived, but even at this distance she can still, like a powerful spirit, provoke fear that — if she and the Christ she quotes were right — should surely be reserved for the living. And yet there is a part of us that loves to our dying day our murderous abusers. We go on trying to think the best of them, and credit them with some of the most exciting and adventurous of our illusions.

Years later at a very different artists' colony, I met a composer who had known James Jones in his last days. On our afternoon walks the composer was smoking the Havana cigars Jim had willed to him, a whole barrel of them. "I was with Jim one evening," he told me. "We walked into the Stork Club, and who did we bump into but Frank Sinatra. He started babbling about how grateful he was to Jim for getting him the role of Maggio in *From Here to Eternity* and Jim was saying it was nothing, but then Sinatra kept saying he wanted to do something to pay back, show his gratitude and all that, and Jim went on saying it was nothing. Then Sinatra leaned close and said, 'Isn't there anyone you want hit?' Jim could not think of a soul, God bless him." Hearing that story, I also blessed Jim.

I can picture clearly what might have happened had Lora and I gone along into the dark countryside outside Williamsport. "It is well known," Milosz writes, "that the same fact observed by two witnesses is not the same thing, and yet the honest chronicler is convinced that his description is exact. His good faith is decisive here, and we should respect it . . . We work at knowing the truth about our lifetime even if its images, derived from various people, are not consistent with each other. We exist as separate beings, but at the same time, each of us acts as a medium propelled by a power we do not know well, a current of the great river."

There is no way to prove that Lowney sent "Ray Maynard" to carry out her threats. But the encounter, following the disappointments and violence of the colony, frightened me so profoundly that when, several years later in Europe, I read in a newspaper of her death, I could not believe it. I was still afraid of her, and even today hesitate to call up some of the details of her obsession with violence. I would prefer to believe in the generous, inspiring, and unique person who rescued me from a squalid rooming house in Tucson. We do not want to believe the dark histories of a Procopius or Suetonius, yet my mentor Lowney would have advised me to think the worst of everyone if I wanted the truth.

Lowney, were you the creator of creators, or were you as grand a bitch goddess as Kali? Were you the destroyer of worlds, the woman with the guts to carry out threats to kill anyone who ever crossed you? Were you bluff or understatement? Were you mother of mercy or small town psychotic with murderous rage that could be triggered by even a sassy moment of disrespect? Lowney, I will never know, though the mention of your name still sets my heart racing like a frightened rabbit's.

SI #100-8828

ADMINISTRATIVE PAGE

Informants

67c
67D

Administrative Data

For the information of the Chicago Division, the Phoenix Division by letter of 6-19-53 entitled, "DAVID EUGENE RAY - Security Matter-C", Phoenix origin, advised that ▓▓▓▓▓▓▓▓▓▓▓▓▓▓▓ advised RAY anticipated leaving Tucson on Friday, April 10, 1953, to attend an un-named writing school in Illinois. ▓▓▓▓▓▓▓▓ advised this writing school was conducted by a Mrs. HAMBY (phonetic) who, in conjunction with JAMES JONES, a well-known novelist, would probably take RAY with them upon return to the school. ▓▓▓▓▓▓▓▓ JAMES JONES recently completed a best-selling novel entitled, "From Here to Eternity." ▓▓▓▓ the opinion JONES was attempting to ready his book for motion pictures.

67c
67D

▓▓▓▓▓▓▓▓▓▓▓▓▓▓▓▓▓▓▓▓▓▓▓▓▓▓ It was subsequently learned one REX BOLLIN, co-owner, Indian Trading Post, Tucson, was also in attendance at the un-named writing school. Inquiry at the Indian Trading Post revealed his forwarding address to be in care of Box 186, Marshall, Illinois.

Leads

CHICAGO DIVISION

    AT CHICAGO, ILLINOIS

67c

Will furnish the Phoenix Division with background data and record of subversive activities, if any, from credit check and indices search on ▓▓▓▓▓▓▓▓▓

- 3 -

David's FBI Files

FEDERAL BUREAU OF INVESTIGATION

Form No. 1 THIS CASE ORIGINATED AT	PHOENIX			
REPORT MADE AT	DATE WHEN MADE	PERIOD FOR WHICH MADE	REPORT MADE BY	
PHOENIX	8-11-53	6-5,23,26;7- 2,16,17,20;	████████████	b7c slb
TITLE		9-5-53	CHARACTER OF CASE	
DAVID EUGENE RAY			INTERNAL SECURITY - R	

SYNOPSIS OF FACTS:

DAVID EUGENE RAY presently believed attending the Handy Writing Colony, Box 186, Marshall, Illinois. ████████ former associate of subject. Efforts to locate JOHN H. WARNER, at Denver, Colorado, and Phoenix, Arizona, unsuccessful.

CLASS. & EXT. BY
REASON-FCIM II, 1-2 4.2
DATE OF REVIEW

P

DETAILS: **AT TUCSON, ARIZONA**

Informants named within the body of this report are of known reliability unless otherwise indicated.

I. BACKGROUND DATA

Residence - DAVID EUGENE RAY as of 7-8-53 was residing care of the Handy Writing Colony, Box 186, Marshall, Illinois.

DAVID EUGENE RAY has resided at the following residences:

342 W. Moreland Street as of 7-5-50.
1005 E. 60th Street, University of Chicago, Chicago, Illinois, as of 6-18-51.
5441 Kimbark Street, Chicago, as of 7-28-51.
5610 Dorchester Avenue, Chicago, as of 2-25-52.
1161 N. Columbus, as of Nov - 1952.
874 E. 3rd Avenue, Tucson, Arizona, June - 1953.

APPROVED AND FORWARDED	SPECIAL AGENT IN CHARGE		DO NOT WRITE IN THESE SPACES
			100-397533-10

COPIES OF THIS REPORT
3-Bureau (100-397533) REGIS.
2-Springfield REGISTERED
3-Phoenix (100-4278)

63 SEP 8 1953

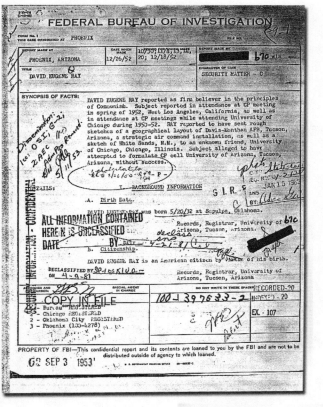

FEDERAL BUREAU OF INVESTIGATION

FORM No. 1 THIS CASE ORIGINATED AT PHOENIX			FILE NO.
REPORT MADE AT	DATE WHEN MADE	PERIOD FOR WHICH MADE	REPORT MADE BY
PHOENIX, ARIZONA	12/26/52	10/3/52; 11/24/52; 20; 12/18/52	670 mls
TITLE		CHARACTER OF CASE	
DAVID EUGENE RAY		SECURITY MATTER - C	

SYNOPSIS OF FACTS:

DAVID EUGENE RAY reported as firm believer in the principles of Communism. Subject reported in attendance at CP meeting in spring of 1952, West Los Angeles, California, as well as in attendance at CP meetings while attending University of Chicago during 1950-52. RAY reported to have sent rough sketches of a geographical layout of Davis-Monthan AFB, Tucson, Arizona, a strategic air command installation, as well as a sketch of White Sands, N.M., to an unknown friend, University of Chicago, Chicago, Illinois. Subject alleged to have attempted to formulate CP cell University of Arizona, Tucson, Arizona, without success.

- P -

DETAILS:

I. BACKGROUND INFORMATION

A. Birth Date.

DAVID EUGENE RAY was born 5/20/32 at Sapulpa, Oklahoma.

Records, Registrar, University of Arizona, Tucson, Arizona. 670

B. Citizenship.

DAVID EUGENE RAY is an American citizen by virtue of his birth.

Records, Registrar, University of Arizona, Tucson, Arizona

ALL INFORMATION CONTAINED HEREIN IS UNCLASSIFIED
DATE ___ BY ___ 4-21-81

DECLASSIFIED BY SP-1 GS KLV/L
ON 4-9-81

APPROVED AND FORWARDED:	SPECIAL AGENT IN CHARGE	DO NOT WRITE IN THESE SPACES
COPY IN FILE		RECORDED-20 100-397533-2 INDEXED - 20
5 - Bureau REGISTERED		EX - 107
2 - Chicago REGISTERED		
2 - Oklahoma City REGISTERED		
3 - Phoenix (100-4278)		

PROPERTY OF FBI—This confidential report and its contents are loaned to you by the FBI and are not to be distributed outside of agency to which loaned.

62 SEP 3 1953

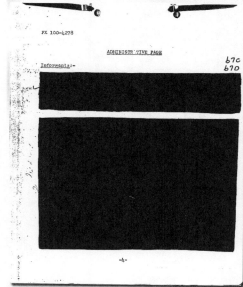

FX 100-4278

ADMINISTRATIVE PAGE

Informants:-

67C
67D

-4-

28.

WHETHER LOWNEY HANDY tried to have me killed or not, there was another who had—the genial guardian who had repeatedly offered me a Luger pistol and suggested what to do with it. For years I hauled with me from place to place Warner's abusive Special Delivery letters. On impulse, one winter night during the time I was teaching at Cornell University, I stashed the beer boxes stuffed with those letters as well as manuscripts and other papers into my green Volkswagen and drove to a hill overlooking Ithaca. I took along the bottle of brandy I had been killing that evening, sprinkled the brandy on the boxes, and threw down a lit book of matches, then stood watching blue and yellow flames whipping in the wind. The papers were soon ash on snow, though altogether too many of the phrases in blue ink still live in my mind.

I had heard nothing from or about Warner for many years until one day a document stapled in a brown folder arrived in the mail. It was a copy of an amendment to his will, in which I was named as a beneficiary, together with a bequest to another David, probably my successor in his life. The amendment to the JOHN KINGSBURY WARNER TRUST read, in part:

> "Section 1.00. If Settlor's friend DAVID EUGENE RAY, now residing in Portland, Oregon, or any child, stepchild, or more remote issue of his shall be living at Settlor's death, there shall be set aside the DAVID EUGENE RAY FUND, which shall consist of one fourth of

the trust estate on hand after satisfying the provisions of Paragraph
7.00. Such fund shall be distributed to DAVID EUGENE RAY,
absolutely, if he shall survive Settlor. . . ."

Some time after that, I received a phone call from Warner telling me
that he would like to be back in my life. He would like to be an uncle
to my children, he said, and be allowed to play Santa Claus at
Christmas. This genial plea in the old recognizable voice triggered such
rage that it must have been fed from far back in our history. Flooded
with anger and protective anxiety for my children, I told him I did not
want him back in my life, and I certainly did not want my children to
have any contact with him.

I hung up on him. But I am not proud to have done so, for I have
learned since how hard it is to try making amends, and how painful it is
if they are scorned.

But at the time it was not in my power to forgive. I still felt that
Warner had ruined my life, though clearly much damage had been
inflicted long before he came along imposing with his manipulations
and brainwashing a battered wife syndrome on a teenage boy. "To be
betrayed by a stranger is one thing. To be morally wounded by one you
have loved is quite another," writes Beverly Flanigan, in *Forgiving the
Unforgivable, Overcoming the Bitter Legacy of Intimate Wounds*. She
goes right to the heart of the matter: "Unforgivable injuries fly straight
into one's heart, into private spaces where hopes and aspirations dwell.
They bring about a kind of finality—the end of a myth . . . or perhaps to
dreams of a long-anticipated future (or an idealized past). When unforgivable injuries are fully experienced, their victims will never be the
same."

For me, the real injury was indeed the shattering of a myth, a belief
system. I had lived through a miserable boyhood with the myth that I
would be happy if my father returned. When Warner offered a home in
Arizona, I thought that a dream had been fulfilled, and therefore I
should be happy. I found it hard to forgive myself for having caved in to
Warner any number or times for the paltry reward of room and board.

Even today, decades after my adolescence spent fighting John Kingsbury Warner, I find it difficult to trust. I may suddenly become aware that I have become too close, too fond, too trusting. A reminder can be as simple as finding myself riding in the passenger seat of a friend's car. It is too much like the old days with Warner, my sitting there, obliged to be charming or to fend off his nagging. It is an unbearable role—that of the sidekick, the second fiddle. I avoid the friend, and soon he is gone like others from my life. Though longing for friends, I choose isolation and grieve that few friendships have survived—the cost not only of my fight or flight migrations but of unbearable associations from the past.

A bipolar condition that may have been present all along merely compounds the ambivalence. A recently diagnosed woman told me recently, "I look back on my whole life and realize that what I always thought was my personality was really my disease." Viewing oneself as a clinical medical case or an FBI object of scrutiny has its dangers. Others do not understand the bitterness.

When I heard of Warner's death I was temporarily elated. The Disney song ran through my head—"The big bad wolf is dead." Like the three little pigs, I felt like dancing wildly around. But the pleasure was short-lived. Nothing, not even his death, could undo the past. His death—like that of my father and my beloved son's—was yet another to grieve. I tried to recall to his credit that Warner had once saved my life and that at times his attention was, despite himself, "more love than hate, however tortured it was"—as Tennessee Williams wrote of his alcoholic father.

In time I undertook the challenge of forgiving. As my Aunt Edris might have said—it is her voice I hear intoning—forgiveness may be too late, far too late for this world, but it will just have to do.

David with Aunt Edris

29.

IN JUNE OF 1966, after a decade of graduate school, teaching at various universities, and writing, with some success in poetry and a few stories published in little magazines, I was surprised by a letter in German, arriving out of the blue. I had been awarded a five-year University of Vienna and Woursell Foundation fellowship—with no strings attached. There was not even the obligation to show up in Vienna. It offered freedom to live anywhere, but on a shoestring budget—the dream of the expatriate Hemingwayesque life.

It was another invitation to mania. The stipend triggered my old response to rescue—leap first, look later! I took a leave from my assistant professorship at Reed College, gave my Volkswagen to my wife's sister, disposed of furniture, stored books, and booked a steamship for Europe. James Jones was already in Paris, but I did not know it at the time.

I had been active in protesting the Vietnam war, and during his visit to the Reed campus, Robert Bly and I had founded the American Writers Against the Vietnam War. Our protest reading in Portland was written up in *The New York Times*, and news clips were broadcast on television around the country, sparking readings elsewhere. One of my poems honoring Oregon's Senator Wayne Morse, who almost alone had spoken out against the undeclared war, was quoted in the *Times*: "Some of us were born in the wrong land to become war criminals." It was tempting to get caught up in the protest movement, but the utopian dream the colony had represented was not dead. I still wanted a place where I could center my life around writing and family, a spiritual and creative center without the distractions of any kind of politics or competitiveness — academic or otherwise.

Just before our departure, a phone call came from my father. He had heard from my sister Ellen that we were leaving the country, and thought we should come through Los Angeles for a visit. He reminded me it had been many years since we had seen each other, and said he would like to meet my family, including his one-year-old grandson, Samuel, and my adopted daughter, Wesley. When I resisted the suggestion, he offered to reimburse me for the extra fare involved.

I had come to regard him as irrelevant in my life. Why give him a chance to hurt me all over again? I had come to regard my family as toxic, an influence I wanted to spare my children. On the other hand, I was proud of the children and wanted to show them off — an urge toward restoration, bridging the abyss, healing. If he really wished to see his grandchildren, what right did I have to stand in the way?

Dad met us at the airport. We shook hands and he patted the heads of the children and led us out past the legs of the great concrete spider to the parking lot. We got into his blue Cadillac and headed onto the freeway toward Long Beach.

"I got two barbers working for me now, and both of 'em is pretty good," he said.

"How's old Ben?" I remembered the shoe shine man, who had given me more attention on my high school visit than Dad had.

"You mean that ol' nigger boy that was shining shoes for me? Aw, he died years ago. Your brother, Sonny, y'know, half-brother, I guess you'd say, he was out here for a while when he was in high school and he worked the shine stand for a while, but he didn't like it much, nigger work."

He had not changed. "The niggers are taking over," he went on, as always, and I shot back with a wisecrack. "It's about time."

He pretended not to hear me, or maybe I had said it too softly, not wanting to get into the issues that had always spoiled visits, not only with him but with others in the family. Like Warner, they blamed everything that was wrong in the world on minority scapegoats. I thought of how *we*

had been snubbed as white trash, Okies, hillbillies, hicks. No matter—
everybody had to have a scapegoat.

"I'm doing good with the barber shop," he said. "The work gives me
a worldly satisfaction." He went on to say his family was very involved
with church work. I recalled that he had become very religious after
coming to California. His third wife may have had led him in that direction, or it could have been Aunt Edris's influence.

By the time we parked in his driveway, he had brought me up to date
on my five half-siblings, two from his second marriage and three from
his third. It was clear that he had little use for any of us but the last three.
He seemed to have it in for the two boys from his second marriage.
When they had come to Long Beach to live with Dad after their mother
died of alcoholism back in Kansas, he soon sent one of them back and
had trouble with the other.

"Billy's wild and I can't let him work for me. He's got his barber's
license, but he's drinking too much. I had to kick him out the last time
he visited. Maybe he'll settle down one of these days."

To hear Dad talk, you would think he himself had never taken a
drink. But on June 19, 1945, when he was in the Seabees, he was tried
before the captain's mast and given one hundred hours of extra duty.
"OFFENSE: Demanded beer at a time when the sale of beer was not
allowed. Cursing another man in the Navy."

On a brighter note, paying little attention to the family I had
brought, Dad filled us in on his youngest son. "Ronnie's the apple of my
eye," he beamed. "You should hear him preach. He's been preaching
since he was knee high to a grasshopper. He's blessed by the Lord. My
girls have both got themselves beautiful voices and they're in the choir,
but they can't keep up with my boy. He's got hisself a quartet."

"Do you still like Bob Wills' music?" I asked. It is always the old days
we come for. There was a fond remembrance buried in our relationship
somewhere.

"He's getting a letter in baseball," my father continued.

"Bob Wills and His Texas Playboys," I tried again. "I still hear them
now and then."

"Your Ma didn't like that music," he said. "It ain't as good as church hymns, that's for sure." He had finally deferred to Mother's opinion on the hillbilly music Bob Wills and His Texas Playboys represented. I remembered the terrible arguments they had over the music on the radio, and the charity concert Bob and his band had given us on Christmas day at the orphanage.

"Aw ha, take it away, Leon," I mocked the old radio call of Bob Wills as he had stepped back to make way for McAuliffe with his steel guitar. My father looked at me and for a moment I thought he was going to shout at me to shut up. Maybe he thought I was making fun of him.

Unwelcome memories flooded me as disappointment sank in—the unhappy visits, the broken promises. On my visit from Tucson in my teens, he had driven us through miles of citrus groves and I had fallen in love with the purring swoop-fendered roadster he owned at the time. He remarked that I could have it when he bought a new car. I had held on to that vision, a gift that would make up for the dime-sized puniness of his others. Now, when I casually asked him what had happened to that roadster, my father indifferently explained, "Oh, I gave that old car to Ronnie a long time ago."

There was something else I could not get out of my mind—the letter I had written to him from a Chicago hospital bed after a suicide attempt. He had not answered, and in time I assumed he had not received it. But years later Ellen told me that he had mentioned the letter to her, commenting, "I didn't know I had a son who was a nut." I never sent him the long letter I wrote after hearing that comment. I put it in a story called "The Thirty-Eight Page Letter Franz Kafka Wrote His Father." Kafka could not put his father on trial, so he wound up putting himself on trial, imposing a death sentence not only on himself by his suicide, but on all his works. His friend and executor Max Brod betrayed him, though, refusing to carry out the sentence against the works. He could not bear to consign great literature to the flames.

At his house that last time I would see my father, though he would live for another twenty-three years, we sat in the living room while one of my half-sisters played the electronic organ under the pastel picture of

Jesus praying in the garden. My father showed me his large soft-leather Bible. "It's all in red, what Jesus had to say." My other half-sister sat on the couch and held Sam on her lap, bending to kiss his cheek and whisper how cute he was.

As our hostess put a platter of fried chicken on the table and stood with her hand in a quilted glove, she said, "That Bible of his is no better than mine. The Lord's word is worth just as much in my dime store Bible."

"It's the same words," my father insisted, "but you'll likely pay more attention to 'em if the important stuff is in red letters. Ain't that right?" He turned to me for support.

"I'm with her," I said. "It's the words that count."

"I'll get you one of these red-letter Bibles if you want," he offered.

"We don't have room in the suitcases," I said. "I'll pick one up after we get over there."

I explained our itinerary again, but he did not seem interested, and it was time to come to the table. There was always a numbness, a space of silence and indifference to any attempt to interest either him or my mother in my ambitions. The expatriate life was just another folly. The only acknowledgement my father ever made of my career was when a customer waiting for a haircut showed him a poem in a copy of *Esquire*. "Here's something about a barber by somebody named Ray," the man said, holding up the magazine. Unconsciously I had probably aimed the poem at my father by sending it to a magazine that always turns up in barber shops.

> THE BARBER
> checks his watch again and again,
> it always has hair under the crystal
> and it always says the day has a long way to go
> to the bitter end.
> And he knows where it ends, in which suburb
> among all the things hair bought—
> so many million hairs it took for a toilet seat

and its fluffed cover, for a cat, for a daughter.
He took time off to send his son a stone
when the boy had cut his wrists and asked for a loaf,
time off from forever cutting hair,
round and round the gentleman's chair,
clipping away so that no man could be Apollo
or Adonis, but just another regular guy . . .

After the first ceremonial sparks during that last visit, everything went flat as hot champagne. Time layers were scrambled in a roiling flux. After dinner we strolled into the backyard and took snapshots, my father holding Sam, Wes standing beside him and all of us smiling. I was sorry that my daughter Wini, back in Ohio, could not be with us.

Like so many who vow not to be like their parents, I had never meant to be a serial monogamist like my father or subject children to the aftermath of broken marriages. R. D. Laing observed that the family script never changes, though the *dramatis personae* are replaced with each generation. I was on the same road my father had taken, his restlessness aflame in my blood, though I tried to believe I had not walked away as he had. I was still seeking a way to rip up the script, hopeful that my children could grow up without the blight of loss.

I was feeling a hollow ache, and was glad I had booked the flight, allowing only one night's stay in California. I was eager to get back on a plane and let it lift us out of the smog. The past was somehow contained in that viscous pool, toxic and oppressive. My family ghosts, survivors of dust bowl and Depression, had been transplanted to a city of ironic name. Uncle Henry was working for the L.A. Parks Department, picking up trash and condoms and cans from the beaches. Aunt Edris labored mornings cleaning toilets and changing light bulbs in the trailer park where they lived, then rode a bus for miles to work in a piecework sweatshop, huddled over a sewing machine.

I should have insisted on visiting with Aunt Edris immediately after arrival, for the next morning my father decided there would not be time. But he wanted to take us by his barber shop so he could give me a haircut and shave. "Don't you want to get rid of that hippy beard?" he asked.

"You can trim it if you like," I said.

"It oughta come off."

An hour before my father drove us to the airport, I sat in his barber chair, wondering if it was the same seat where the manicurist had received her double massage. As his wrist reached past my eyes, I saw a stray hair under the crystal of his watch and wondered if it was the same one I had noticed at my sister's wedding.

My heart was racing. I closed my eyes to submit to the worst, not wanting to look at the bare blade. He clipped my beard and shaved it close, drawing blood though no one was more skillful with scissors and razor than he was. When he was finished, I looked in the mirror and realized that he really had, as he had joked, "lowered my ears." The rough treatment was a reminder that he had once had power over my life.

He seemed as eager to drive us to the airport as I was to get there, to escape the freeway traffic and most of all the suffocating sadness that had descended as if it were a part of the smog filtering sunlight into a dull yellow dust. He parked the Cadillac and still had not said anything about the expenses he had promised to cover.

"You said you could help us with the plane ticket," I said, at the last minute.

He had it ready, was just waiting to see if I asked. He pulled fifty dollars from his pocket and handed it to me. "Is that enough?" he said.

"Close enough," I said, and put the money in my pocket. It had cost considerably more to change the ticket to include the detour to Los Angeles. I regretted letting him talk me into it. We had just stirred up the bitter past, the old hunger.

> Once when I was five
> quite early one morning
> in a streetcar diner
> he lifted me up on the counter,
> said to the waitress,

"This here's my boy,
ain't he a dandy?"
Six decades I've kept
his words in my mind
to comfort the fatherless years.
So I lied when I cursed him,
said he gave me nothing,
a stone each time I asked for bread.

One of my half-brothers summed it up in a telephone call after my father's death. "Daddy never ever did come back," he said. "The main thing I remember about him was that nothing was worth remembering."

In my brother's voice I heard my own sadness—what Richard Rhodes called "the hole in the world." And Rilke's lines echoed: "So cloudy that I cannot understand / this figure as it fades into the background."

Ellen told me of a visit to our father she had made when she was fourteen. "Dad was living in Long Beach with Aunt Edris and Uncle Henry. I went out there for a month, took the train by myself. I was kind of a scared little kid. Coming back, Dad only gave me five dollars and it was the only money I had to buy food for three days on the train. I remember calling Mother collect from Kansas City. I just hinted, I didn't say, 'Mom, I don't have any money to eat,' I just hinted. I had 35 cents. And she didn't send me any money. I got a glass of milk for the 35 cents and that got me through. Mother was upset. She said, 'Why didn't you tell me?' I said, 'I didn't know if you had any.' We didn't have much. Very little."

We had very little.

But life could still deliver surprises that could leave us with even less.

"I'd love to have a better story to tell," F. Scott Fitzgerald lamented, "but it is the only story I have to tell."

He was wrong. He had, and I have, other stories that must be told. Ancient griefs merge with fresh ones. If Ellen and I were back in that Children's Home and someone turned up on visiting day, who would it be, which ghost? We just wanted someone—anyone—to show up. Would the good people bother to come, making the journey through the years and wilderness? Or would we once again face the abusers, the predators, the brainwashers? Would they simply drop by to entrap us again—and to demand that we forgive and even love them?

David after his poetry reading at the
Library of Congress, 1971

Robert Bly and David, 1971